CONTENTS

Quality Comprehension

A Strategic Model of Reading
Instruction Using Read-Along Guides,
GRADES 3–6

SANDRA K. ATHANS

DENISE ASHE DEVINE

INTERNATIONAL
Reading Association
800 BARKSDALE ROAD, PO BOX 8139
NEWARK, DE 19714-8139, USA
www.reading.org

Executive Editor, Books   Corinne M. Mooney
Developmental Editor   Charlene M. Nichols
Developmental Editor   Tori Mello Bachman
Developmental Editor   Stacey Lynn Sharp
Editorial Production Manager   Shannon T. Fortner
Design and Composition Manager   Anette Schuetz

Project Editors   Stacey Lynn Sharp and Rebecca A. Fetterolf

Cover   Design, Linda Steere; Photographs, Bolivar Road Staff

Library of Congress Cataloging-in-Publication Data
Athans, Sandra K., 1958-
  Quality comprehension : a strategic model of reading instruction using read-along guides, grades 3-6 / Sandra K. Athans and Denise Ashe Devine.
     p. cm.
  Includes bibliographical references and index.
  ISBN 978-0-87207-464-4
  1. Reading comprehension--Study and teaching (Elementary) I. Devine, Denise Ashe, 1967- II. Title.
  LB1573.7.A84 2008
  372.47--dc22
                                                                                          2008006544

It is with grateful appreciation that we dedicate this book
to our families, colleagues, and students.

Sandra K. Athans is a fourth-grade teacher and has provided instruction at this level for eight years within the Chittenango Central School District in Chittenango, New York, USA.

Having earned a Bachelor of Arts in English from the University of Michigan, Ann Arbor, USA, Sandra entered the field of publishing where she worked in New York City and White Plains, New York. She excelled in this field for nearly 10 years before pursuing a career in education. Sandra earned her Master of Arts in teaching from Manhattanville College in Purchase, New York, in 2000 and is currently completing the requirements for her Secondary English Certification.

In addition to this teaching experience, she has also taught at the preschool level and the sixth-grade level, and she recently served as an adjunct professor within the English Department at Cazenovia College in Cazenovia, New York, where she provided reading and writing instruction.

In addition to assisting students in her role as a classroom teacher, Sandra also introduced and provided instruction in many engaging after-school programs that encouraged students' authentic reading and creative writing activities.

Quality Comprehension is Sandra's first book and is based on her experience studying and working with intermediate-level students in the areas of guided reading, reading comprehension, and motivation. She has been awarded numerous grants through the Central New York Teaching Center and enjoys sharing her experience at reading and writing conferences throughout the United States.

Sandra grew up in Westchester County, outside of New York City, and currently resides in Chittenango.

Denise Ashe Devine received her Bachelor of Science in elementary education in 1989 and her Master of Science in reading from the State University of New York–Oswego in Oswego, USA, in 1993. She has been teaching for 19 years, and in that time she has provided instruction at various elementary grade levels within several school districts in the central New York area.

In addition to this experience, Denise was involved in a summer instructional program for at-risk students and their families. In this capacity, Denise provided reading instruction for elementary-level students together with their parents. Denise also serves as the fourth-grade chairperson on the Chittenango Central School District's Elementary Curriculum Council, representing the curriculum concerns of all nine fourth-grade classroom teachers.

Over the past several years, Denise has actively been involved in researching critical issues in education such as guided reading, comprehension, and motivation at the intermediate levels and has been awarded numerous grants on these topics.

In addition to these roles, Denise is an active after-school instructor, offering creative programs in Readers Theatre and creative writing.

Denise is also a frequent speaker at conferences and workshops throughout the United States. *Quality Comprehension* is her first book.

Denise grew up in Liverpool, New York, and currently resides in Cazenovia, New York.

Author Information for Correspondence and Workshops

Sandra and Denise welcome questions and feedback from readers.
Sandra can be reached at athanss@ccs.cnyric.org.
Denise can be reached at devined@ccs.cnyric.org.

Our objective to *significantly* improve student reading comprehension began nearly 10 years ago. We had come together as a small group of third-, fourth-, and fifth-grade classroom teachers, realizing that we were providing instruction within grade levels where *learning to read* was supposed to have flip-flopped into *reading to learn*. The fact that this wasn't happening gracefully suggested we needed to intervene. To this end, our intent was to glean the best practices we could find and then refine them for classroom use at the intermediate-grade level. A focus on guided reading seemed the best avenue to take to launch this objective; it was an approach that not only had been successfully integrated at the lower elementary grades for many years but also was gaining acceptance as one suitable to adapt to the intermediate levels.

During the initial stages of our journey, we read books and articles, attended seminars, and even arranged site visits to other schools to observe classroom teachers who had been spotlighted by peers and colleagues for their successful practices. Always, we would try out these new ideas in our own classrooms—to the best of our ability. The logistics of meeting with multiple student reading groups, the lack of materials, and even our method of teaching, which was strategy-based instruction, seemed slow, cumbersome, and foreign. Although difficult for us, we were seeing small signs of improved comprehension skills in our students. So we persisted and continued to meet and develop what was clearly becoming a very different approach to reading instruction.

As time passed, we continued to be guided by the ideas and wisdom of those authorities who shared their practices in books and seminars. However, we also began to develop our own tools, such as our Read-Along Guides and our unit assessments, and we began to integrate our own practices, such as the use of Literacy Bins, to build background knowledge as well as to motivate students who intrinsically lacked this skill. Collectively, all of these efforts enabled us not only to tailor instruction but also to strengthen what we perceived as "needs" or "weak areas" that needed to be addressed within our classrooms. As a result, our students continued to demonstrate significant gains in their reading comprehension, which also put to rest our initial feelings of uneasiness and uncertainty.

Today, we (Sandra and Denise) have synthesized what we feel to be the most effective elements of guided reading and other best practices in order to meet our objective to create specific solutions that match our unique needs as intermediate-level teachers. In doing so, we've crafted a strategic form of reading comprehension instruction, which we call the Quality Comprehension Model.

Today we also seem to have come full circle in our quest; we are often asked to provide workshops and informational briefings at other school districts, for our regional teaching center, and even at major state and national reading conferences. Many of the classroom professionals who attend our workshops liken our approach to one in which key features of guided reading and differentiated instruction are blended. Perhaps this is true. We have always felt that our approach works because we shaped it to work with what we had—and, even more importantly, what we *didn't* have. As classroom teachers, we were painfully aware of our lack of materials, time, and support, among other things. Yet because of this, we came to rely on each other as our greatest resource so that we could share our strengths, tackle our challenges, and accomplish our goals within our district and within our individual classrooms. The closing line we often included as we informally passed feedback, suggestions, and materials back and forth—which we did very often—was, "Use this as you wish." These words best capture the spirit of our collective effort in a way that only a teacher-driven effort can. We think this, too, is why we continue to refine, build, and shape our approach. This collective effort seems to make it work!

In this book, we provide other teachers with a model of reading comprehension instruction that is based on sound foundational and classic practices and also on tried and tested classroom innovations. All have passed the rigors of extensive classroom use.

Who Should Read This Book

This book will be an asset to intermediate-level classroom teachers, whether they are new to the teaching profession and seek assistance building their instructional methods or whether they are skilled veterans who seek to broaden their masterfully crafted practices. In addition, discussions on ways to integrate content area reading within the Quality Comprehension Model will greatly help all intermediate-level teachers incorporate the demands of their content curriculum while they provide instruction in reading comprehension. Reading specialists and resource teachers will also benefit from the book by gleaning creative classroom-tested tips for providing strategy-based instruction to struggling intermediate-level readers.

Organization of This Book

In the Introduction, "Our Journey: The Development of the Quality Comprehension Model and the Read-Along Guide," we share key points of our journey as a way of offering a path to implement the Quality Comprehension Model. We describe our approach to reading comprehension instruction, highlighting the research-based theory that guided it as well as the unique features contributing to its success. Also included are key steps we took on our journey, which may serve as a useful guide during a start-up implementation plan.

Chapter 1, "Using the Quality Comprehension Model to Meet the Needs of Intermediate-Level Learners," discusses the specific needs of the intermediate-level learner and describes how these needs can be addressed through the use of small-group instruction, independent practice, and the Read-Along Guides. Suggestions on the logistics of implementing the approach, including scheduling and grouping students, are also provided as are helpful hints for instructional planning. The chapter concludes with guidelines on creating instructional unit plans and activities that help address two critical issues that challenge a student's ability to successfully use the strategies: lack of motivation and insufficient background knowledge.

Chapter 2, "Instruction in Key Comprehension Strategies: The Foundational Eight," includes in-depth discussion on eight comprehension strategies that teach critical foundational skills and seek to establish strong reading behaviors in students. Some help students avoid common pitfalls and problems that could result in confusion and misunderstanding, while others delve into ways of building meaning and understanding. Many of these foundational skills need to be in place before other, more complex skills can be developed. Chapter 3, "Instruction in Key Comprehension Strategies: The Skill-Building Nine," includes additional strategies we feel may be best thought of as outcome skills. Versions of these key strategies may be familiar to many of us in education. In both chapters, we've provided essential information on providing instruction on the strategies; the discussion of each strategy includes a difficulty rating for its use by students, teacher tips for strategy instruction, text suggestions, student-friendly chats, on the importance of the strategy, practice with prompts for the Read-Along Guide, key indicators of successful student performance, connections to other strategies, and test-taking tips.

Chapter 4, "Understanding, Creating, and Using the Read-Along Guide," shows you how the prompt pages for strategies shown in chapters 2 and 3 all fit together to form complete Read-Along Guides. The chapter provides thorough step-by-step instructions and a systematic approach to constructing Read-Along Guides, beginning with your text selection and continuing through tailoring your Guide to specific books and strategies. Within these steps we provide guidelines for many issues, such as format, inclusion of the written response section, and others, in order to aid you in the process.

Chapter 5, "The Written Response Section of the Read-Along Guide," defines and discusses the written response section of the Read-Along Guide. Here, teachers are guided through how to encourage their students to use this section to demonstrate their comprehension, extend their thinking, and monitor their own learning.

Chapter 6, "Reading Selections: Locating Materials for Use With the Read-Along Guide and Comprehension Strategy Instruction," shows you how to locate and build collections of reading materials for strategy instruction. In this chapter, we demonstrate that although you might not have a diverse and well-rounded selection of multiple-copy sets of books, this should not be a barrier that prevents you from getting started. We provide the essential steps that will help guide your initial actions toward building your collections, whether or not you have been given a budget to begin your strategy-based instruction.

Chapter 7, "Methods of Monitoring and Assessing Your Students' Small-Group and Independent Activities," offers guidelines for and methods of assessing students' group and independent work. Sample assessment tools are featured with discussion on how to best use them to communicate effectively with students as well as for teacher accountability issues.

Chapter 8, "The Quality Comprehension Model: Frequently Asked Questions" provides answers to some of the most frequently asked questions we receive during our workshops as well as some of the more puzzling questions we struggled with while shaping our Model. We have always allowed time for a question-and-answer period at our workshops, as we typically find that participants are at various stages of exploring or implementing their own comprehension improvement initiatives (even when participants are from the same district), and many have specific questions they need addressed so they can continue moving forward.

Appendixes provide a collection of aids or resources for teacher use. Appendix A, "Reproducible Read-Along Guides," offers blank reproducible Guides. Appendix B, "Reproducible Planning and Assessment Charts," provides reproducible charts for organizing reading groups, assessing student groups, and assessing students' independent work, among others. Electronic versions of the reproducible materials in Appendixes A and B can also be found online at www.reading.org on the webpage for this book (found in the Publications section of the site).

Acknowledgments

We consider ourselves extremely lucky to have been surrounded by many supportive and enthusiastic people during the entire process of preparing this book. We are particularly thankful to the following people:

- Everyone who over the many years assisted with our journey of research and discovery, including those teachers who have since retired or moved on to other grade levels

- Those theorists, authorities, pioneers, and practitioners who provided us with a solid foundation as a starting point and encouraged us, through the simple act of sharing their expertise, not to recreate the wheel

- Our long-time friends at the Central New York Teaching Center who, over the course of numerous years, supported and encouraged our continued work in this area by awarding us with numerous action research grants

- Our colleagues who enthusiastically participated in our studies and provided us with invaluable data, anecdotes, and information and to whom we remain grateful

- The Chittenango Central School District, including our administrators and board members, who encouraged us and provided start-up funds as well as green lights to move forward

- Finally, our readers

If you've picked up this book hoping to find some answers, a plan, or perhaps a little of both in your quest to improve student reading comprehension, we pass along these words to you in keeping with the spirit that enabled us to write it: *Use this as you wish!*

Our Journey: The Development of the Quality Comprehension Model and the Read-Along Guide

"Using the Read-Along Guide, together with the small-group instruction and independent practice, allows the teacher a lot of flexibility and control. The teacher can decide what books will be used, what strategies will be taught, and how those strategies will be taught. They can determine when, where, and how they should emphasize their instruction. They are in charge."

—Mrs. Stietz, fourth-grade teacher

"I think my reading comprehension has improved because I understand a lot more now than I did at the beginning of the year. The skills were easy to learn in small groups and my Guide let me practice until I got it right."

—Alexandra E., fifth-grade student

The Quality Comprehension Model, our four-part approach to reading comprehension instruction, is the product of a nearly 10-year journey and represents our answer to the question "How do we help our intermediate students become better readers?" To many, 10 years might be considered a long time to pursue an idea. Worse still, our concern—how do we help our students become better readers—was as old and tired as the nearly forgotten excuse "My dog ate it." Add to this the fact that answers were already out there; methodologies and best practices existed that authorities said "for sure" would help. In fact, the real idea we seemed to be considering was how we could integrate these best practices and our classroom instruction.

As classroom teachers, we knew that we didn't have much spare time, we couldn't afford significant errors, and any errors we made must be remedied quickly. Unlike in many other fields, an allowable learning curve in education is severely limited. Because of this, we prefer to call our lengthy pursuit of an idea to solve a long-existing problem a journey. Certainly, that sounds more enticing, with stumbling blocks and false starts inherently expected and a final destination perceived to exceed even the happiest of endings. Though we have traveled far, we are still on our journey.

We hope our journey might serve as a path for you to trace if you wish—though our hope in writing this book is that you will be able to benefit from our experience and achieve success much more swiftly than we did. We also want to provide encouragement (especially during the rocky start-up phase), and lastly, we wish to provide proper credit to the pioneers who cleared the way for our journey and laid the solid foundation upon which our approach is based.

As we near the end of a decade in our journey, we have organized our thoughts in three sections based on important events or activities that took place: our initial efforts in the first few years, significant gains in our progress spanning the next five years, and moving beyond as the journey continues. We then discuss what our approach looks like today and also provide some data on its success.

Initial Efforts: The First Few Years

Our initial efforts were largely based on the guided reading practices which, at that time, were mostly directed toward the lower elementary grades. We were interested in this approach as the elementary grades within our district and elsewhere were finding the practices beneficial. The landmark text *Guided Reading: Good First Teaching for All Children*, authored by literary mavericks Irene C. Fountas and Gay Su Pinnell (1996), was a resource we worked with, trying to modify and tailor the practices to the intermediate-level learner. We were especially pleased with the later publication of *Guiding Readers and Writers, Grades 3–6: Teaching Comprehension, Genre, and Content Literacy* (2001) also by Fountas and Pinnell. This confirmed the relevancy of the practices, with modifications, for intermediate learners and provided us with further direction.

We also attended a seminar by Joanne Monroe titled *Guided Reading: Teaching Strategies for Grades 3–8*, where we were introduced to the concept of a "bookmark" that was to be used by the student and was defined as "a sheet of paper folded into quarters" to be used as "a note-taking tool" (Monroe, 2002, p. 19). While quickly agreeing that many of the practices offered by these sources would work in the classroom, silent guided reading—a practice supported by Fountas and Pinnell (1996) as well as Monroe (2002)—was not as easy to grasp, and we wondered if this would work for all of our intermediate-grade readers.

Nonetheless, we tried out what we liked and even what we questioned; we placed students in groups and selected three different texts we leveled ourselves—high, medium, and low. Then, using strategies suggested by Monroe, we began, creating simple bookmarks, an early version of what later became the Read-Along Guide. Our first bookmark was a single, folded sheet of 8½ × 11 paper that we distributed to students along with sticky notes. Students used sticky notes to mark areas in their books that aligned with the strategies they were practicing—so as not to interrupt their reading—which they could return to later and then record on their bookmark. The four strategies students practiced were making connections, asking questions, figuring out vocabulary, and using fix-up strategies when they were confused.

Our single greatest error at that time was that we used works of fiction that were each over 100 pages long as our guided reading texts, including George Selden's *The Cricket in Times Square*, Roald Dahl's *James and the Giant Peach*, and Barbara Park's *Skinnybones*. For example, Figure 1 depicts a student's bookmark created during the reading of *The Cricket in Times Square*. As is evident, there were few components to this first bookmark. We provided some basic prompts, which were designed to assist students in applying the comprehension strategies. For example the prompt, "When I read page ____, I thought about..." was designed to help students make connections. Generally, we provided very basic prompts and encouraged students to include page numbers so we could return to the source when we discussed their strategy practice. We quickly agreed that our instruction was lengthy, cumbersome, and plodding—not at all what we had intended. We realized it would be too time-consuming to practice the four strategies and complete the reading. Pacing was an issue with these lengthier texts. (We have since become skilled using longer works but would caution against using them to launch this instructional approach.)

Another event that shaped our approach was a site visit we arranged with a neighboring school district. The teachers used a form of guided reading in their instruction and students had been increasing their performance on standardized state tests. We wanted a closer look. Although we envied their well-stocked and diverse collections of leveled texts, we marveled much more at the journal writing their students produced. Journal-writing activities happened elsewhere in our curriculum and were not purposefully a part of our guided reading instruction because it seemed that practicing comprehension strategies was somehow mismatched with reflective writing. Also, we thought it would be impractical for students to carry a separate journal to their small-group instruction when they already had to tote their book, their bookmark, a pencil, and sometimes a packet of sticky notes. Still, guided

FIGURE 1
Early Bookmark Created by Student During the Reading of *The Cricket in Times Square*

Bookmark for *The Cricket in Time Square*
When I read page _____, I thought about...

pg. 1 When I read page 1 a mouse is looking at Mario, it made me think about when I played Super Mario Brothers on Nintendo.

pg. 10 "A cricket he exclaimed!" It reminded me of when I caught a cricket.

pg. 18 This page made me think about living in a subway station. I don't think I'd like it.

pg. 21 "Especially around rush hour" made me think of when I saw the movie Rush Hour.

pg. 50 When Sai Frong asked Mario if he wanted a fortune cookie reminded me of when I went to a Chinese restaurant and we got a bunch of fortune cookies with our meals.

Words That Are New to Me—Clues Used:

pg. 1 scrounging- context

pg. 2 murmured- punctuation clue

pg. 12 sheen- thought what would make sense

pg. 20 haunches- context

pg. 21 liverwurst-context

pg. 27 frantic- context

pg. 73 smuggled- made sense

Questions I Would Ask and Answers to Those Questions

Chapt. 1 (pg. 3)- What is a shuttle train? A shuttle train is a subway train.

Chapt. 2 (pg. 12) What did Mario use the Matchbook for? He used it for a bed for the cricket.

Chapt. 4 (pg. 36) What was the counterman's name? His name was Mickey.

Chapt. 9 (pg. 81) What problem does Mario think his cricket has? He thinks it eats money.

Chapt. 11 Why did Mario's mom think the cricket was a jinx? She thought that because there was a fire and she blamed the cricket.

A Reader Might Be Confused When...

pg. 4 A reader might be confused when they read "the station of Time Square."

pg. 12 A reader might be confused when he reads "a tissue of Kleenex."

pg. 15 A reader might be confused when they read "a Sunday Times."

pg. 20 A reader might be confused when they read "He loved to hear stories". They might wonder who loves stories?

pg. 82 they read the word "tlee"

by our instincts and what we had witnessed, we added a response section to the bookmark. We had no idea then that the written response section would become as important as we consider it to be today.

Last, our small group was given start-up funds to purchase guided reading books, as our principal who accompanied us on the site visit was equally impressed with their book collections and encouraged us to begin building a collection of our own. We wanted to make good and equitable use of these funds for each of three grade levels represented in our building (grades 3 through 5) and first needed to get a quick inventory of what we had and what we needed. As a result, in one afternoon we leveled nearly all of the books in our collections using *Leveled Books for Readers Grades 3–6: A Companion Volume to* Guiding Readers and Writers (Fountas & Pinnell, 2002), identified gaps, and located publishers who were creating the small paperbound texts that were used for guided reading. We even e-mailed Joanne

Monroe and asked her opinion on the types of works we should purchase. She advised that we buy nonfiction materials to supplement our fiction-dominant current collections and that the shorter works would help with our pacing and start-up difficulties (personal communication, May 3, 2002). We followed her advice and bought three boxed sets, one intended for each of the three grade levels. We also ordered five-pack sets of nonfiction titles from another publisher, trying to fill content gaps with works that aligned with our science or social studies curriculum. These books would eventually become the focus of the next step of our growth.

Significant Gains: The Next Five Years

Although we continually worked with many texts and circulated journal articles from the International Reading Association, the Association for Supervision and Curriculum Development, and others, we also became familiar with *Strategies That Work: Teaching Comprehension to Enhance Understanding* (Harvey & Goudvis, 2000). This work captured exactly what explicit instruction in a selection of five comprehension strategies looked like through an array of case studies. The studies included teacher instruction, student activities, prompts, and pictures. This became another important source for us to help guide our approach.

In addition, *Reading is Thinking: A Metacognitive Approach to Reading With an Emphasis on Non-Fiction Texts* was a seminar we attended by presenter Debbie Ashmore (2003). Here, critical points were confirmed, such as the idea that providing explicit instruction in the comprehension strategies is integral (Ashmore's list of comprehension strategies was similar to others) and that a focus on nonfiction was key in the intermediate grades. By the end of her seminar, we had sketched a bookmark that featured a set of eight key strategies we had amassed from our collective sources, including those suggested by Fountas and Pinnell (2001); Harvey and Goudvis (2000); and Strickland, Ganske, and Monroe (2002):

1. Using fix-up methods when meaning is challenged
2. Finding word meaning and building vocabulary using context clues
3. Using visual text clues to figure out meaning
4. Asking questions to engage in the text
5. Making connections
6. Visualizing to support the text
7. Making predictions
8. Synthesizing to gain new meaning

This original list of eight comprised those that were most often cited by experts, except for the third, which we identified on our own. This bookmark, which Monroe (2002) referred to earlier as a "simple sheet of paper folded into quarters" now had a response section attached to the back as well as room to practice eight strategies. The bookmark was evolving into what we would eventually call a Read-Along Guide (which would be even further shaped over time).

Our idea behind this first Read-Along Guide was to introduce students to many things all at once—all eight strategies, using the Guide as an instructional practice tool, working comfortably in small groups and working independently doing "seatwork." If we could simply expose students to all this in the very first bookmark—swiftly—we would have a foundation upon which to build as we moved forward. In essence, we adjusted our expectations and began.

Surprisingly, this Introductory Read-Along Guide has changed little since its creation many years ago. We still feel that launching the instruction through quick-paced, brief exposure is a good way to begin, with subsequent Guides featuring slower-paced practice in fewer strategies. We even encourage students to create posters while working through these eight strategies and contribute examples of their use of the strategy. When we refer back to the posters, perhaps six months later, students easily call to mind their contribution and connect it to the overall strategy. Figure 2 shows two students contributing ideas to a strategy poster.

Although there were many theorists who had identified critical comprehension strategies, there was not an overabundance of guidelines for providing direct in-

FIGURE 2
Students Contributing Ideas to a Strategy Poster

struction in them. Though these strategies came automatically to skilled readers, we were still struggling to determine the best way to teach them through direct instruction. Ultimately we broke down these processes into discrete steps and gave students the opportunity to practice the steps and to learn and internalize them.

It is an understatement to say that the comprehension strategies were difficult to break apart and teach, yet it is even more of an understatement to express the degree of difficulty students had in their attempts to learn and perfect the use of the strategies when this skill does not come naturally. Harvey and Goudvis's (2000) work pointed us in the right direction, but we recognized that we would have to create activities and prompts for our own collection of strategies.

The prompts we devised and included in this book (see chapters 2 and 3) are ones that have stood the test of time. By listening to our students and through trial and error, we have constructed some that are very complex and others that are basic and forthright. Are there or could there be more? Of course! However, in this book you will find the activities and prompts that we found to be the most effective for revealing student understanding and targeting improvement in key comprehension strategies.

In addition to having created the Introductory Read-Along Guide, we also began to explore use of the small-format guided reading texts we were able to purchase with our start-up funds. Not only did these nonfiction books keep the pace of our instruction moving but they also enabled us to investigate how to integrate our content curriculum comfortably within our language arts instruction. Figure 3 features the cover of one of these small-format texts, *Cherokee Heroes: Three Who Made a Difference* (Hirschfield, 2001) alongside the early nonfiction Read-Along Guide created by a student based on that text. This Read-Along Guide featured a practice page and prompts that encouraged students to look for visual text clues of features they might find in a nonfiction text, together with the page number on which they found them to reference in follow-up discussion and instruction. Next, a written response section intended as a journal entry was included as an assessment activity. Lastly, building vocabulary and working with word meaning featured a prompt asking students to list difficult words. Methods of figuring out meaning for these difficult words were also included.

Moving Beyond: The Journey Continues

Witnessing a couple of years of success with our early Read-Along Guides, we grew convinced that they could become even more valuable if we extended their use more fully into the content areas, especially social studies where the curriculum was demanding. Based on our earlier successes, we were awarded a grant to create content-based Read-Along Guides that would align with our social studies curriculum. Using multiple works of historical fiction or informational nonfiction, we created the Guides and provided differentiated instruction to meet the needs of individual students while simultaneously covering topics mandated by our curriculum, such

FIGURE 3
Book Cover and Student Read-Along Guide for *Cherokee Heroes*

A. Cover of *Cherokee Heroes*

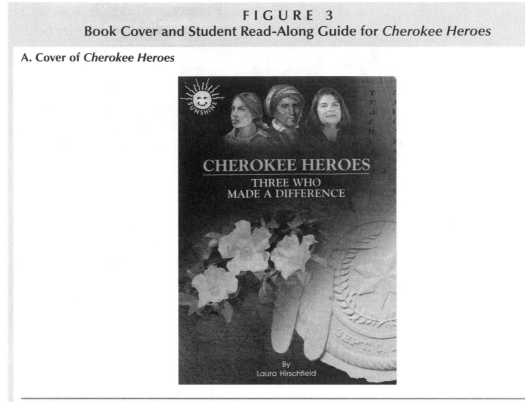

Cover from *Cherokee Heroes: Three Who Made a Difference* by Laura Hirschfield. © 2001 by Wright Group/McGraw-Hill. Reprinted with permission.

B. Early Read-Along Guide Created By Student Based on *Cherokee Heroes*

(continued)

Special Features of Nonfiction
Help Us Understand What We Read
During your reading, locate these special features and write down the page numbers where you found them. Be prepared to discuss how they helped you understand what you are reading.

Subheadings pg. 5, 17. 17
Photographs pg. 4, 7, 14, 15, 19, 21, 23, 27, 28
Captions pg. 7, 13, 14, 15, 19, 27, 28, 29, 31
Maps pg. 5, 13
Sidebars pg. 17, 25
Bold/Italics _____
Title pg. 5
Content & Glossary and index pg. 32
Chapter title pg. 12, 20, 20, 26
Symbols pg. 14, 12, 20

Possible Ideas For Your Journal
Entries Could Be:

1. What was going through your mind as you read this?
2. What questions did you have when you finished reading?
3. What would you do if this happened to you?
4. How did you feel while reading this part?
5. What was the most important idea?
6. How are you similar to one of the characters?
7. What predictions do you have about the next reading.

1-18 My response to today's reading is that I thought it was very fun because I love learning about Indians and history. I can't wait to read the rest of the story. I want to know what happens to the three main Cherokee Indians. I wonder why the Europeans were so selfish. They

should not have taken their land.

1-19 My response to today's reading is that I think it would be pretty hard to motivate the warriors to win because the other Indians could probably kill you. I can kind of believe that Nancy was that brave to motivate the warriors, so she deserves the reward of the beloved woman. I don't know if she had all of her bravery. Hey, maybe I could have done that. I wonder what the boys are named. It is definitely, positively beloved boy.

1-22 My response to today's reading is that this is the best chapter I have read yet! It really shows me I should never give up. I mean, it took Sequoyah 125 years to make the alphabet. Even though people called him crazy and a fool he never gave up. I can hardly believe it. He probably went through a lot of hard work just to help his fellow Cherokees.

Words or concepts that were difficult for me—Page # word
Pg. 6 voluntarily
retrieve

Some strategies to help with difficult words are:
1. Use context clues
2. "Chunk" the word
3. Link the word to a known word
4. What makes sense
5. Look for smaller words
6. Other

as immigration (see Appendix B for a reproducible version of the instructional unit plan).

Although daunting at first, creating a collection of Read-Along Guides helped propel us forward and even gave us the impetus to step into the spotlight where we shared our work with teachers and other professionals outside of our district through workshops, seminars, and local and national conferences. Initially, we were surprised that many of the practicing professionals attending our discussions enthusiastically referred to our Read-Along Guide as "the missing link" in their own small-group reading instruction. Yet for those who had not witnessed its evolution, it was easy to see how it could be likened to a missing link. It was a device that enabled students to not only practice a "thinking" skill but also at the same time provide teachers with written insights on a student's level of understanding. Without it, much was left unknown.

Although we had been working for several years as a self-guided, self-motivated pair with our group, our district had taken an active interest in small-group, differentiated reading instruction from the start. Then, beginning in 2004, our district required all teachers at the elementary levels to incorporate guided reading with their reading programs, using leveled texts and a small-group configuration for instruction. They also required that benchmark assessments be performed on all students to determine beginning and year-end reading levels. These initiatives were to take place at the end of that academic year and carry into the 2005–2006 year. Training was provided and numerous in-house offerings were made available to explore this approach. Likewise, we were also asked to adopt a collection of 12 comprehension strategies that had been published in *Strategies to Achieve Reading Success* (Curriculum Associates, 2000b):

1. Finding main idea
2. Recalling facts and details
3. Understanding sequence
4. Recognizing cause and effect
5. Comparing and contrasting
6. Making predictions
7. Finding word meaning in context
8. Drawing conclusions and making inferences
9. Distinguishing between fact and opinion
10. Identifying author's purpose
11. Interpreting figurative language
12. Distinguishing between real and make-believe

In order to provide a starting point for those teachers who had not integrated guided reading into their reading programs, while still permitting those of us who had years of experience to move forward from where we were, the district allowed flexibility in how we conducted our instruction. As a result, we incorporated these 12 and our original 8 into one group and, after eliminating duplicates, now work comfortably with the following 17:

1. Using fix-up methods when meaning is challenged
2. Finding word meaning and building vocabulary using context clues
3. Using visual text clues to figure out meaning
4. Asking questions to engage in the text
5. Making connections to aid understanding
6. Visualizing to support the text
7. Making predictions
8. Synthesizing to gain new meaning
9. Finding the important or main idea
10. Identifying facts and details
11. Telling fact from opinion
12. Understanding sequence
13. Comparing and contrasting
14. Interpreting figurative language
15. Recognizing cause-and-effect relationships
16. Drawing conclusions and making inferences
17. Summarizing

These strategies will be discussed in greater detail in chapter 1 and will be explored fully in chapters 2 and 3.

We were also fortunate in having received two additional grants that enabled us to study the success of our approach through the preparation and analysis of formal assessments (which we discuss later in this chapter) and to investigate methods to address students who lacked the motivation to apply themselves and benefit from this successful approach (and academic success, in general). We have included information on some of the activities related to these grants.

Today: The Quality Comprehension Model— A Four-Part Approach to Reading Comprehension

Over the course of nearly a decade of classroom research and experience, our reading comprehension instruction progressed and evolved as outlined in the previous sections. Today, we describe the process as a four-part approach called the Quality Comprehension Model, and it was developed from the classroom trials and experiences of providing the most effective strategy-based comprehension instruction for intermediate-level students that we could conceive. The components of the Model are as follows:

1. Teacher-led **instruction in key comprehension strategies** incorporates the use of teacher-selected materials including basal readers, newspapers, guided reading books, or other types of literature. This instruction is often provided in homogenous small groups—in other words, groups where students share similar reading levels or struggle with the same comprehension strategies.

2. A **Read-Along Guide**, which is a writing component used by the student, is used to support the reading instruction.

3. **Independent activities** allow students to practice the strategies they have learned through direct instruction, reading on independently, or writing in the journal component of their Guide.

4. **Assessments** follow each unit of instruction, allowing teachers to determine if a student has achieved an acceptable level of competency with a skill and also enabling students to demonstrate in writing what they have learned.

In chapter 1, you will learn more about each of these components of the Model, and the chapters that follow thereafter are devoted to further explorations of each component.

Strengths of Our Approach

When asked what makes the Quality Comprehension Model unique from those already described in other texts, our response comes quickly:

- We have successfully used the Model with a variety of reading materials, including basal readers, content area texts, small-format guided reading books, fiction and nonfiction, content area literature, and more.

- We have developed a multiple-page tool, the Read-Along Guide, which enables students to practice what they've learned from their instruction. In the Guide, students can also extend and support their own learning in the written response section.

- We have designed the Model to encourage, suggest, and allow for easy integration of modified instructional methods so that instruction can be tailored to meet the needs of individual students.

- We have provided experience-based prompts and guidelines that aid users in delivering successful instruction while also avoiding common pitfalls.

- We have built into our Model suggestions for blending test-taking concerns with comprehension-building instruction—a concern aligned with recent mandated testing requirements.

- We have devised project-based and more traditional assessments to be used during and following each unit of instruction and included sample formats and guidelines.

- We are classroom teachers and have shaped our approach in our classrooms, pooling our collective insights as well as our ability to troubleshoot typical problems.
- We have identified key barriers that stall or threaten progress—such as a lack of student motivation or minimal background knowledge—and have devised methods to remedy these barriers within the approach.
- We have used as a foundation a collection of best practices from a variety of leading authorities, unburdened by having to confine our practices to one way of doing things or one specific philosophy.

Just as these unique features contribute to the success and strength of this approach, so, too, have those best practices mentioned earlier and as the final item in the list above. These practices we adopted from knowledgeable, respected authorities, many noted earlier in this chapter. Additionally, a must-have list of suggested texts on best practices for intermediate-level readers appears in Table 1. Many are probably already among your reference collection and dog-eared from use. Just as many guided us, we trust they will be helpful for you as well.

Measures of Our Success

There are many ways we have measured the success of the Quality Comprehension Model. An informal but powerful indicator of our success is the positive reactions we have received from students and teachers who have used our Quality Comprehension Model and the Read-Along Guide. Throughout our journey, we have collected many students' thoughts and reactions to various components of our approach, using them originally to alter or tweak what we were doing. Their voices also touted their successful learning and thus the success of our approach. We have included some of their comments in the chapter-opening pages of this book. It's an interesting task to ask students to reflect on their own learning. And at first, listening to their responses takes some getting used to. "Do you feel comfortable making connections with events you've never actually experienced? Are you able to make pictures in your mind of places you've never been based on descriptive passages in the text? Which methods did you use to figure out the meaning of difficult words? Can you support your prediction using details from the text? Which strategy helped you better understand this passage and why?" These are the types of questions and discussions that students and teachers engage in during instruction. Student and teacher voices throughout the book clearly confirm that we have affected them and, likewise, that they have affected us, too.

Together with these informal indicators of success, we also conducted several action research studies, funded by the Central New York Teaching Center, to investigate multiple aspects of our approach. One year, several classroom teachers we worked with specifically undertook a study to determine the success of the approach. In this study, 26 students were selected from three separate fourth-grade classrooms

> **TABLE 1**
> **Recommended Text Sources for Strategy-Based Reading Comprehension Instruction at the Intermediate Level**
>
> Curriculum Associates. (2000). *Strategies to achieve reading success: STARS series books 3, 4, & 5.* North Billerica, MA: Author.
>
> Fountas, I.C., & Pinnell, G.S. (1996). *Guided reading: Good first teaching for all children.* Portsmouth, NH: Heinemann.
>
> Fountas, I.C., & Pinnell, G.S. (1996). *Teaching for comprehension and fluency: Thinking, talking, and writing about reading, K–8.* Portsmouth, NH: Heinemann.
>
> Fountas, I.C., & Pinnell, G.S. (2001). *Guiding readers and writers, grades 3–6: Teaching comprehension, genre, and content literacy.* Portsmouth, NH: Heinemann.
>
> Harvey, S., & Goudvis, A. (2000). *Strategies that work: Teaching comprehension to enhance understanding.* York, ME: Stenhouse.
>
> Harvey, S., & Goudvis, A. (2007). *Strategies that work: Teaching comprehension to enhance understanding* (2nd ed.). Portland, ME: Stenhouse.
>
> Keene, E.O., & Zimmermann, S. (2007). *Mosaic of thought: The power of comprehension strategy instruction* (2nd ed.). Portsmouth, NH: Heinemann.
>
> McLaughlin, M. (2002). *Guided comprehension in action: Lessons for grades 3–8.* Newark, DE: International Reading Association.
>
> McLaughlin, M., & Allen, M.B. (2002). *Guided comprehension: A teaching model for grades 3–8.* Newark, DE: International Reading Association.
>
> Oczkus, L.D. (2003). *Reciprocal teaching at work: Strategies for improving reading comprehension.* Newark, DE: International Reading Association.
>
> Strickland, D.S., Ganske, K., & Monroe, J.K. (2002). *Supporting struggling readers and writers: Strategies for classroom interventions, 3–6.* Portland, ME: Stenhouse; Newark, DE: International Reading Association.
>
> **Text Sources for Leveled Books at the Intermediate Level**
>
> Fountas, I.C., & Pinnell, G.S. (2002). *Leveled books for readers grades 3–6: A companion volume to Guiding Readers and Writers.* Portsmouth, NH: Heinemann.
>
> Fountas, I.C., & Pinnell, G.S. (2006). *The Fountas & Pinnell leveled book list, K–8.* Portsmouth, NH: Heinemann.
>
> Fountas, I.C., & Pinnell, G.S. (2006). *Leveled books, K–8: Matching texts to readers for effective teaching.* Portsmouth, NH: Heinemann.
>
> Weaver, B.M. (2000). *Leveling books K–6: Matching readers to text.* Newark, DE: International Reading Association.

based on their "near or below grade level" or "inconsistent" performance on reading comprehension assessments. They were provided with instruction in eight comprehension strategies in a small-group environment using Read-Along Guides. The study was based on two separate pre- and postassessments: the *Comprehensive Assessment of Reading Strategies II* (Curriculum Associates, 2000a) and a New York state reading comprehension sample test (McGraw-Hill, 1998). Additionally, pre- and post-Rigby PM Benchmarks (Nelley & Smith, 2000) were administered to each participant to identify student reading performance level.

At the end of the study we learned that over a seven-month period, student comprehension increased an average of 23.8%, while student reading performance increased an average of two levels. Likewise, we learned that students also progressed in their ability to demonstrate in writing their reading comprehension. These data were based on the written essay component of unit assessments. Here, student average performance of 69% in September rose to 75% in March. Certainly these results were encouraging.

We also relied on our standardized state test results to provide a further measure of our students' performance over time. Located in a primarily rural area in the northeastern part of the United States, our district comprises a large and economically diverse population in which over 25% of the students, on average, are eligible for free or reduced-price school lunches. The number of students who passed our standardized fourth-grade English language arts test within the same classrooms participating in the earlier study over four consecutive years (during the time when our approach was taking shape) are as follows: in 2004 83% passed, in 2005 100% passed, in 2006 97% passed, and in 2007 94% passed. The three fourth-grade classrooms averaged 20 students per class and represented a typical and randomly grouped student population. We believe that our approach to reading comprehension instruction described in this book contributed to this success.

Your Journey: A Beginning

As you move forward with implementing the Quality Comprehension Model in your classroom, know that we are cheering for you, especially during those times when you might make mistakes or grow frustrated when your plans don't turn out the way you had expected. We found it was helpful to remember and celebrate our successes along the way, no matter how little or insignificant they seemed. We continue to do this today as we further refine, shape, and extend our own journey.

Using the Quality Comprehension Model to Meet the Needs of Intermediate-Level Learners

"My students come to me bringing what often seems like more differences than similarities. Their experiences, understandings, and attitudes vary greatly, just as the range of skill among them can seem to be anywhere from one to four grade levels apart. Despite these differences, I must deliver one curriculum that's been set by state and district standards. It seems that having the ability to address each student's unique needs and finding the means to strengthen for each student any unique areas that need attention, is what's essential to make my task challenging, and not simply impossible."

—Ms. T., fourth-grade teacher

"I like that the things we practice in our reading group can help us with all of our reading."

—Hunter B., third-grade student

While intermediate-level readers strive to improve reading fluency and comprehension as a way of increasing their knowledge, many are nonetheless hindered by their struggles to read. Students in the intermediate grades must be able to read proficiently in the content areas in order to continue to build their knowledge. When reading difficulties interfere with this process, readers struggle to create and build foundational knowledge. Over time, the impact of this problem is so far reaching that it affects all academic areas and widens the gap between successful readers and those who perpetually struggle. The Quality Comprehension Model addresses these struggles. In essence, we wanted a blending of the right practices, the right materials, and the right focus and direction to best support instruction for students at this level. The Quality Comprehension Model provided this blending.

Challenges in Meeting the Needs of Intermediate-Level Learners

When we informally asked a group of teachers of grades 3 through 6 what generalizations they could make about their students' abilities to ease into the intermediate-grade curriculum, the following were the responses most often repeated:

- The curriculum seemed, at times, challenging for many students, in both scope and depth, and background knowledge seemed a critical factor affecting this.
- The absence of foundational skills now posed significant stumbling blocks for building new knowledge.
- Parental assistance with homework and academic support showed some signs of weakening although their encouragement may have remained steady.
- Students who were building their organizational skills, independence, and self-monitoring abilities met with a smoother transition than those who weren't.

When asked this same question in terms of how students transitioned into the language arts curriculum, especially reading, the following are some of the typical responses we heard:

- Reading informational or nonfiction text (typically in the content areas) posed some degree of challenge for most students, especially struggling readers.
- The range of reading ability among individuals in a class was great and was apparent even as students read works of fiction (students generally seemed more comfortable with works of fiction than with informational or nonfiction works).
- Those students who did not have strong foundational reading skills struggled with many reading tasks that fell outside of the language arts curriculum.

• Students' attitudes about reading differed greatly, with some expressing and showing great interest and others demonstrating the opposite.

The final question we asked these intermediate-grade teachers was what they viewed as their single greatest obstacle to helping all students succeed academically. The typical response we heard was that students had different needs, and it was difficult, if not impossible, for one person (even with assistance from aides or resource specialists) to address all of those needs, especially when facing the challenge of having to provide a demanding curriculum. Although this informal discussion took place with a group of teachers in our district, it would not take a great stretch of the imagination to assume that the same concerns would be voiced within school districts everywhere.

Although these concerns are ones that have been echoed over time, there were others that seemed more current. Addressing intermediate-grade students' academic needs today—in general terms as well as within the language arts curriculum—seems different, more challenging, than it was years ago, and it appears there may be several reasons for this.

One possible reason is that state and national standards have established criteria specifying what all students are required to know in all subject areas. Most teachers would agree that the standards are rigorous, requiring all elementary-level students to perform challenging skills and achieve a degree of proficiency with them. For example, New York state standards (New York State Education Department, 1996, p. 1) require that elementary-level students exhibit reading, writing, listening, and speaking skills across the following four broad spectrums:

• For information and understanding

• For literary response and understanding

• For critical analysis and evaluation

• For social interaction

The state also recently provided an increased level of specificity for each of the learning standards (New York State Education Department, 2005), of which a selection for fourth-grade students states that they will

• Collect and interpret data, facts, and ideas from unfamiliar texts

• Select books independently to meet informational needs

• Make inferences and draw conclusions, with assistance, based on information from text

• Use text features, such as captions, charts, tables, graphs, maps, notes, and other visuals, to understand and interpret informational texts

• Recognize, with assistance, how the author uses literary devices, such as simile, metaphor, and personification, to create meaning

• Analyze ideas and information on the basis of prior knowledge and personal experience

- Identify, with assistance, different perspectives, such as social, cultural, ethnic, and historical, on an issue presented in more than one text
- Make predictions, draw conclusions, and make inferences about events and characters

Impressive standards like these are paralleled in many locations, and although members within our discussion group did not argue the benefits of setting high standards, the challenge to do so successfully was most often the root of their concern.

In addition, addressing intermediate-grade students' academic needs today seems more challenging because changes in technology and information sources put additional literacy demands on all readers. Not only is there simply more information but it is also easily accessible and always changing. Though few will argue the benefits, the information boom has placed new demands upon our students that must be addressed. New literacies, representing the Internet and other information and communication technologies (ICTs), broadens the implication of what constitutes literacy and has added to our already full curriculum the need for instruction in their use. According to Leu (2001), teachers' concerns must be directed at a new definition of literacy and at ways in which they can help children to continuously become literate. The implications of developing ongoing and changing proficiencies with ICTs adds to what some teachers might consider an already fast-paced and full curriculum. Still, the benefits and necessity of doing so are not questioned.

Furthermore, two additional major obstacles we identified through our research that jeopardized a student's ability to succeed are lack of motivation and insufficient background knowledge. When our comprehension improvement effort was well underway, data we collected and then analyzed on student performance led us to conclude that although the approach was clearly successful with most, there remained a small percentage of otherwise capable students who showed little gain in their reading comprehension skill development as a result of these issues. Just as we had launched our approach by reviewing and addressing the needs of our students, we quickly added these two obstacles to that list, recognizing that they, too, must be addressed in order to enable all students to succeed.

Finally, another challenge is that each student follows a different path in learning. Teachers know instinctively that not every student is taking away the same thing from whole-class instruction. According to some experts, when a teacher tries to teach the same thing to the entire class at the same time, chances are some of the students will already know it, some will get it, and some won't. Therefore, it could be possible that many of your students are not benefiting from instruction. This reality is largely based on the fact that students are at different levels of readiness to learn and, subsequently, will require different assistance to realize the objective of a lesson. According to Tomlinson (1999), differentiation requires that teachers possess a true understanding of the fact that all students differ and must do whatever it takes to get the whole range of students interested in learning.

Collectively, these ideas helped forge our plans to create an instructional approach for intermediate-level learners that would not only address concerns for covering the curriculum but also address the unique literacy needs of our students. We wanted to create a model that would encourage reading skill development and minimize obstacles that prevented students from making gains in that development. In order to do this, we reshaped and adapted the guided reading program that had been used and is still used at the lower elementary levels within our district. In essence, we borrowed and kept the idea of providing direct, small-group instruction in select comprehension strategies (though we included more strategies); however, we added to this our need for a program that would align with the rigorous curriculum and would address the needs of intermediate-level learners and their teachers. The Quality Comprehension Model is the outcome of our efforts. It blends best practices such as guided reading and differentiated instruction with proven methods of instruction such as strategy-based comprehension. Likewise, it takes into account the unique circumstances of intermediate-level students, such as their need to meet the challenge of rigorous standards, to grasp new and complex ideas that span the scope of their content area curriculum, and even to explore new literacies. In addition to this, the Model is purposefully flexible and thus it is able to support teachers as well as students in the manner in which each will benefit most. It is a model that promotes quality—quality comprehension.

The Components of the Quality Comprehension Model

The Quality Comprehension Model comprises the following four components, or critical factors, that we found most effective in enabling us to reach our goal of helping our students become better readers:

1. Instruction in Key Comprehension Strategies
2. Use of a Read-Along Guide
3. Independent Reading and Practice Activities
4. Assessments

In essence, these four components represented the outcome of our work to integrate best practices and instructional methods within a flexible framework in which we could target the unique needs of intermediate-level students. In some way, either collectively or independently, these components allowed us to address nearly every area of concern expressed by teachers at the onset of this chapter, no matter if the concerns were ones that had been echoed over time or if they were based on more contemporary issues.

Instruction in Key Comprehension Strategies

Instruction in key comprehension strategies is vital to our reading instruction. Teachers meet with small groups of students who share similar reading skill and ability. During this instructional time, teachers typically provide direct instruction, monitor student progress, and then assign independent work. Key comprehension strategies comprise the content taught during direct instruction.

As mentioned in the Introduction (see pages 5–11), the 17 strategies we focused on have been collected from a variety of sources and, in essence, represent the activities or skills that good readers come to use instinctively. Versions of these strategies are so familiar to those of us in the teaching profession that it's difficult, if not impossible, to credit any single source as their originator. Likewise, we found it difficult to remain "pure" to any single specialist's strategies because our experience suggested that we pick and choose from all in an attempt to use what is most useful. As a result, we added to our list and also pulled from it over the course of our investigation.

For the purpose of including a selection that would be useful to as wide a readership as possible, we included all of the strategies we worked with extensively and could thoroughly and credibly comment on. Today, it is generally agreed by authorities that it is most productive to teach a few strategies so that they are learned well (Gambrell, 2007; Trehearne, 2007). However, we were also aware that many of the strategies needed little or brief instruction (Willingham, 2006/2007). We balanced these ideas, being able and ready to provide instruction in all as necessary, always taking our cues from the direction in which our students pointed us. Table 2 provides a list of these 17 strategies and descriptions of the skills involved in their use.

Detailed suggestions for providing instruction in each of these strategies appear in chapters 2 and 3. We clustered the strategies into two groups: the foundational eight and the skill-building nine. The first set of strategies, the foundational eight, are critical foundational skills and seek to establish strong reading behaviors in students. The skill-building nine, on the other hand, are outcome skills, in that they represent successful skills proficient readers are capable of demonstrating. The distinction among the two collections seems less important than determining which among them will best help your students. Certainly you can select and choose those strategies you deem appropriate for your classroom and student needs.

The Read-Along Guide

The Read-Along Guide is a multipage booklet used by the student during small-group instruction and independent reading and practice. The Guide is indisputably the most critical component used within our approach. It serves to reinforce direct instruction in a selection of the comprehension strategies by providing prompts, or cues, that help students apply and practice the strategies while they read. In essence, the Guide seeks to replicate actions that skilled readers use automatically to construct meaning.

TABLE 2
Comprehension Strategies—Skills Good Readers Use

Comprehension Strategies	Description
1. Using fix-up methods when meaning is challenged	1. When meaning is lost, students must become aware and take action—reread a passage, review earlier sections, or read on for about two sentences.
2. Finding word meaning and building vocabulary using context clues	2. Coming across new and unknown words is common. Sounding out, chunking, and linking words are tools to aid us while using context clues to make meaning of words or phrases.
3. Using visual text clues to figure out meaning	3. Text features such as punctuation, type font, spacing, titles, and subtitles give clues to aid meaning.
4. Asking questions to engage in the text	4. Engaged readers ask and answer who, what, when, where, and how questions as they read.
5. Making connections to aid understanding	5. Prior knowledge and experience help us connect to our reading and in turn build our knowledge.
6. Visualizing to support the text	6. Readers make pictures in their mind of the people, places, or events they're reading about.
7. Making predictions	7. Engaged readers often make logical predictions about what will happen next in the story.
8. Synthesizing to gain new meaning	8. Students construct new meaning to build their knowledge and even create new understandings.
9. Finding the important or main idea	9. The important idea is the point or message conveyed in the passage.
10. Identifying facts and details	10. The facts and details provide substance to a reading passage and support important and main ideas.
11. Telling fact from opinion	11. Distinguishing fact from opinion helps readers build a deeper understanding of their reading.
12. Understanding sequence	12. Making sense of the order in which ideas are presented enables students to build comprehension.
13. Comparing and contrasting	13. Considering ways in which ideas relate to something else—either through similarities or differences—is an avenue to develop understanding.
14. Interpreting figurative language	14. Understanding creative techniques authors use to convey meaning—such as similes, metaphors, personification, and more—helps aid comprehension.
15. Recognizing cause-and-effect relationships	15. Understanding relationships between ideas helps students grasp meaning by linking outcomes to causes.
16. Drawing conclusions and making inferences	16. Students often use a "sixth sense" or their inferential skills to interpret actions, events, or characters' motives or feelings.
17. Summarizing	17. Providing a brief description of critical information is one way students can hone their comprehension.

Guides are typically used during small-group instruction, where they support the teacher as he or she introduces, models the use of, and monitors student progress with each strategy. For example, a teacher may ask students in a small group to follow along in their own Guides as she reads the description of a strategy that appears in the Guide and then discusses how the students will practice using the strategy with the prompt (also supplied in the Guide). Next, she might model use of that strategy through a think-aloud while reading a short passage from a text and then demonstrate how she would record her use of the strategy in the space provided on the Guide. The teacher might ask students to copy her example so they can refer to it as they independently practice using the strategy and recording their use in their Guides. Last, the teacher might ask students to then read quietly and try applying the strategy on their own, which the teacher will review before that small-group instruction concludes. When used in this manner, the Guide becomes the primary device that teachers use to launch and build student knowledge and skill with the comprehension strategies during small-group instruction.

The Guides are also used independently by the students most often following the small-group instruction for further strategy practice and skill development. Here, students may return to their seat, where they will practice applying the strategies while they read, recording their experiences in their Guide. Everything they need to succeed with their independent practice is available in their Guide: descriptions of the strategies, examples provided by their teacher, practice examples they completed with their teacher, prompts to launch their practice, and space to accommodate their practice.

Guides may be used flexibly to address the independent needs of the students. For example, they can be used either during small-group instruction, whole-class instruction, or as students work independently at their seats. In essence, they can be used to support extensive direct instruction provided by the teacher, or they can be used with little direct instruction. In addition to this, teachers can determine how much or how little practice may be necessary with any given strategy. This, too, is another flexible feature of the Guides that aligns the independent needs of the student with the focus of the instruction.

The Read-Along Guide will be discussed in depth in chapter 4, and chapter 5 focuses specifically on the response section of the Guide. Guides that may be reproduced for classroom use appear in Appendix A. Electronic versions of these reproducible Guides can also be found online at www.reading.org on the webpage for this book (found in the Publications section of the site).

Independent Reading and Practice Activities

Although students are provided with small-group, teacher-led direct instruction in specific comprehension strategies, in the Quality Comprehension Model students are also given the opportunity to work independently. The type of independent work and the length of time allowed for this activity will vary among reading groups. It is often based on what occurs during the small-group, teacher-led activity. For example, a group may end up needing more support with a teacher, which would then cut into their independent work time. Although the teacher's objectives were set before instruction began, adjustments may need to be made based on the monitoring that took place during the instructional activity.

During this independent time, students might practice applying the strategies while they read and record their experiences in their Guide. They might also be writing a journal entry about their reaction to their reading. Alternatively, they could be reviewing teacher notes in their Guide and making adjustments to entries they made earlier in their strategy practice. This independent time is critical for many reasons. It allows students practice time to reinforce their understanding. It also provides them with time to examine and record their thinking or to consider how to express their ideas concisely. Allowing students the time to do this sends a clear message that this process is valued. Another benefit is that the teacher is able to meet with other small groups, provide direct instruction to others, or assist struggling students as necessary; in essence, the teacher can use the opportunity to effectively make best use of his or her time.

Assessments

Each unit of instruction, which may last 5 to 15 days, is typically followed by an assessment. Over time, we developed two types of assessments. One is patterned after our state language arts test and relies on the use of multiple-choice questions as well as short- and extended-response questions. The other is project-based. Though different in format, the objective of both is twofold. First, they assess a student's ability to demonstrate use of the skills and strategies that were taught during the instructional unit. Second, they assess comprehension of the topic or genre presented in the unit. Teachers decide which format they would like to use. Chapter 7 includes a thorough discussion on assessments and includes samples of both types.

The Model in Action: The Big Picture of Small-Group Instruction and Independent Work

Generally, all students—no matter which group they are in—will be instructed on the same comprehension strategies. Typically, each group will be using a text that is appropriate for their reading ability (though adjustments may be made through varying degrees of teacher support as necessary, which is discussed in chapter 4). Each student will be required to read some of their text independently, with more support offered to the students with greater need. Likewise, after being instructed on comprehension strategies, the students who are able to complete the Read-Along Guide with little guidance will be encouraged to do so and will be challenged with extension activities, while those needing more guidance may be given extra prompts, examples, more direction, and more overall support. Throughout the process, all students will come to a reading group to share insights, responses, and ideas. Also during this small-group instructional time, students may read aloud to the teacher or the group, and extensive teacher modeling as well as peer modeling of the use of strategies takes place. Teachers also monitor student progress and adjust direct and independent instruction as appropriate. (Further information detailing some specifics on instructional lesson styles—from methods of conveying daily assignments to ways in which small-group instruction may be launched—are discussed later in this chapter.)

Guiding Questions to Consider When Deciding on Instructional Settings and Grouping

A variety of configurations for instruction may be used with this approach, including whole-class, small-group, and independent work. When and where to use each one is best determined by the teacher or teachers providing instruction and may depend on a number of factors. Consider the following questions and how they apply to your classroom:

- Is support available through a reading teacher or aide? If support is available, how often and for how long?
- What is your class size, what are your students' needs, and what is the range of their abilities?
- How much material do you have, and are you limited in space?
- What strategies are planned, and are some more difficult than others?
- How many days will be needed for the instruction?

Answers to many of these questions may not be simple. For example, you may have support but only for three days per week; you may have ample materials on some subjects but not on others; and some students may need a lot of support to build background knowledge on a subject prior to reading instruction. These demonstrate just a few of the situations that need to be addressed when trying to plan instruction. Recognizing that your needs and your students' needs change depending upon these types of factors, you should understand that you can approach your grouping and instructional setting decisions with an open mind and remain flexible. What will work for one instructional unit may need to be changed for another, and what worked one year with one class may not work another year with another class. Although this may be difficult to consider at first, we found that it becomes easier with time. However, we identified some pointers that might be helpful with each of these concerns.

Is Support Available Through a Reading Teacher or Aide? If so, How Often and for How Long? If support is available, following the format presented in the Read-Along Guide—and adjusting the instruction and expectations to students' needs— makes it relatively easy for a classroom teacher and a reading specialist to juggle multiple groups as their schedule permits. Also, the reading specialist can aid in all components within the Quality Comprehension Model; he or she can deliver instruction and monitor students' independent work, all the while providing immediate assistance as necessary. They can also help administer assessments. In our experience, some years we were fortunate to have the support of a reading specialist through our Academic Intervention Support (AIS) services and were able to rely on the expertise of another professional. Typically, the AIS teacher worked with one group of students throughout the duration of class instructional time, while we provided instruction for two other groups, either by dividing up the class time evenly or otherwise. Depending on how many days per week AIS support was available, we provided whole-group instruction at times, while at other times we relied on independent skill practice and one-on-one monitoring. You may consider doing the same, knowing the flexibility of the Model will easily accommodate this.

What Is Your Class Size, What Are Your Students' Needs, and What Is the Range of Their Abilities? Students can be clustered into groups according to your responses to these questions. Although literacy experts agree that smaller group sizes are better, teachers often must group students according to more practical criteria such as available teacher and support resources and time (not to mention available materials and classroom space). We initially grouped our students according to multiple performance indicators: the Rigby Benchmark Program (Nelley & Smith, 2000), state test results, and classroom assessments and performance. Of course, grouping is flexible, and students may change groups from one unit to the next. We tried to work with groups of four to eight students and typically had three to four groups in each class with a range of reading levels from M–T (Fountas & Pinnell, 2001), which loosely translates to below, on, or above grade level. We tried to meet with each group every day for anywhere from 10 to 30 minutes.

How Much Material Do You Have, and Are You Limited in Space? Although you may not like it, at times the quantity of materials you have might dictate whether or not you have multiple groups meeting simultaneously or not. If students must share reading materials, this might be the criteria you use to determine how you cluster students for instruction, and that's fine. Keep in mind that accumulating a supply of materials is ongoing and takes time, which is a topic discussed in chapter 6. Likewise, if you are limited by space—your classroom might be small or a specialist, if available, doesn't have a separate room—you might have to rely on a whole-class setting that better addresses your inability to break up into small groups. If this is the case, providing individual student support might mean stopping at each student's work area and spending several minutes with that student.

As you may not often have enough leveled material in some content areas, you might decide to use one text for the whole class and vary the teacher support provided during instruction. Similarly, at one time we did not have enough material and students had to share. In these cases, we adjusted our groupings so that students paired up for reading or students shared materials. Additionally, the six fourth-grade classrooms in our buildings might have been working with the same materials at the same time (as they may align with instruction in a particular content area). As such, we were often sharing texts between classes, and we alternated the times that we provided reading instruction across the grade level. Although we had no insurmountable difficulties with space, we held some instruction in the cafeteria or the library as necessary.

What Strategies Are Planned, and Are Some More Difficult Than Others? Some strategies appear more complex than others (see chapters 2 and 3 for further discussion). Based on this, you might choose to break up daily reading assignments into smaller clusters so that you can spend more time working with students as they practice the strategy instruction in their Guide or model the instruction numerous times during small-group instruction.

We found that some strategies are tougher for some students to grasp, and we tried to build more time, prompts, modeling, or practice into our planning for those strategies. Monitoring student performance during group instructional time and monitoring student performance in their Read-Along Guides will easily provide teachers with insights to adjust the pace or delivery methods of their instruction.

How Many Days Will Be Needed for the Instruction? Units of instruction generally last from one to two weeks. We have found that this range works well for two reasons: it allows us to juggle all of the content that needs to be covered in the intermediate-level curriculum, and many of the reading materials we now use can easily be covered in this timeframe.

If we find that we're crunched for time we might temporarily alter our grouping configurations. For example, if all groups are working with the same text, we might provide whole-group instruction in place of meeting with multiple groups. Although this might be more difficult to do as you attempt to end a lesson (as groups will most likely be at different points in their reading), it might be easier to consider beginning your new unit using a whole-group approach.

If you are fortunate enough to have the support of a reading specialist, you can make best use of this assistance on days when you launch a new lesson or when you are giving an end-of-unit assessment. Should this be the case, you might decide not to meet with one your groups on a day the specialist is unavailable and instead provide instruction for the group that otherwise meets with him or her. Working together with the specialist is key.

You might also find that juggling the pacing of multiple groups takes some practice. Still, there are extension activities such as building vocabulary that can easily be built into the Model. Likewise, there are methods to quicken the pace of other groups (such as those discussed previously), if need be.

Small-Group Instruction

Working together with students in a small group gives us special instructional opportunities that we don't have during whole-class instruction. Strickland et al. (2002) make clear the benefits of small-group instruction noting that teachers are "better able to observe, monitor, and attend to the needs of individual readers" (p. 57). Examples of some suggested small-group activities as well as instructional pointers we share while working in our small-group setting are outlined below.

Tailored Direct Instruction. Teachers determine the emphasis needed on direct instruction and modeling, checking this against student participation and performance in the small group. Instructional adjustments can be made on the spot.

Discussion. Small-group time allows for a targeted exchange of ideas, and engaging dialogue between the teacher and students and among the students. Students benefit not only from the teacher's insights but also from the thoughtful ideas and concerns expressed by peers.

Peer Modeling. Although direct instruction is provided and the strategy is then typically modeled by the teacher, peer modeling is another important technique many teachers use during their small-group instruction.

Use of Sticky Notes. Many teachers have sticky notes handy during the small-group instruction so students who wish to alter their Guides or mark pages in their book (based on events during instruction) can do so quickly and independently.

Active Engagement. Small-group time makes more practical the chance of engaging all students by keeping a lively pace and encouraging intermittent student involvement.

Writing Needs. As Read-Along Guides rely greatly on students' written responses, teachers must monitor struggling writers' comprehension, which may not necessarily align with the quality of what he or she has written. Teachers can adjust the writing demands, and they can also adjust their dialogue and discussions with these students during small-group instruction.

Working Independently

Previously in this chapter, we clarified the importance of having students work independently so they can read silently on their own, practice their comprehension strategies, prepare a written response to their reading, and demonstrate their understanding clearly and concisely. In sum, this opportunity affords students the time to consider, apply, and extend what they've learned during their small-group instruction. Students are also able to identify areas where they may still need assistance or support and can seek help to thus begin to take charge of their own learning. Some pointers for making the best use of this independent activity are described in the following sections.

Posting Assignments. Teachers may want to record and display the assignments students are to complete independently on a white board or chart paper so students can refer to it and check they have completed all tasks. Although many of the assignments will be given at the end of the small-group instruction (many teachers have students write assignments in their Guide before disbanding the group), having the information posted ensures that students will not interrupt the teacher—who typically will be providing instruction to another small group—with a question about the assignment.

Student Ability to Work Independently. Many teachers found that some students had trouble working independently, especially at the beginning of the school year. Students are transitioning into a new grade and are adjusting to meeting new expectations. Working independently is a skill that, for most students, may require instruction and practice. Providing a lesson on your expectations for students as they work independently and then providing a visual reminder such as a poster may be helpful especially early in the school year.

Pacing. Some students may struggle with pacing their time with the activities they've been asked to complete during their independent work, especially as students may have anywhere from two to four types of tasks to complete, and each task will likely require a different amount of time to complete. Although students may develop a sense of pacing, they might still need help and additional support in terms of extra time to complete their work.

Teachers may want to carefully monitor students' pacing early in the year, noting those who have trouble and determining how best to help them. A student who is unable to complete work because of off-task or unfocused behavior will need different support than a student who struggles because he or she is confused by what they have read. Determining when to provide students with extra time, when to modify expectations for the amount of practice a student may be asked to complete, and when to work with students to build their skill at working independently are issues teachers may need to address by observing student behavior during their independent activities.

Quality of Work. Some students may think that the expectations for the quality of their work might be different for independent work and group work. Clearly establishing that the expectations are the same may be necessary. Teachers may wish to quickly check through students' independent work regularly and provide comments on student work periodically. Reviewing students' independent work to determine the focus of instruction and to monitor student performance is ineffective if the student's work does not reflect his or her best effort.

Self-Sufficiency and Peer Assistance. Allowing students who are working independently to rely on peer assistance when questions arise helps avoid disruptions during small-group instruction. Also, encouraging students to seek solutions (and allowing them a degree of error), while also establishing a routine and an environment that supports independence, is important for this type of instruction. All factors allow for uninterrupted instruction as well as independent learning.

Inefficient Use of Time. As the teacher can readily monitor this issue during his or her small-group instruction, being aware of what students are doing as they work independently at their seats is another issue. Catching glimpses of observable on-task behaviors becomes second nature for teachers as they monitor all students in the classroom, including those to whom they are providing instruction.

What the Settings and Groupings Look Like in the Classroom

The following three vignettes represent different approaches and grouping configurations we used for our instruction. The first vignette presents a whole-class introductory lesson, while the second and third vignettes demonstrate simultaneous instruction taking place with one class of students who are receiving instruction by two teachers in two different locations. As the Quality Comprehension Model is fluid and allows for much flexibility, these vignettes will help you determine how to make the Model work according to your own needs.

Whole-Class Introductory Lesson

The 22 students in Miss Wiley's class sit at desks configured in multiple paired rows. The students just shared some of their favorite nonfiction books—a biography of a champion athlete, the story of Harriet Tubman, a collection of true pet stories, and others. They return their attention to their Read-Along Guide and read with Miss Wylie as she introduces the three strategies featured on the cover—Finding the Important or Main Idea, Identifying Facts and Details, and Finding Word Meaning and Building Vocabulary Using Context Clues. She gives the students a minute to share their ideas on the strategies with elbow partners. Which do they know? Have they used any before? Can they give examples? After some whole-class idea sharing and discussion, she instructs students to turn the page and read the descriptions aloud so they can build their understanding of the strategies and see how they are going to practice them in this unit. Three separate stacks of books are ready on a side table. Shortly, Miss Wiley will introduce each of the three books with a quick (yet enthusiastic) one-minute talk and then distribute them as planned to students. Tomorrow the students will break up into their groups and begin reading.

Small-Group Instruction in Regular Classroom Setting

The classroom teacher provides instruction to two reading groups while a specialist works with a third group in a separate location. Ms. Smith, the regular classroom teacher, sits at the back table with six students. Each student has a Guide, a pencil, a book (in this case a small-format guided reading text such as depicted in Figure 3 in the Introduction), and some sticky notes containing ideas he or she had sketched out the day before following their group instruction. As the students open their Guides to page 3, where they have been practicing how to find important ideas and key facts and details, Ms. Smith glances across the room at the nine other students who sit at their desks working independently in their Guides. These students are reading the next three chapters in their book—historical fiction—and are also practicing identifying important ideas and key facts and details, as well as hunting for new vocabulary words. Instructions for all three groups appear on the board. Ms. Smith works with her first group for 20 minutes. Then, she will gather the second group and work with them for 20 minutes. Mr. Josling, the reading specialist, has pulled out five other students and will work with them for the entire 50 minutes.

Small-Group Instruction With Reading Specialist

Mr. Josling sits with five students. He explains that today they will begin as usual: taking turns reading their written response to yesterday's reading (which they completed independently) and then reviewing the last entry they prepared together on the important idea on page 3 in their Guide. After that, they will continue reading—a chapter book that contains a few sketched illustrations—and work on identifying the main idea and key details in that chapter. They will also work on finding the meaning of the content vocabulary and recording definitions of two difficult words on the back page of their Guide.

Pointers on the Big Picture

As is clear from the vignettes, there may be many activities occurring in a classroom simultaneously. For example, while groups might be meeting at various locations in the room, another group may be leaving for or arriving from a specialist's classroom, and there could also be students working independently at their seats. Although this environment may at first seem intimidating to manage from a teacher's perspective or confusing and disruptive from a student's point of view, the classroom environment not only becomes very manageable but also routine. Keeping the classroom running smoothly during instruction while also focusing on individual student progress is what might be considered the "big picture." In addition to the pointers for small-group instruction and working independently provided earlier in this chapter, the following pointers will help you keep the big picture in check.

Daily Assignments. During small-group activities teachers can assess the quality of a student's work and take measures immediately so small gaps don't become gaping holes over time.

The Need for Quiet. Although each student and each teacher has their own comfort level with classroom "noise," this becomes a critical concern with small-group instruction, as many activities occur simultaneously. Monitoring noise level—from the small group(s) and the students working independently—may become necessary.

Missed Class. Establish a system for students who have missed class that does not involve pulling the teacher from instruction. Encouraging students to "partner up" may be helpful in these circumstances.

Assignments. Instructions for all students must be clearly displayed so that the teacher is not needed to clarify. Most teachers will begin their lessons by reviewing instructions that are prepared on a board. Figure 4 shows instructions for three groups of students as they appear on a whiteboard. The teacher adds to the instructions

---

FIGURE 4
Sample of Daily Instructions for Groups

New York's Melting Pot Culture
(Thomas, Alison, Regan, Ben, Kyle, Jamie, Grace)

5/29	(pp. 5 + 7)	1. Main/important idea 2. 3–5 vocabulary words 3. Journal entry 4. Independent reading (pp. 6–20)
5/30	(pp. 9 + 11)	1. Main/important idea 2. 3–5 vocabulary words 3. Journal entry 4. Independent reading (pp. 21–34)
5/31	(pp. 13 + 15)	1. Main/important idea 2. 3–5 vocabulary words 3. Journal entry 4. Independent reading (pp. 35–44)

If Your Name Was Changed at Ellis Island
(Alex, Trenton, Keith, Sarah, Alyssa, Jen W., Michael, Sam, Nathan, Victoria)

5/29	(pp. 12–20)	1. Main/important idea (pp. 8 + 9, 12 + 13) 2. Vocabulary words—2 per section 3. Journal entry—1 for both sections
5/30	(pp. 25–30)	1. Main/important idea (pp. 25 + 26, 29 + 30) 2. Vocabulary words—2 per section 3. Journal entry—1 for both sections
5/31	(pp. 37–40)	1. Main/important idea (pp. 37, 38, + 40) 2. Vocabulary words—1 per section 3. Journal entry—1 for both sections

Ellis Island
(Noah, Breanna, Ethan, Jeff, Matty, Jen S., Matt)

5/29	(Re-read Irish Immigration) 1. Graphic Organizer for Letter
5/30	(Mrs. Dean's Room for Instruction—Ellis Island)
5/31	(Mrs. Dean's Room for Instruction—Ellis Island)

---

daily, enabling students to check their progress, catch up if they missed class, or clarify verbal instructions that were given at the onset of the instruction.

Homework. Depending on your personal views or your district's guidelines, you may or may not have existing thoughts on homework. Still, we mention here that the use of the Read-Along Guide has also made it easier for us to send work home with a student who missed class or was unable to complete assignments during class time. As it provides an easy-to-follow format and often includes modeled examples, the Read-Along Guide allows parents to quickly grasp how they can assist their children, if necessary, with homework. Although in our experience this was not done often, it was helpful when assigning homework did become necessary.

Instructional Unit Plans

Remaining flexible is key when planning your instructional configuration—whether it be whole-class or small-group instruction, independent work, or even as you assign individuals to various groups. Keeping this in mind, you should plan each unit to address as many of these variables as possible by using an instructional unit plan as shown in Figure 5, a completed instructional plan for our unit on the Revolutionary War, in which three different leveled texts are used. (See Appendix B for a reproducible version of the instructional unit plan; electronic versions of the reproducibles in this appendix can also be found online at www.reading.org on the webpage for this book, found in the Publications section of the site.) Instructional units tend to run about 10 days. For example, in our Revolutionary War unit, we broke out into three groups, with instruction lasting for approximately 6 days. If support services are not available, the classroom teacher might provide longer segments of whole-class instruction and meet with the three groups for a much shorter period of time.

In addition to noting our book selection and time frame, we also included other information in the instructional unit plan that helped us with smooth instruction (see Figure 5 for an illustration of these components of the instructional unit plan):

- The strategies that are covered in the Read-Along Guide
- The daily assigned reading sections
- Prereading "before" instruction activities that might be covered in a minilesson or during the introduction of an instructional unit using a whole-class configuration
- "During" instruction activities (for example, in the Revolutionary War unit students are developing their comprehension skills to compare and contrast by practicing adding ideas to the Venn diagrams in their Read-Along Guides as they complete assigned reading)
- "After" instruction activities, such as any special preparation that might be needed for the assessment that will follow instruction—whether it is project-based or traditional (discussed further in chapter 7)

FIGURE 5
Instructional Unit Plan for Unit on Revolutionary War

Instructional Unit Plan

Title/Theme _Revolutionary War_ _____ Level(s) _M,Q,T_

Approximate Time _6 days_

Strategies: 1. _Comparing & Contrasting_ _____

2. _Drawing Conclusions & Making Inferences_ ___

3. _Finding Word Meaning Using Context Clues_ ___

4. _____

Chapter Breakout: _(Title/Level)_

1. _Toliver's Secret (T)_   2. _Samuel's Choice (Q)_ ^M   3. _Revolutionary War on Wednesday & Res. Guide (M)_

Chap. 1–2 pp. 1-31	pp. 4-9	Prologue & Chapt. 1–2 pp. 1-15
Chap. 2–5 pp. 32-66	pp. 10-15	Chap. 3–4 pp. 16-31
Chap. 6–8 pp. 67-106	pp. 16-21	Chap. 5–6 pp. 32-47
Chap. 9–10 pp. 107-134	pp. 22-27	Chap. 7–8 pp. 48-59
Chap. 11–13 pp. 135-166	pp. 28-33	Chap. 9–10 pp. 60-69 & back matter
	pp. 34-40	
	Historical note	—Resource Guide— before/during/after

Instructional Plans

Before	During	After
1. Introduce topic 2. Introduce books/ Read-Along Guide	1. Follow through strategies (use Venns accordingly) 2. Monitor responses 3. Share vocabulary	Rev. War Assessment

Notes on Read-Along Guide Use: _____ _1. Group 1 to pull own vocabulary_

2. Two Venn diagrams for groups 1 & 2; 1 for group 3.   3. Reader response

size difference.   4. Group 2 Strategy 2 = some 2x per reading

Attachments: _none_ _____

*Suggestions for Venn diagrams: group 1—2 characters on cover, group 2—
slaves-free/patriots-loyalist, group 3—patriots-loyalist

- "Notes on Read-Along Guide Use" that provide notes to classroom teachers and support reading specialists on the instruction (For example, the Revolutionary War unit plan in Figure 5 shows that group 1 will need to pull their own vocabulary out of the text, as it has not been provided by the teacher; there are two Venn diagrams for groups 1 and 2 and only one for group 3; the reader response size is different for the groups; and the amount of practice in the drawing conclusions and making inferences strategy is different. Suggestions for topics for the Venn diagrams have also been provided.)

Planning instruction in this manner is often done at the same time you prepare a Read-Along Guide. Further information on selecting texts, creating and using Read-Along Guides, coordinating the activities of multiple groups, and determining strategies for which to provide instruction is presented in chapter 4.

Although the instructional unit plan provides a great deal of information on the content and structure of the lesson, there is much leeway for interpretation, and the style of instruction is as varied as are the teachers who provide it. Certainly, typical techniques of modeling, teacher think-alouds, peer support and demonstration, and others all come into play. Likewise, teachers may certainly choose to use any instructional tools they deem appropriate, such as chart paper, markers, whiteboard, or sticky notes.

Figure 6 features a section of a sample planning page from a week-long reading unit in which three different reading groups met every day. Two groups are instructed by the classroom teacher, while another is instructed by a reading specialist. As is evident from the planning page, the teacher models extensively and relies on student discussion during her work with vocabulary. She has her students work with sticky notes and fluctuates between using a whiteboard and chart paper. Certainly, other teachers may choose to plan different activities and deliver instruction using different methods. Others may sketch out a few details right on their instructional unit plan and rely almost exclusively on the Read-Along Guide for instruction.

Activities to Increase Student Motivation and Background Knowledge

Some students need a great deal of help building background knowledge, and although this tricky issue is often tied to environmental factors as well as to maturity and other developmental issues, we nonetheless feel that there are clusters of students within our classes we can help. We have an altogether different take on the matter of motivation, having redefined our original intent on what we thought was a pretty clear-cut dilemma. Though we initially identified motivation as a "need" for the unengaged or disengaged student whose minimal efforts produced minimal outcomes, we broadened our definition, believing after careful consideration that it

FIGURE 6
Sample Planning Page From a Week-Long Reading Unit

One-Week Overview
Three Groups

Day 1: Minilesson (whole group)
        Review comprehension strategies
                1. Drawing Conclusions and Making Inferences
                2. Comparing and Contrasting
                3. Finding Word Meaning Using Context Clues

        Discuss Theme: The Revolutionary War

Day 2: Postreading assignments (each group will have some required independent reading)

Group 1 (struggling readers): Instructed by reading specialist (50 minutes)

Review Read-Along Guide, page by page.

Students will read to themselves, while one at a time the teacher will select a student to read aloud (check for pacing, fluency, voice).

After reading, discuss any vocabulary that students marked (using sticky notes) as being difficult; compare with vocabulary from last page of guide.

Model (using chart paper or whiteboard) how to explain the meaning of a quote using inferencing. Group will complete this together.

Reader response—Discuss responses before writing.

Group 2 (middle readers): Instructed by classroom teacher (20 minutes)

Review Read-Along Guide, page by page.

Students will read to themselves, while one at a time the teacher will select a student to read aloud (check for pacing, fluency, voice).

After reading, discuss any vocabulary that students marked (using sticky notes) as being difficult; compare with vocabulary from last page of guide.

Model (using chart paper or whiteboard) how to explain the meaning of a quote using inferencing. Do one quote together; complete independently.

Reader Response—Briefly discuss responses before writing.

Group 3 (middle/high readers): Instructed by classroom teacher (20 minutes)

Review Read Along Guide, page by page.

Students will read to themselves, while one at a time the teacher will select a student to read aloud (check for pacing, fluency, voice).

After reading, discuss any vocabulary that students marked (using sticky notes) as being difficult; compare with vocabulary from last page of guide.

Model (using chart paper or whiteboard) how to explain the meaning of a quote using inferencing. Do one quote together; complete independently.

Reader response—Briefly discuss responses before writing.

was an issue affecting all students—even high performers. For these students we not only wanted to encourage their high-level performance *consistently* and *routinely* but we also wanted to extend their skills and to challenge them, hoping they would become intrinsically motivated. Though improvement in both background knowledge and motivation remains an area of study in which we are currently involved, we found that we could easily integrate methods of addressing them within the framework of the approach so that all students would benefit according to their individual needs. Though these activities are still under study, we have received enough positive support to feel that they are deserving of mention should you wish to incorporate them with your plans at the start.

Collectively, these activities seek to build motivation as well as background knowledge, some more aptly suited to one than the other. As the link between the two cannot be overlooked or underestimated, our bundled and intertwined approach to addressing them together appears supported. Though it is clear that we are trying to provide some concrete learning experiences, we are also doing so within an environment that is conducive to meeting other student needs, such as a sense of community, belonging, and connectedness.

Literacy Bins

Providing a different twist on Literacy Work Stations (Diller, 2005), Literacy Bins contain activities that support the reading comprehension instruction in two ways: they are thematically aligned to reading instruction (such as the Revolutionary War unit discussed earlier in this chapter) and they include a variety of practice activities that may be strategy or comprehension based. These activities are typically performed independently by students at their desks (as opposed to stations) or in small two- or three-person groups to minimize noise. Because students who are not involved in their small-group instruction often have independent seatwork in their Read-Along Guides, selecting Bin activities occurs only after they have completed their other work (Figure 7 shows students selecting activities from a Literacy Bin).

Some of the types of literacy activities that we have used for the Bins include the following:

- Creating minibooks (see Figure 8 for an example of a student's minibook based on a unit on tall tales), posters, comics, or other drawings
- Building vocabulary through word searches, crossword puzzles, and jumbles
- Performing text or character analysis using well-known graphic organizers, such as Venn diagrams
- Completing T-Charts, cause-and-effect charts, and other charts
- Doing creative writing activities such as writing poetry, plays, and critiques

Resources for locating these types of activities are plentiful, though adaptations may be necessary for alignment with instructional themes.

FIGURE 7
Students Selecting Activities From Literacy Bin

Tic-Tac-Toe Boards

The nine-block template used in the popular tic-tac-toe game provides a useful structure with which to organize the Literacy Bin activities to maximize student motivation. For example, by selecting from among the nine choices available on the board, students assume responsibility and are in control of their learning (Atkinson, 2000). Teachers may also vary the activities, providing a type of differentiated choice in terms of key factors that include content, process, or product (Tomlinson, 1999). Further, varying the activities to address the different learning styles espoused by Gardner (2006) in his well-known multiple intelligence theory is another way to bolster motivation. The possibilities are limitless. We built strategy practice activities into our board, which may mimic the prompts used in the Read-Along Guide—especially for those strategies we know are often more complicated for students to grasp (difficulty levels based on our studies are provided in chapters 2 and 3). Figure 9 provides an example of a tic-tac-toe board used in our instructional unit on tall tales, in which students are encouraged to complete three in a row.

FIGURE 8
Student's Minibook Created for Unit on Tall Tales

Name Grace   Date 10/27/06

CREATE A MINIBOOK

DIRECTIONS: In this activity, you will need to read a tall tale from the book bin and then create an 8 page minibook that retells the story. Be sure to include a title page. Each page after that should tell something important about the story. Write a sentence or two that tells what is happening and then illustrate your page. Make certain you put the events in the correct order.

John Henry was born with a hammer in his hand.

Before he was 6 he was carrying stones for the railroad.

By the time he was 10 he was hammering steel from dawn to dusk.

John Henry had to keep a bucket nearby to cool his hammer down!

One day a man came and said "Come See Everybody!" Here a steam drill can go...

A worker decided to have a contest to see who could go faster, John Henry or the steam drill.

John Henry hammered hard. In the end John Henry...

John Henry died after that. John Henry died but his legend lives on forever.

FIGURE 9
Tic-Tac-Toe Board for Unit on Tall Tales

Name_____

Unit **Tall Tales**_____

Word Search Tall Tales Find and highlight all of the words from the word bank. Get ready to s-t-r-e-t-c-h your imagination! Extra Credit Crossword Puzzle, too!	**Figurative Language** Can you find some creative and colorful similes, metaphors, idioms and personification in the packet of tall tales?	**Batter Up!** "Casey at the Bat" is an American tall tale about a talented baseball player. Here, the story is presented as a choral reading. This means you find a buddy or two and read it aloud. Practice, practice, practice and then record your reading!
Comic-Book Writers Wanted! Create and illustrated a mini-comic book about your favorite tall tale character and his or her dashing escapades.	**READ Read At Home!** Have your parent sign your reading list of a minimum of five tall tales. Bonus points awarded for special research challenge.	**Truth OR Exaggeration!** You Be the Judge... Use a T-Chart and list as many truths and exaggerations as you can in the sample story.
Drama! Try out some of these tall tale Readers Theatre plays. You can find some friends who would like to read with you. Practice, practice, practice, and perhaps you'll get a chance to perform! **Library Pass Needed**	**DARE To Compare!** Compare and contrast two tall tales using a Venn diagram	**Author For Hire!** Write your own tall tale! Be the main character or make up a character! A prewriting graphic organizer will help guide you. **Be Creative!**

100% Effort Celebrations

To encourage overall good effort, it is beneficial (and fun for students) to incorporate monthly 100% Effort Celebrations into your activities. When we did this, the six fourth-grade classes in our building participated. Students helped to define what 100% effort looked like by completing all assignments, following directions, offering good citizenship, participating in class, following school/classroom/bus rules, and showing respect. Children received an invitation to meet in a specific location (classroom, outdoors, library, etc.) during their lunch period where they participated in an activity and played games. Examples included making ice cream sundaes, decorating cookies, and creating bookmarks. The students were given a certificate noting their accomplishment, often handed out by the principal. Their pictures were also displayed on the 100% Effort bulletin board.

In addition to displaying student pictures, we also created Hall of Fame bulletin boards where we could display students' achievements. These were examples of exceptional work or work deemed to be a student's personal best.

Teacher–Student Coaching and Student–Student Peer Coaching

Sometimes students benefited from a little help or guidance from a friend, either a teacher (or adult) or a peer. Pairing students with a contact person on whom they can count for guidance may provide the extra support needed. Also, if students are pulled from class due to music lessons or are absent due to other circumstances, having a contact person or a buddy to collect missed work, explain directions, or share notes is beneficial.

Parental Involvement

Parental involvement can be the key to keeping a student motivated. Creating a simple checklist that the student, teacher, and parent review daily may help a student improve their organizational skills or work habits (see Appendix B for reproducible versions of these checklists). Many students only rely on this for a few weeks until they master the skills independently, whereas others may need a lengthier timeline for support. These checklists can easily be tailored to the needs of your students.

Unique Hooks

You should always remain on the lookout for the perfect book or book-type product that will be just the thing to hook an otherwise "unhookable" student. With the increasing variety of materials available, it is not difficult to find books or other materials that will excite a reluctant reader, such as Readers Theatre scripts, comic books, e-books, or graphic novels appropriate for intermediate readers.

Aligning the Quality Comprehension Model With Your Curriculum

Decoding, fluency, and comprehension skills need to be taught and practiced, yet teachers cannot afford to jeopardize their responsibility for building student knowledge in the content areas. If one was sacrificed for the other, surely this would unleash further trouble for students as they progressed into higher grade levels. The Model has not only been successful in language arts lessons, but it is also easily adaptable for instruction in the content areas. Likewise, the Model enables teachers to vary the level of difficulty based on the range of skills in their classrooms. The Quality Comprehension Model is strategic and precision-directed, making it easy for teachers to target the focus of their instruction.

To resolve this dilemma, we often selected reading materials that aligned with the curriculum, and we created instructional reading units to incorporate their use. For example, we selected a variety of reading materials based on the Revolutionary War, immigration, Native Americans, and other topics covered in our fourth-grade social studies curriculum. Though we also covered topics falling more traditionally within a reading curriculum, such as genre studies or author studies, many of our instructional units covered issues of relevance to social studies and even science. Table 3 features a selection of instructional reading units from fourth grade together with the multiple texts we have used for instruction over time. (Additionally, many of the student examples appearing throughout chapters 2 and 3 are from texts that coincide with instruction in the content areas.)

TABLE 3
Selection of Curriculum Texts for Various Instructional Reading Units

Native Americans
George, L. (2003). *Native Americans in New York*. New York: Rosen Publishing Group.
Levine, E. (1998). *If you lived with the Iroquois*. New York: Scholastic.
Waters, K. (1996). *Tapenum's day: A Wampanoag Indian boy in Pilgrim times*. New York: Scholastic.

Colonial Period
Dalgliesh, A. (1954). *The courage of Sarah Noble*. New York: Simon & Schuster.
Edmonds, W.D. (1941). *The matchlock gun*. New York: Dodd, Mead & Company.
Waters, K. (1993). *Sarah Morton's day: A day in the life of a Pilgrim girl*. New York: Scholastic.
Waters, K. (1996). *Samuel Eaton's day: A day in the life of a Pilgrim boy*. New York: Scholastic.
Wilmore, K. (2000). *A day in the life of a colonial blacksmith*. New York: Newbridge Educational.
Wilmore, K. (2000). *A day in the life of a colonial innkeeper*. New York: Newbridge Educational.
Wilmore, K. (2000). *A day in the life of a colonial printer*. New York: Newbridge Educational.
Wilmore, K. (2000). *A day in the life of a colonial schoolteacher*. New York: Newbridge Educational.
Wilmore, K. (2000). *A day in the life of a colonial silversmith*. New York: Newbridge Educational.
Wilmore, K. (2000). *A day in the life of a colonial wigmaker*. New York: Newbridge Educational.

Revolutionary War Period
Berleth, R.J. (1990). *Samuel's choice*. Niles, IL: Albert Whitman.
Brady, E.W. (1976). *Toliver's secret*. New York: Random House.
Griffin, J.B. (1977). *Phoebe the spy*. New York: Scholastic.
Moore, K. (1997). *If you lived at the time of the American Revolution*. New York: Scholastic.

Growth of Government
Levy, E. (1992). *If you were there when they signed the Constitution*. New York: Scholastic.
Swain, G. (2004). *Declaring freedom: A look at the Declaration of Independence, the Bill of Rights, and the Constitution*. Minneapolis, MN: Lerner.
The Constitution of the United States of America

Immigration
Maestro, B., & Ryan, S. (1999). *Coming to America: The story of immigration*. New York: Scholastic.
Wilson, N. (2003). *New York's melting pot culture*. New York: Rosen Publishing Group.

Though a broad generalization, intermediate-level learners, like all learners, have academic needs, as well as needs that some might argue extend beyond the traditional boundaries of a typical educator. Even further, each intermediate-level learner, like all learners, has individual needs, which might also challenge existing instructional norms. Still, we tried to pair all of these needs with solutions. At times we used grouping configurations or the creation of instructional materials such as the Read-Along Guide, while at other times we assigned a buddy to help a student or we advised a parent how to best support his or her child. Though we continue to seek solutions to these needs-based problems, we are resigned to the fact and accept the challenge that our troubleshooting skills on this front will forever be on call. These skills are, after all, both the cause and effect of any change. We remind ourselves every now and then that—especially when we are daunted by the challenge of enabling intermediate-level students to transition to proficiency with higher-level reading skills—it is also vital to present reading as a means of recreation and enjoyment. That is the prize.

CHAPTER 2

Instruction in Key Comprehension Strategies: The Foundational Eight

"The strategies had things for me to do that helped me understand, like make predictions and figure out new words."

—Max S., fourth-grade student

"It's interesting to listen to the kids talk about the strategies. They actually call the strategies by name and discuss them. During one of my third-grade classes, we were discussing connections. One student was explaining to another how she could tell the difference between a text-to-world connection and a text-to-self connection: 'I knew that if I had seen it on the news, it would be a text-to-world connection.' This tells me that they're getting it."

—Mr. Bethune, reading specialist

This chapter is devoted to the first component of the Quality Comprehension Model: providing teacher-led instruction of key comprehension strategies, most often delivered in a small-group setting. Specifically this chapter offers guidelines and recommendations for providing instruction on the following foundational eight comprehension strategies:

Strategy 1: Using Fix-Up Methods When Meaning Is Challenged

Strategy 2: Finding Word Meaning and Building Vocabulary Using Context Clues

Strategy 3: Using Visual Text Clues to Figure Out Meaning (fiction and nonfiction)

Strategy 4: Asking Questions to Engage in the Text

Strategy 5: Making Connections to Aid Understanding (fiction and nonfiction)

Strategy 6: Visualizing to Support the Text

Strategy 7: Making Predictions

Strategy 8: Synthesizing to Gain New Meaning (fiction and nonfiction)

These eight strategies are critical foundational skills and seek to establish strong reading behaviors in students. The foundational eight are featured in our Introductory Read-Along Guide, which is often the method by which we launch our initial instruction. Typically, it is necessary to provide formal instruction in each strategy only once except for Strategies 2 and 8, which are repeated for additional student practice. Likewise, Strategies 3, 5, and 8 have unique features when applied separately to works of fiction or nonfiction. As a result, it is often best to provide formal instruction for each genre. Informal instruction—through teachable moments—is provided throughout the balance of the entire school year for the other four strategies.

For each comprehension strategy, we have provided a wealth of helpful information that is intended to be used by teachers in a variety of ways. First, each comprehension strategy is given a difficulty rating. Each strategy is rated for difficulty on a scale of 1–5 (with 5 being the most difficult). The difficulty rating is based on our experience providing instruction in the strategies for nearly 10 years, our analysis during a two-year action research study, and our analysis of standardized test data over several years. Rarely is there a strategy that all students master with extreme ease; as such, we have been reluctant to assign a difficulty rating of 1 to any of the 17 strategies. Keep in mind that these ratings are simply a guide. An explanation of each strategy and the skills employed when the strategy is used opens the discussion, and the following information is included for each:

- *Teacher Tips for Strategy Instruction*. This section provides general instructional recommendations on teaching the strategy; insights we have gained while working with a particular strategy, such as areas of common difficulty for students; and pitfalls to avoid.

- *Text Suggestions*. This section provides experience-based pointers for choosing texts, such as genres, size, features, and others, that might best support a strategy.

- *Student-Friendly Chat on the Importance of the Strategy*. To aid you in your direct instruction in each strategy, a student-friendly dialogue excerpt is provided, specifically written in language that teachers can use as a prompt in dialogue or within written materials to explain the strategy and its importance to students. It reflects the type of language that will be used in the Read-Along Guide (see chapter 4 for more detailed discussion on the Read-Along Guide).

- *Practice With Prompts Using the Read-Along Guide.* In this section, how students will actually apply and exhibit their skills for each strategy is shown. Prompts, which are simple written cues meant to help guide students in their strategy practice, were designed to mimic the authentic thinking processes performed automatically by skilled readers. The prompts in this section are actually reproduced sections from the Read-Along Guide, which will be explored in greater detail in chapters 4 and 5 (reproducible versions of the Guide appear in Appendix A). By using the prompts in this section, you will be able to see exactly how students will be asked to practice each strategy through the Guides. In the cases where we had prompts that specifically addressed features of fiction and nonfiction text, we have provided those as well. For example, the following prompt is used with Strategy 6, Visualizing to Support the Text:

When I Read (Page #)	I Could Picture...

Here, students are guided by the written cue "I Could Picture..." as a way to guide their thinking toward the practice of visualizing (when readers make pictures in their mind of the people, places, or events they are reading about).

- *What to Look For: Key Indicators of Successful Student Performance.* Selected sample responses from students are analyzed here. Highlighted beneath the samples are significant points and benchmarks teachers can look for as they provide instruction in a particular strategy. Also, ways in which to coordinate student independent work in the Read-Along Guide and teacher-supported small-group instruction are also suggested.

- *Strategy Connections.* This section reveals connections between the strategies and any strategies that might best be featured together.

- *Test-Taking Tips.* A section featuring ways in which a comprehension strategy may be expressed as a test question concludes each strategy. Also, this section provides teachers with insight on typical errors students might make with a specific strategy and offers suggestions on how these might be minimized.

Using Fix-Up Methods When Meaning Is Challenged

When a reader becomes confused or is unclear about the meaning of a passage, some type of corrective action is needed. Encouraging students to use fix-up methods when meaning is challenged is critical. Providing them with the following three methods to clear up comprehension problems is one way to provide instruction in this strategy:

1. Reread the passage.
2. Go back to other parts of the text.
3. Read on for no more than two sentences.

Teacher Tips for Strategy Instruction

- Students need direct instruction in practicing the three fix-up methods. This is best done through think-alouds during small-group instruction, where teachers can first demonstrate confusion or misunderstanding and then a trial-and-error process of using the fix-up methods. After modeling the various methods and encouraging students to independently practice while remaining in the small group, discussions on how students used the methods to clear up their confusion are critical. Obviously, initial direct instruction can later be replaced with occasional teachable moments once students internalize this process and become proficient.

- Of the methods presented, the second, which that requires students to scan earlier paragraphs, pages, or chapters, is the one most resisted by struggling as well as proficient readers. Simply reading on and ignoring misunderstandings may be so routine to some students that it becomes a hard-to-alter habit. Using think-alouds and modeling to provide students with quick ways to scan other places in the text, such as by hunting for keywords or referring back to the table of contents for a page range where they might find the detail they need, may be helpful.

- At times, students will be unable to clear up misunderstandings, as they may be unable to understand words or phrases used in the passage. For example, in the student example on page 51, "getting on his good side" is an idiom. If a student doesn't understand the idiom, he or she may not be successful at gaining meaning no matter which fix-up method is used.

- When providing instruction in nonfiction or informational text, students may be confused by new information that could challenge prior knowledge they gained from another source. For example, during an instructional unit, a student encountered information from two sources that was contradictory. Here, teachers may advise the student to (a) check the credibility of the sources, (b) seek other sources to either confirm or refute the information, or (c) state that there was contradictory information and keep it as an ongoing question to resolve during future studies.

Text Suggestions

While providing instruction in this strategy, it is critical to have a text that provides a "just-right" amount of challenge. If the text is too easy, students may indicate they don't have an authentic opportunity to try using the fix-up methods. Likewise, if the text is too complicated, students will be overburdened trying to grasp meaning and become frustrated with recording all of their experiences. Working with nonfiction small-format guided reading books might present more authentic opportunities for students to try the fix-up methods. Even using carefully selected passages within these small-format texts is a workable plan.

If necessary, support the instruction you're providing in this strategy by using passages from different texts. In other words, if you've clustered this strategy with others and thus far you've worked with one text, simply take a break from that text and use varied materials during small-group instruction.

Student magazines such as *Weekly Reader, Time for Kids,* or *National Geographic for Kids* would be good alternatives to nonfiction texts. Perhaps your library has a subscription and keeps back issues. Using nonfiction magazine articles, even if they are from different issues, in a small-group setting is a workable solution.

As students progress in their ability to work with the fix-up methods, consider exposing them to other opportunities to use the methods. Sometimes students don't think of reading as a skill that is developed outside of the instructional time provided for it during the day. Using think-alouds during teachable moments, teachers can demonstrate the use of the fix-up methods while reading school fliers, notes, or even a lunch menu.

Student-Friendly Chat on the Importance of the Strategy

When providing instruction on using fix-up methods when meaning is challenged, you can use the following dialogue as a way to explain the importance of this strategy to your students:

> Good readers pay attention to their ability to understand what they're reading. At times, even the best readers may be unsure of what they've read. Their thoughts might wander or maybe they get distracted by noises across the classroom. Before they know it, they're at the end of a page and can't remember what they've read. Other times, even the best readers might become confused by what they've read. "This doesn't make any sense," they might think silently. No matter which problem happens, whenever good readers don't understand what they've read, they take action and do something to help fix this problem. They *don't* keep reading. Three good fix-up methods are the following:
>
> 1. Reread the passage. Rereading the passage after you've regained your focus might solve the problem. Also, if you read something incorrectly, rereading the passage might help correct the problem. Even rereading it aloud might help.
>
> 2. Go back to other parts of the text. Quickly scanning an earlier paragraph, page, or chapter might help you find just the right detail that clears up a misunderstanding or confusion.
>
> 3. Read on for no more than two sentences. Often, a misunderstanding might become clear through something else that you read in the text. In this case, reading on might fix the problem. Still, you have to be careful you don't keep reading

and never clear up the problem. It's best to go only about two sentences before you stop and try another fix-up method.

Remember it's not only important to use one of these fix-up methods, but it's also just as important to recognize when you don't understand something and take action!

Practice With Prompts Using the Read-Along Guide

This strategy will typically be introduced and covered only in the Introductory Read-Along Guide, which features only the foundational eight strategies covered in this chapter (see chapter 4 for more information on the Read-Along Guide). After this initial instruction, students may be offered further instruction using teachable moments. Here, students may be asked to refer back to their experience with the strategy in the Introductory Guide and then encouraged to simply transfer the skill as they work with new texts. Determining how often to formally cover this strategy in a Read-Along Guide is a decision best left to the teacher.

You can use the following dialogue as a way to explain to students how they should begin their practice in the use of the strategy:

> Let's practice using these fix-up methods during our reading. Use the prompt in your Read-Along Guide to record any confusing parts you read, and be sure to include the method you used to help fix the problem.
>
> To learn and practice this strategy, you'll be asked to pay close attention to your reading. When something doesn't make sense, try fix-up method 3 and read on for no more than two sentences. If you're still not getting it, stop reading. Then you can try out another fix-up method. If you just lost focus and don't remember what you read, try fix-up method 1. If something doesn't make sense, fix-up method 1 might help here, too. For example, maybe you read *snake* for *snack*. If you're confused and can't remember a character's name or certain events, try fix-up method 2. Go back to other sections in the passage.

Figure 10 illustrates how students will respond in the Guide to prompts about their reading as a way to monitor their use of Strategy 1. In this example, a fourth-grade student responded to prompts about using fix-up methods while reading *Skinnybones* (Park, 1997). Featured excerpts from the book provide insights on how the student applied the strategy while reading.

While providing instruction in fix-up method 1 where students will be practicing rereading sections of a passage and recording their activities in their Guide, struggling and proficient readers will often fix the problem and want to keep reading instead of recording it in their Guide. For example, the student whose response is featured in Figure 10 was able to swiftly fix his misunderstanding caused by the transposition of words in the idiom "getting on his good side." Still, encouraging students to record some examples that demonstrate their ability to use the strategy is important, as it is the only insight teachers have on their mental processes. Also, remind proficient readers who may automatically correct themselves through rereading that this will be a one-time lesson.

FIGURE 10
Fourth-Grade Student's Responses to Read-Along Guide Prompts for Strategy 1

A. Excerpts From *Skinnybones*

When I first discovered the news that T.J. was in my class, I went straight to my mother. I was hoping that she would call the school and have me switched. (p. 16)

Last year, T.J. Stoner grew to be the biggest kid in the whole fifth grade. When I began to notice how gigantic he was getting, I decided it might not be a bad idea to try to get on his good side. But T.J. didn't seem too interested. When I asked if he wanted to be friends... (p. 17)

It's too bad my mother wasn't there. Maybe she could have told me how to ignore someone's Nike in your mouth. (p. 17)

From SKINNYBONES by Barbara Park, copyright © 1982, 1997 by Barbara Park. Used by permission of Alfred A. Knopf, an imprint of Random House Children's Books, a division of Random House, Inc.

B. Student Response

When I Read (Page #)	I Was Confused Because...	The Fix-Up Method I Used Was...
p. 17	I read that T.J. was in 5th grade, but I thought Alex was in 6th grade. This didn't make sense.	#2, when I checked back to page 12, where it said both boys were in 5th grade, I knew the event took place last year and the author had switched time.
p. 17	I didn't understand what "getting good on his side" meant.	#3 & #1, where I first read on and still didn't get it. Then I reread it, and I knew it should have been "getting on his good side." That made sense.
p. 17	When I read Nike, I thought it was a name and it didn't make sense.	#3, when I kept reading I was able to figure out Nike was the sneaker.

What to Look For: Key Indicators of Successful Student Performance

• *Students question preexisting information that no longer makes sense.* In the first entry in the sample prompt, the student is confused by the grade level of a main character. In essence, preexisting information he thought he knew about a character is challenged by new information. Here, the student decides the way to clear up his misunderstanding is to go back to the passage where he first learned of the character's grade level. Certainly, he could also have first reread the passage on page 17 to make sure he didn't misread information and then tried fix-up method 2.

• *Students question the sense of something unclear or illogical.* In the second entry, the student is confused because he cannot make sense of what he has read. After reading on for a short period of time, hopeful that his misunderstanding would be corrected, he abandoned fix-up method 3 and reread the passage. His second attempt to correct the problem was successful as he realized he had transposed the words.

• *Possibilities other than those found in the text are explored.* For the last entry, the student correctly identifies that *Nike* is a proper noun, yet incorrectly assumes it is another character's name. While reading on, he realized his understanding didn't make sense and adjusts his thinking.

- *Students demonstrate ease using multiple methods as necessary.* When students demonstrate a trial-and-error process of using all three fix-up methods in any order that seems correct to them, this is a good measure of mastery of this strategy.

Strategy Connections

This strategy can easily be grouped with numerous others. Additionally, working closely with Strategy 2, Finding Word Meaning, and Strategy 14, Interpreting Figurative Language, may provide support for Strategy 1. Determining how to help students in certain cases, by either providing answers or encouraging them to try other strategies, may be based on where you are in your instruction. If Strategy 1 is introduced, perhaps it would be best to assist students by providing an answer (such as by helping them interpret the meaning of an idiom) rather than directing them to another strategy. However, if you've already provided instruction in Strategies 1, 2, and 14, you might consider reminding students so that they consider using them. Having a variety of strategies to work with will eventually become routine.

Test-Taking Tips

- Unlike many of the other strategies where test questions can be directly linked to assessing a student's ability with a skill such as identifying the main idea, sequencing events, and so on, using fix-up methods is one that is indirectly tested through all other question formats. For example, did the student misunderstand the main idea or the sequence of events in a story? Assessing a student's ability to use fix-up methods becomes a very tricky issue to isolate and practice as a part of test-taking preparation.

- Adding to the problem discussed above, multiple-choice selections on standardized tests often contain incorrect responses that represent common or anticipated misunderstandings. As such, they can trick struggling as well as proficient readers.

- Cautioning readers to take action when their comprehension is challenged and to be wary of questions that seem too easy, include something from the passage where they encountered comprehension trouble, or seem not to have a correct answer may be ways to assist students. In all cases, students might want to go back to the passage and reread, or they should carefully consider possible responses.

- Always encourage students to read all selections, even if they are convinced that the first answer is correct. Discussing this in terms of these trick questions might heighten their awareness in test-taking situations, despite having heard this advice repeatedly.

- Finally, encouraging students to eliminate wrong answers, and being just as certain that answers are incorrect, may cause them to reconsider their interpretation of something and arrive at a new conclusion. Certainly, having a student second-guess himself is not a favorable outcome. However, there is a distinction between reconsidering and second-guessing (the former may be supported through other evidence in the passage), and it might be worthwhile to discuss this test-taking strategy with students.

Finding Word Meaning and Building Vocabulary Using Context Clues

Instruction in this strategy encourages the use of context or other clues to glean meaning for new or unfamiliar words as they are encountered in a passage. Providing students with the following seven methods for using context clues is one way to focus instruction in this strategy:

1. Sound out the word.
2. "Chunk" the word.
3. Link the word to a known word.
4. Look for smaller words that you recognize.
5. Use context clues.
6. Think about what makes sense.
7. Consult other sources.

This strategy seems straightforward and critically important to teachers and most other adults, so developing it as a skill would seem intrinsically rewarding. However, evidence suggests that most intermediate-level students don't share these views; if left unmonitored, most students would not fully use this strategy. Oddly, it seems to be one of the most resisted strategies of all—at least in terms of our experience while working with intermediate-level students. These findings appear consistent with struggling readers as well as proficient readers.

Teacher Tips for Strategy Instruction

• Students need direct instruction in working through the seven methods of determining word meaning, especially struggling readers who may not have a solid grasp of phonics. This is best done in your authentic reading activities during group instruction. Discussions on how students figure out the meaning of a word are critical, yet they are also very abstract and difficult. This is largely because students are not often asked to describe these types of thinking processes. In essence, students need to retrace what is often a very rapid mental process, which may or may not include numerous trials and errors. Providing step-by-step discussions can be complex and even lengthy. Still, it is a worthwhile process as students begin to grasp and then strengthen their ability to use the seven methods. Obviously, initial direct instruction can later be replaced with occasional teachable moments once students internalize this process and become proficient. Additionally, the distinction between the seven methods becomes less important (there are only subtle differences among several) than the students' abilities to use some of them to figure out meaning.

• Teachers may choose to provide words from a text, have students select new or unusual words, or opt for a combination of the two. If words are selected in advance, they can be included in the Guide, or students can be asked to simply write them in their Guide during group instruction. If students are selecting their own, they might be given some parameters, such as three to five words per chapter. No matter which method is used, monitoring student activity will be needed.

- If you allow students to self-select words and they claim they didn't find any (which often happens with the highly proficient readers), ask them to note interesting or difficult words, or even slang, and provide a thoughtful, well-developed definition. Also, you might ask them to note synonyms or antonyms as a way to extend the activity. Alternatively, if you're suspicious about their claim, you might want to assign words. If you have selected words in advance, you might consider having students mark where they appear with a sticky note prior to reading. This way, students use the methods to figure out meaning authentically (as they come upon the word) and record this in their Guide. When students have to go back to a passage after the fact, recording their effort becomes cumbersome.

- Spelling the word correctly (if students are responsible for writing them) is critical. In the students' definitions, we allow more leeway, especially if students are extending their effort and refining their understanding by providing more than one-word definitions.

- Some students may rely on the use of a dictionary and neglect other methods, while others may take wild guesses (especially if they did not record their practice in their Guide as they read). Monitoring student activity will greatly help with this, as will sharing and modeling during small-group instruction.

- For English-language learners (ELLs), you may also wish to provide words in two languages. Another useful device is tape recording words to provide further assistance with vocabulary development. However, some teachers prefer not to focus too much attention on individual vocabulary words for ELLs. Instead, comprehending the overall meaning of ideas is more important than struggling with the meaning of a word in isolation. So, too, is grasping the natural flow of the language. You can best determine the approach you would like to take with these readers.

Text Suggestions

Depending on the text selected, this strategy may or may not be difficult for students. Teachers wishing to minimize the difficulty should select leveled texts that align with a student's reading ability. Likewise, teachers who greatly support instruction in vocabulary development may choose a text that is more challenging for students.

Small-format, informational guided reading texts may be one way to begin work with this strategy, especially if you wish to link the subject to a content area such as social studies or science. This type of text may include support for students who are introduced to this strategy. For example, new vocabulary words are often highlighted in boldface and also appear in a glossary where there may be a pronunciation guide and other aids. Students could independently check their understanding and discuss the outcomes during group instruction. These texts often include visual aids, illustrations, or pictures, which could further help students. Use of the visuals is a logical transition for intermediate-level students, who are already familiar with picture walks.

Historical fiction would be a good choice after students have practiced the methods used in this strategy and have gained some proficiency. These works are engaging due to their sense of story, plot, character, and so forth. Informational textbooks and trade publications are also a good source for vocabulary work. Both often provide additional support for students. Stories that originated from oral retellings, such as tall tales, fables, pourquoi tales (a folk tale that explains why or how something happens) and even fairy tales, may include colorful language, rich in dialect and slang. For example, tall tale characters are often known to "wrassle" wild animals (West, 1998, p. 34) and always "come out on top" (Kellogg, 1992, p. 20). You might want to save these types of works to extend and playfully challenge students once they have reached a comfortable level of proficiency with the word-meaning methods.

Student-Friendly Chat on the Importance of the Strategy

When providing instruction on finding word meaning and building vocabulary using context clues, you can use the following dialogue as a way to explain the importance of this strategy to your students:

Finding word meaning is a critical skill that will help you better understand what you're reading. Although it's one of the hardest strategies to master, it's also one of the most helpful. Being able to figure out new or unfamiliar words is kind of like good detective work. Often there are clues within the passage, and it's simply a matter of decoding them. Although it takes a lot of practice, it's a skill that will come in handy. Also, it will make it possible for you to read and understand just about anything! Imagine never being stumped by a word again!

Seven good methods are

1. *Sound out the word.* You might know the word but not recognize it in print.

2. *"Chunk" the word.* Break up the word. Is there a root word, a prefix, or a suffix?

3. *Link the word to a known word.* Do you know other words that look or sound like this one? (For example, *studious—studious* sounds and looks like *study*.)

4. *Look for smaller words that you recognize.* Is the word made up of a smaller word you know? (Example: compound words)

5. *Use context clues.* Use clues from the sentence or surrounding sentences.

6. *Think about what makes sense.* Ask yourself, "What would make sense in the sentence?" This method should serve as a final check no matter which method is used. The meaning you've assigned to an unfamiliar word must make sense in the sentence where it appears.

7. *Consult other sources.* Ask a teacher, use a dictionary, or use a glossary.

Practice With Prompts Using the Read-Along Guide

As this strategy is critical, teachers may opt to include this in many Guides (we typically feature this in the last one or two pages). If students run out of room on the pages in the Guide, large sticky notes (3 × 5) can be attached, or a separate sheet with just this prompt and lots of space for response can be used. Still, formal instruction using the methods is usually provided once, with the expectation that the methods will be used from that point forward.

You can use the following dialogue as a way to explain to students how they should begin their practice in the use of the strategy:

> Let's practice using these methods for finding meaning from context during our reading. To learn and practice this strategy, you'll first be introduced to many different ways you can help yourself identify new or unfamiliar words. Then you'll be asked to practice using these methods to track down or construct the meaning of your troublesome words. Be assured that you won't be asked to use a dictionary every time you come across a new word. It'll be OK to save that method until last. After all, it's pretty frustrating when you have to stop all the time to look up a word, right? By the time you find a word's definition, you've forgotten what you were reading! Plus, sometimes you might find more than one definition in a dictionary. There's a better plan.
>
> Use the space on the Guide to write your new or unfamiliar word, and try to use one or more of the seven methods to figure out the meaning of the word. Be sure to list the number of the method or methods you used and give a definition of the word.

Figure 11 illustrates how students will respond in the Guide to prompts about their reading as a way to monitor their use of Strategy 2. In this example, a fourth-grade student responded to prompts about finding word meaning while reading the historical fiction text *The Courage of Sarah Noble* (Dalgliesh, 1954). Featured excerpts from the book provide insights on how the student applied the strategy while reading, and this example illustrates all of the methods suggested for use.

What to Look For: Key Indicators of Successful Student Performance

- *Students may note minor details in their word definitions.* In Figure 11, for the word *cloak*, the student worked hard to use phrases and a comparison to give a thorough definition. She did the same for the word *wilderness*. This careful attention should be encouraged, as students quickly grow to appreciate subtle differences in word meanings.

- *Students clearly demonstrate that they understood the word.* For the word *fastening*, the student whose work was featured in Figure 11 was initially misled and had an incorrect definition despite using correct word-identification methods (2, 3). Once this student was reminded that method 6 (making sense) should serve as a final check for all other methods, she changed her definition. Students should also correct definitions or review contextual use of a definition when they have found that their responses differ from those discussed during small-group instruction.

- *Students are able to use multiple methods to confirm word meaning.* The student whose example is featured in Figure 11 gave two methods of figuring out word meaning. This will make for great discussions during small-group instruction. Learning and practicing the methods, which are in many ways similar, is more

FIGURE 11

FIGURE 11
Fourth-Grade Student's Responses to Read-Along Guide Prompts for Strategy 2

A. Excerpts From *The Courage of Sarah Noble*

The spring night was cold, and Sarah drew her warm cloak close. That was comfortable, too. She thought of how her mother had put it around her the day she and her father had started on this long, hard journey. (p. 1)

"Keep up your courage," her mother had said, fastening the cloak under Sarah's chin. "Keep up your courage, Sarah Noble!"

And, indeed, Sarah needed to keep up her courage, for she and her father were going all the way into the wilderness of Connecticut to build a house. (p. 2)

Against a tree Sarah's father sat, his musket across his knees. (p. 2)

Reprinted with the permission of Atheneum Books for Young Readers, an imprint of Simon & Schuster Children's Publishing Division from THE COURAGE OF SARAH NOBLE by Alice Dalgliesh. Copyright 1954 Alice Dalgliesh and Leonard Weisgard; copyright renewed © 1982 Margaret B. Evans and Leonard Weisgard.

B. Student Response

Page #	New or Unfamiliar Word	Method(s) Used	Definition
p. 1	cloak	5, 6	blanket-like jacket, wrap
p. 1	journey	1, 6	a long trip
p. 2	fastening	2, 3, 6	~~speed~~ put together
p. 2	~~Curege~~ courage	6	bravrey
p. 2	wilderness	4, 6	wild area like a forest
p. 2	musket	6, 7	rifle, gun

important than distinguishing differences among them. Method 6, however, should always be used as a final check.

- *Selection of words appears thoughtful.* If the student whose work is featured in Figure 11 selected these words independently (see Teacher Tips for alternative methods), this would be considered a good selection: there are no sight words (students sometimes try to sneak in easy words), proper nouns (such as the name of a place, although we often permit yet limit place names), or interjections. For example, you might determine that *Connecticut* (on page 2 in this text) would be acceptable to list, while *Wooo—oooh* (a noise by an animal, which also appears on page 2 in this text, although not featured in Figure 11) might not be.

- *Student shows some consideration for spelling.* The student initially spelled *courage* incorrectly and was reminded to check the spelling. We typically required the words be spelled correctly but not necessarily the definitions, as is evident from the misspelled word *bravrey.*

Strategy Connections

This strategy may become closely connected to Strategy 14, Interpreting Figurative Language, as some unfamiliar words may comprise figurative language, including idioms, similes, metaphors, and personification. You can determine how students treat these crossovers.

This strategy is also closely connected to Strategy 3, Using Visual Text Clues to Figure Out Meaning. Still, there are discernible differences; Strategy 3 relies on nonverbal clues such as formatting or punctuation, whereas this strategy relies on contextual-based verbal clues. Students need proficiency in both.

Test-Taking Tips

- In addition to using informational and other nonfiction works, consider using other genres as well. State and other high-stakes assessments ask word-identification questions about passages within many genres, suggesting that building student proficiency across the genres is beneficial.

- Word-identification questions may be asked in several ways. In all cases below, the word represented by a blank line, would appear italicized in the test. It may or may not be italicized in the passage.

    The meaning of _____ is the same as_____.

    The meaning of _____ most likely means the opposite of_____.

    As it appears in the passage, the word _____ means _____.

    The best meaning of the word _____ as it appears in the passage is _____.

- The word might be used in context with a character or an event from a passage:

    The main character, Tom, was *inquisitive*. This means he _____.

    A mother chimpanzee will routinely feed and clean her young. The word *routinely* means _____.

- Word identification questions may be straightforward, but students must be careful to rely on the contextual meaning of a word. This is especially true for homophones, words with multiple meanings. For example:

    When Tom, the main character, *retired* for the evening, he _____.

    A character *retiring* for the evening is quite different than his or her action of *retiring* from an occupation. Often, the selection of answers from which students must choose includes a meaning that although correct is not contextually correct. Students who do not go back to the passage to check their meaning may select an incorrect answer.

- The word appearing in the passage might also be used in a word web, clustered with synonyms or antonyms. As students are encouraged during their word-identification practice to provide thoughtful definitions, they should be skilled in considering word meaning.

- For any type of word-identification question, students increase their ability to select the correct answer if they return to the passage, "read" their answer into the place where the word appears, and check that their answer makes sense. This test-taking strategy relies on method 6—making sure your understanding of the word makes sense—which serves as a final check on all other methods.

Using Visual Text Clues to Figure Out Meaning

Using visual text clues encourages students to notice and make sense of punctuation, formatting, and other text features that appear on a page and have meaning. Fiction and nonfiction text may each have unique features and therefore are discussed separately in the Practice With Prompts Using the Read-Along Guide and corresponding What to Look For sections that follow.

Teacher Tips for Strategy Instruction

- Unless students have had prior instruction and practice detecting atypical features on the printed page, they often ignore them. As a result, considering why these unusual features appear on the page and how they might affect meaning in the story may never be an authentic concern for students. However, after a brief time working with the strategy, students are quick to grasp that there are usually meanings in these features and that uncovering what they are becomes a worthwhile endeavor.

- Most fiction-based text clues are detected quickly by the students, whose attempts to uncover their meaning soon become routine. This is not true, however, when working with the punctuation. Although quick to find and correctly name the various types of punctuation, students require continual reminders to pay attention to the punctuation as they read aloud (which also might mimic what they do while reading silently). When this strategy is introduced, teachers might want to have students in all groups read aloud frequently so students can practice their fluency and expression.

- When working with nonfiction texts, many students are not familiar with how to read columns and other nonfiction features and may need some instruction with this. Also, they may be confused about when to read artwork, captions, sidebars, and other special elements that interrupt the text. Although there may not be a clear-cut answer to this, a thoughtful discussion enables students to feel comfortable making a decision, knowing there may not be a right or wrong answer. Having a choice and recognizing that it might be different than someone else's choice makes for a great lesson.

- Although it becomes easy for students to identify text clues, they may require help explaining the importance of the clues. Teachers might want to cluster pages together or they may choose to discuss each clue independently. Determining how best to address the explanation will depend on a multitude of factors. For example, Is the clue used in the same manner repeatedly throughout the text? Does it happen rarely? Is it used to mean the same thing consistently? Answers to these questions will assist teachers in knowing when and how to address them.

Text Suggestions

When this strategy is introduced, it is important to locate texts that include as many features as possible. Shorter texts are often most suitable for instruction in this strategy, as students are quick to grasp the idea that text features are clues to meaning. Therefore, short chapter books are often ideal, provided that they include multiple features. Students need to develop an understanding of the style used in the publication—whether the work is fiction or nonfiction—which they can achieve without listing every detail.

As we formally provide direct instruction in this strategy only in our Introductory Read-Along Guide, this concern for selecting ideal works of fiction based on the quantity of features they include and their size is temporary. The texts students responded to within the example student prompts featured with Strategies 1 and 2, *Skinnybones* (Park, 1997) and *The Courage of Sarah Noble* (Dalgliesh, 1954) are both relatively short and also provide a good assortment of text features for practice in this strategy. Other texts that have been used within various intermediate-level grades include *The Kid in the Red Jacket* (Park, 2004), *Danger on Panther Peak* (Wallace, 1989), *Revolutionary War on Wednesday* (Osborne, 2000), *The Chocolate Touch* (Catling, 1988), *Freckle Juice* (Blume, 1990), and *Muggie Maggie* (Cleary, 1990).

Following this introductory instruction, we often select works of fiction based on authentic literary themes such as friendship or coming-of-age stories. You might also select texts for author studies, such as multiple-leveled texts by Barbara Park, Sharon Creech, or Roald Dahl. Thus, text selection based on literary criteria soon replaces text selection based on accommodating instruction in this strategy.

You may also want to use Readers Theatre scripts, which often include stage directions that appear in italics, parentheses, or in other formats. Likewise, changing character roles are often featured in bold—and sometimes in color in some of the new leveled Readers Theatre scripts. Using this type of literature might be helpful for students who may have difficulty recognizing changes in fonts or other stylistic formats.

Student-Friendly Chat on the Importance of the Strategy

When providing instruction on using visual text clues to figure out meaning, you can use the following dialogue as a way to explain the importance of this strategy to your students:

> Good readers pay attention to any features of the page or the text. For example, good readers pay attention to when a character is speaking because of the quotation marks and the indented space. Also, good readers look at punctuation and read expressively (even silently to themselves) using the punctuation clues. For example, when coming across a comma, good readers will pause. Or, when seeing an ex-

clamation mark, good readers know to add enthusiasm. Likewise, really good readers will notice that something has been written in boldface or italicized type and wonder why that is so—there is usually a good reason.

Practice With Prompts Using the Read-Along Guide—Fiction
This strategy is typically introduced and covered only in our Introductory Read-Along Guide (see chapter 4). After this initial instruction, we often provided instruction using teachable moments and referred back to our experience with the strategy after students demonstrated they could easily transfer the skill as they worked with new texts. Likewise, as practice with fluency was ongoing within all components of our reading instruction and also spanned the curriculum, we continually revisited this activity despite not including it in another Guide. Determining how often to formally cover this strategy in a Read-Along Guide is a decision best left to the teacher. Certainly, the Guide can be adjusted to include any features that may be unique to any text.

You can use the following dialogue as a way to explain to students how they should begin their practice and use of this strategy when working specifically with fiction texts:

> There are many clues that will help you make sense of what you're reading. To learn and practice this strategy, you'll be looking for four different types of clues: (1) punctuation, such as commas and quotation marks; (2) print features, such as boldface type and formatting; (3) spacing features, where the spacing might look funny; and (4) chapter titles, which might stand out. Perhaps you'll even spy other things that might look unusual.
>
> Before reading, scan the pages and try to find as many of these features as you can on the page and write down the page numbers where you find them. Then, try to figure out their importance.

Figure 12 illustrates how students will respond in the Guide to prompts about their reading as a way to monitor their use of Strategy 3 with fiction. In this example, a fourth-grade student responded to prompts about using visual text clues to figure out meaning while reading *Skinnybones* (Park, 1997). Featured excerpts from the book provide insights on how the student applied the strategy while reading.

What to Look For: Key Indicators of Successful Student Performance—Fiction
• *Students recognize and accurately identify all features.* Teachers can decide to cluster pages and scan for text clues prior to reading, as was done with many of the text clues in the example. Here, the entire chapter was scanned before the teacher opened up discussion on the importance of any clues.
• *Plausible reasons for unusual text features can be provided.* For font changes in the second row of Figure 12, the student explained two ways she used these clues to gain meaning. The first explanation shows she is aware of a character's action, which is "writing," and the second refines her understanding that the character is writing information on an order form, which "looks" different on the page.

FIGURE 12
Fourth-Grade Student's Responses to Read-Along Guide Prompts for Strategy 3 (Fiction)

A. Excerpts From *Skinnybones*
chapter one
ME AND THE KID WITH THE WOODEN NOSE

MY CAT EATS KITTY FRITTERS BECAUSE...

If she didn't eat Kitty Fritters, she would die of starvation.
　　Kitty Fritters is the only cat food my mother will buy. She buys it because she says it's cheap. She says she doesn't care how it tastes, or what it's made out of. (p. 1)

After I finished writing my comments, I went to the closet and took the bag of Kitty Fritters off the bottom shelf. I turned to the back of the bag and read the rest of the directions. It said:

COMPLETE THIS SENTENCE;
MY CAT EATS KITTY FRITTERS BECAUSE....
Then print your name and address on the entry blank enclosed in this bag. Mail your entry to:

KITTY FRITTERS TV CONTEST
P.O. BOX 2343
Philadelphia, Pennsylvania 19103 (p. 2)

Finally, I got so frustrated, I dumped the entire twenty-five-pound bag of cat food out onto the kitchen floor. Even then, I must have sifted through about a million fritters before I found the stupid thing.
　　At last, I put it on the table and began to fill it out.

NAME: Alex Frankovitch
ADDRESS: 2567 Delaney Street
CITY: Phoenix　　　STATE: Arizona　　　ZIP: 85000 (p. 3)

From SKINNYBONES by Barbara Park, copyright © 1982, 1997 by Barbara Park. Used by permission of Alfred A. Knopf, an imprint of Random House Children's Books, a division of Random House, Inc.

B. Student Response

Text Clue (Fiction)	Page #	Explain the Importance
Punctuation (. , ; : " " ... ! ? –)	1–9	This helps tell us how to read: when to pause or stop and what expression to use. It also tells who is speaking and how they're feeling.
Boldface Text/Italics/Capitals	1, 2, 3, 4, 5	These help me understand what's happening in the story. For example, Alex is writing an order form, which even looks different from the text.
Spacing Features or Unusual Spacing	1, 2, 3, 9	These help us figure out different things in a story.
Titles or Subtitles	1, 10	These give us clues that a chapter is beginning. It gives us clues about the chapter and when a new chapter and new idea is coming.
Other		

• *Students can discuss the significance of unique features and their overall importance.* When discussing spacing features, the teacher may have covered each of the unique uses from the pages listed. However, he instructed students to identify a sample and then summarize their importance with the explanation, "These help us figure out different things in a story," so the process of recording each use wouldn't be time-consuming. Deciding when to discuss this feature and record responses is best left to teachers. Determining through discussion or written example that the student understands the meaning of the feature is critical.

Practice With Prompts Using the Read-Along Guide—Nonfiction

As previously mentioned in the Practice With Prompts section for fiction texts, this strategy is typically introduced and covered only in our Introductory Read-Along Guide (see chapter 4). After this initial instruction, we often provided instruction using teachable moments and referred back to our experience with the strategy as students demonstrated they could easily transfer the skill as they worked with new texts. Likewise, as practice with fluency was ongoing within all components of our reading instruction and also spanned the curriculum, we continually revisited this activity despite not including it in another Guide. Determining how often to formally cover this strategy in a Read-Along Guide is a decision best left to the teacher. Certainly, the Guide can be adjusted to include any features that may be unique to your text.

You can use the following dialogue as a way to explain to students how they should begin their practice and use of the strategy when working specifically with nonfiction texts:

> There are many visual text clues that will help you make sense of what you're reading. Although you'll recognize many features found in nonfiction (because many are also found in fiction), there may be other things that are new to you. For example, words might be printed in two columns instead of across the entire page. Or maybe there are maps, pictures with captions, or even sidebars that contain extra information that is set apart from the text. Chances are, you'll also see other components such as a glossary or an index. Paying attention to these and knowing how to use them to help construct meaning will become automatic.
>
> Before reading, scan the pages and try to find as many of these features as you can on the page and write down the page numbers where you find them. Then, try to figure out their importance.

Figure 13 illustrates how students will respond in the Guide to prompts about their reading as a way to monitor their use of Strategy 3 with nonfiction. In this example, a fourth-grade student responded to prompts about using visual text clues for meaning while reading the nonfiction text *Cherokee Heroes: Three Who Made a Difference* (Hirschfield, 2001). Featured excerpts from the book provide insights on how the student applied the strategy while reading.

Fourth-Grade Student's Responses to Read-Along Guide Prompts for Strategy 3
(Nonfiction)

A. Excerpts From *Cherokee Heroes*
History of the Cherokees
Like all Native Americans, the Cherokees were among the first people to live in what we now call the United States. At one time, they live in an area that today stretches across eight southeastern states. Wooded mountains and valleys shaped the land.... (p. 5)

One of Nancy's nicknames was Wild Rose, because she had rosy skin. No one knows what Nancy Ward looked like. This picture is one artist's idea of how she looked. (p. 13, photo caption)

The Black Drink
A role of the Beloved Woman was to make a special tea called the "black drink." She made it by boiling the leaves of the holly tree. All warriors drank this tea before they went to war. Drinking the tea was part of how the warriors got ready for battle. (p. 17, sidebar)

From *Cherokee Heroes: Three Who Made a Difference* by Laura Hirschfield. © 2001 by Wright Group/McGraw-Hill. Reprinted with permission.

B. Student Response

Text Clue/Feature (Nonfiction)	Page #	Explain the Importance
Boldface Text/Italics/Capitals	0	There are many boldface titles on a lot of pages. It's good to see them, but we listed them in the next row.
Titles or Subtitles	4, 5, 8, 11, 12, 17, 20, 26, ??	These let us know that what we are going to read about. They are like clues. Also, we know when there will be a change in the idea we're reading about.
Photographs/Illustrations	4–11, 13–15, 17, 19, 20, 21, 23, +	There are a lot of pictures, like a picture book. Some are photos and some are drawn. Some photos are old and in black and white. Others are in color. All of them help me understand what I'm reading about.
Maps	5, 9, 10, 11	These helped me learn more about things that I read. I know where some things took place a long time ago, and I also know about where things are today.
Captions	4, 7, 8, 13, 14, 15+	These help me figure out what the pictures mean. Sometimes they also give a lot more information about something, too.
Sidebars	17, 25	I learned more information from these.
Table of Contents/Glossary/Index	3, 32	The contents help me see what the book is about and how things will be covered. The index tells me where (the page) I can find things.
Other _____		

What to Look For: Key Indicators of Successful Student Performance—Nonfiction

• *Students recognize format styles and distinguish whether or not a style is important as they construct meaning.* As was done with the fiction passage, teachers can decide to cluster pages and scan for text clues prior to reading. As students become comfortable with this, they will begin to distinguish when a text feature is or isn't important. For example, during one group discussion, it was decided not to list page numbers for the titles and subtitles although they appeared in bold. The students agreed it was better to ignore this feature and instead include mention of the subtitles in that area marked "subtitles," as the function they served seemed more critical than the style used.

- *Students are aware of specialized nonfiction features, such as subtitles, that provide clues about meaning.* The student whose work is featured in Figure 13 was aware that subtitles serve a useful purpose and provide a glimpse of what would be presented in the text that followed. Initially some students might overlook them entirely as they may be unfamiliar with their function.

- *Although there may be some questions, students begin to distinguish different types of illustrations (photos, drawings, maps, etc.).* Although many teachers do not initially make a distinction among the different types of illustrations, especially when they do not affect meaning, there may be times when they do become important. For example, when students view maps, they may have to interpret keys, scales, and other features. At other times these features may be absent and so, perhaps, they serve a different purpose. These fine-tuned details make for good discussions.

- *Students recognize the importance of captions and their relationship to the artwork they accompany.* At times, students will pass over a caption and may struggle to interpret the artwork on their own or pass over other information provided in the caption. Recognizing that captions can be helpful is critical, just as understanding that when one is absent may allow more room for interpretation.

- *Subtle differences among nonfiction features may be detected.* Sidebars, which provide additional information related to a topic discussed in the text, often add the "wow" appeal that students readily pick up. Identifying sidebars in various texts and determining how they differ from captioned artwork gets students thinking about the types of information presented, the length of the sidebar, and how it directly relates to the main topic.

- *Students are able to identify other aids, and they can show that they understand how to use them.* Nonfiction works often include unique features, yet students will quickly learn that whether or not they are included is not something that is consistent. Hunting for these devices either in a contents listing or by scanning the book is a good lesson during small-group discussion time so students can masterfully tackle nonfiction, using all devices available to them.

Strategy Connections

This strategy can be grouped with numerous others. For instance, this strategy may be closely connected to Strategy 16, Drawing Conclusions and Making Inferences, because format clues are often deliberate methods used to get into the mind of a character. For example, if a character's dialogue appears in full capital letters and is followed by an exclamation point, this suggests the character is greatly excited. Still, understanding this relationship through inferencing is a skill some students need to develop. This strategy may also be connected to Strategy 2, Finding Word Meaning and Building Vocabulary Using Context Clues. For example, if students are attempting to uncover word meaning, they might need to interpret a character's actions or state of mind based on text clues.

Test-Taking Tips

- Most questions about text clues are inferential and require that students read between the lines to explain something. For example, following a reading passage, students might encounter the following types of multiple-choice questions:

  In paragraph 3, the sentence "*Oh no...I don't know which key to try,* I thought to myself" is partly written in an italic font because _____.

  Here a correct answer could simply be that the character is thinking this silently to himself. Still, some students may not correctly interpret this connection.

  In the last paragraph, the main character claims he is a STAR. Why do you think the word *star* is in capital letters?

  Here a correct answer might be that the use of all capital letters highlights or dramatizes the importance of being a star.

- For nonfiction passages, test questions might ask students to explain the meaning behind the use of a word that is enclosed in unusual punctuation, such as in the following example:

  Read this sentence from the article.

  Ravens often "talk" to each other....

  In this sentence, why are there quotation marks around *talk*?

  Some students may answer this question incorrectly, selecting an answer like, "To tell what someone said about ravens." The correct answer is, "To explain that ravens do not have the ability to talk like humans." Here, the quotation marks were not used as they typically are to indicate dialogue. Even proficient readers may not answer this correctly, as they may not carefully consider that there might be other possibilities for the use of quotation marks.

- For nonfiction passages, test questions might ask students to determine the best meaning for a difficult word where a definition may actually have been provided using some form of a call-out style (for example, the difficult word was highlighted in the passage with a definition provided in a footnote at the bottom, in a box, or using an asterisk alongside where it appeared in the text). If students were not paying attention to text clues or were unable to interpret the clue's meaning, they may have missed this question. Over the years, New York state standardized tests have used multiple methods of call-out styles.

Asking Questions to Engage in the Text

When students silently ask themselves questions about the content of their reading material, they are actively participating in the reading process. They are constructing meaning as they build their understanding. The questions they are asking in this process aren't necessarily ones where an immediate answer may be available. Instead, they are often larger questions, where students explore events for deeper meaning or underlying issues.

Teacher Tips for Strategy Instruction

- A student's level of engagement with the text varies and will affect their desire to ask questions. If students are not naturally asking questions, it may be because they simply don't like the story or characters or they are having trouble comprehending information. Determining which obstacle is causing the interference—through methods such as teacher observation and student assessment—will be important.

- As teachers provide instruction in the use of this strategy, the authenticity of a student's natural questioning is altered. Monitoring students when they are engaged in authentic reading activities may be necessary to determine if students are challenged by this strategy.

- At times, students may become sidetracked by their personal experiences, which could interfere with their natural inclination to ask relevant questions. As a result, students may lose track of events in the story, lose meaning, and become disengaged. Students could also get sidetracked by placing an exaggerated significance on a minor event and become lost in questions that aren't linked to the text. Here, too, the result is that the student loses track of meaning and may eventually disengage from the text. In these instances, teachers may remind students to refer back to the original prompt in the Read-Along Guide (see page 226) or offer them the opportunity to hear another student's response.

Text Suggestions

Teachers may want to avoid introducing this strategy with works of nonfiction or informational texts. Such works might jeopardize students' abilities to witness how they authentically ask questions when they are simply enjoying a good book. Students are used to asking questions about informational or content-based information and may try to transfer this type of questioning to works of fiction. Yet the authentic types of questions students typically wonder about while reading fiction may be very different. For example, where students may have easily found answers to questions asked in informational text, in works of fiction the answer might not be present. As a result, it may take students some time to get used to discussing and describing vague or ambiguous questions.

Therefore, beginning with various types of fiction is an easy way to introduce this strategy. Realistic fiction and texts with action-based plots that may also contain interesting twists or suspenseful events are good choices. Mysteries and science fiction are also good choices, as these genres are written to intentionally pique the reader's curiosity. Works of historical fiction are other good texts to consider, as they often have strong plots, atypical conflicts, and numerous opportunities for students to ask and answer questions as they learn about events and times that have passed. Such works provide a great opportunity to introduce content information and also to challenge students once they demonstrate proficiency with this strategy.

Student-Friendly Chat on the Importance of the Strategy

When providing instruction on using the strategy of asking questions to engage in the text, you can use the following dialogue as a way to explain its importance to your students:

> Good readers ask silent questions (to themselves) before, during, and after reading. They question the content, the author, the events, the issues, and the ideas in the text. Sometimes your questions are answered immediately. Sometimes they are answered by the end of the book. Still, other times you may need to research a little bit more to find an answer to your questions or you may need to think of them as open questions and hold onto them for the future. No matter when your question is answered, using this strategy makes you a better reader.

Practice With Prompts Using the Read-Along Guide

This strategy is typically introduced and covered only in the Introductory Read-Along Guide (see chapter 4 for more detailed discussion on the Read-Along Guide). After this initial instruction, we often furthered our instruction using teachable moments. We began by referring back to our experience with the strategy in our Introductory Guide and then encouraged students to simply transfer the skill as they worked with new texts. Determining how often to formally cover this strategy in a Read-Along Guide is a decision best left to the teacher.

You can use the following dialogue as a way to explain to students how they should begin their practice in the use of the strategy:

> As you practice this strategy, you'll be asked to pay close attention to your thoughts as you're reading. Whenever you ask yourself a question, just write it down. It can be a specific question, such as one that is likely to be answered in the text. On the other hand, it may address a larger issue that may or may not get answered in the text. Using the keywords *who, what, where, when, why,* and *how* or *if* will help you avoid simple yes or no questions.

Figure 14 illustrates how students will respond in the Guide to prompts about their reading as a way to monitor their use of Strategy 4. In this example, a fourth-grade student responded to prompts about asking questions to engage in the text while reading *Skinnybones* (Park, 1997). Featured excerpts from the book provide insights on how the student applied the strategy while reading.

FIGURE 14
Fourth-Grade Student's Responses to Read-Along Guide Prompts for Strategy 4

A. Excerpts From *Skinnybones*

T.J.'s smirk got bigger. "Hey, Frankovitch. How'd you like to make a little deal?" he said.

I shook my head and started to walk away. "Nope. Sorry, T.J. No deals. I'm gonna have to tell you what I've been telling everybody else today. No matter how hard you beg, I cannot pitch for your team. My coach made me sign a contract...."

It's not like I've never tried it before. Just last week, I practiced pitching with my dad. It didn't actually work out that good, though. Most of the balls I threw didn't make it to the plate. The one that did, beaned my father on the head.

"What kind of stupid pitch do you call that?" Dad yelled.

"That would be my bean ball!" I yelled back. (p. 33)

Anyway, T.J. kept on bugging me and bugging me. "Come on, Alex," he pleaded. "Just listen to my deal. What have you got to lose?"

By this time a bunch of kids had started to gather.

"Okay. Fine. Tell me your deal, T.J. But make it snappy. It's almost time for Brian to massage my pitching arm."

...Oh, geez, what a mess! If I said no, everyone would know I was a liar. But if I said yes, everyone would be able to see how weak I threw. Somehow I had to get out of this. (p. 34)

B. Student Response

When I Read (Page #)	I Wondered <u>Why</u>, <u>What</u>, <u>When</u>, <u>How</u>, <u>Who</u>, <u>Where</u>, or <u>If</u>...
p. 33	I wonder what the little deal is T.J. wants to make with Alex.
p. 33	I wonder if Alex's dad was mad after he got hit in the head. I wonder what Alex meant by a bean ball.
p. 34	I wonder why T.J. keeps bugging Alex about the deal. I thought T.J. wanted Alex to pitch for his team, but now I'm unsure.
p. 34	I wonder how Alex will try to get out of the pitching contest.

What to Look For: Key Indicators of Successful Student Performance

• *The questions should be relevant to the plot.* In Figure 14, all of the practice-response questions are significantly linked to activities taking place in the reading passages. The student's questions do not exhibit that his thoughts are wandering from the action.

• *The student's awareness of significant issues in the reading should be demonstrated through the questions.* In all of the sample responses in Figure 14, the student has meaningful questions that show he is aware of important matters in the text. He does not consider questions that would place an exaggerated sense of importance on minor issues—such as wondering where Alex and his dad practiced pitching.

• *Questions exhibit that the reader is using information gained earlier in the text.* The last question this reader considers on page 34 is how Alex will "get out of the pitching contest." Here, the reader shows he clearly knows that Alex tries to avoid uncomfortable situations because Alex has acted this way earlier in the story.

- *Most readers will be curious at similar points in the story.* The first entry in Figure 14 shows a typical question most students will ask at this point in the story. This response is typical as students encounter events that seem masterfully placed by talented writers to build suspense. Just as the appearance of these typical questions during student practice indicates success with this strategy, so too might their absence indicate that some comprehension may be challenged.

- *Some questions may simply lead to new questions.* Two separate entries show that this reader continues to ask questions about T.J.'s plan. He obviously had to alter his previous understanding, which was based on the first answer he thought he had in the text: T.J.'s deal must not have been to have Alex pitch. Monitoring when readers can suspend their need to know or readjust their answers to questions—instead of becoming confused—is a useful indicator of success with this strategy.

- *Although some questions may be based on a student's individual experience, they should not detract from the story.* In the second entry of Figure 14, the student originally asked a question about the meaning of *bean ball*. During instruction, the teacher suggested the student try Strategy 2 to see if context clues might help him figure out the meaning of the phrase. He then added a new question to his Guide, asking if Alex's dad was mad after he was hit. Obviously, this student's question is based on a typical reaction that perhaps his dad, a coach, or a sibling had from getting hit with a ball. Though this question seems almost contradictory to the indicators discussed above, it nonetheless reflects a very critical way in which students engage with a text. Ensuring that these types of questions are not too plentiful and that they don't sidetrack a reader is something the teacher will casually monitor.

Strategy Connections

This strategy is closely related to Strategy 5, Making Connections to Aid Understanding, and Strategy 7, Making Predictions. For example, students may ask questions based on predictions or their own experiences. If teachers want to feature all of these strategies in one Read-Along Guide, they may want to provide initial instruction separately and then have students discover the connections among them as they practice independently.

Test-Taking Tips

- Unlike many of the other strategies where test questions can be directly linked to assessing a student's ability with a skill, such as identifying main idea, sequencing events, and so on, asking questions is one that is indirectly tested through other question formats. The primary purpose of this strategy is to help students comprehend what they're reading.

- Some test questions that could indirectly rely on use of this strategy might be ones involving predictions. For example, a question could be "What might happen to the main character based on the way the story ended?" Although these types of questions may not have been ones students asked while reading the passage, students nonetheless could benefit from this skill by understanding and having a comfort level with the process of asking themselves questions.

- Another benefit students may get from this strategy, although not directly tested in it, is they may be able to ask themselves a *what* or *when* question if they're having difficulty responding to a question. In essence, they can use their skill at questioning to rephrase a problem question. For example, students might have to complete missing events in a sequentially ordered graphic organizer. Asking themselves the question, What happened after the main character...?—reading into their question the completed information provided in the graphic organizer—could direct their effort in scanning the reading passage for the correct answer.

Making Connections to Aid Understanding

When readers are able to connect to people, places, or events they're reading about through a shared experience, they have a powerful starting point upon which to further build their comprehension. This strategy—which requires students to make text-to-text, text-to-self, and text-to-world connections—is effective for works of fiction and nonfiction. A sample of each is provided in the sections that follow.

Encouraging students to reflect on their past experiences as they read is similar to the prereading technique of activating prior knowledge—only here, it is ongoing. Helping students recognize when they are automatically doing this is the main method of working with this strategy. Encouraging them to stretch their experiences when this isn't automatically happening, such as with works of nonfiction where prior knowledge and background knowledge may be weak, is another way of working with the strategy.

Teacher Tips for Strategy Instruction

- The amount of background knowledge students bring to their reading experiences affects their ability to comprehend. Some readers may have more trouble than others making connections. Teachers may need to assist students in recognizing connections, no matter how inconsequential or stretched they might initially seem, keeping in mind that their objective serves as a springboard for further development and refinement. Therefore, sometimes students may need to rely on indirect experiences or less concrete feelings to make connections. These might be through text-to-text or text-to-world connections. However, remind students that text-to-self connections can also be indirect, meaning they might know someone, such as a family member, who shares an experience with a character or who may have traveled to a place discussed in a book. These connections are often overlooked by students.

- Differences among the three types of connections featured with this strategy are not necessarily important. One benefit, however, is that students may recognize relationships that they might not otherwise consider. For example, some students may not automatically associate a passage read during "reading" time with a topic they recently covered in social studies using their textbook. For instance, students might not automatically relate a passage from a picture book like *Phoebe the Spy* (Griffin, 1977) with a textbook section covering events leading to the Revolutionary War. Distinguishing the connections helps readers connect all curriculum areas and pull information from multiple sources.

• Teachers might want to assist struggling readers by providing supplementary materials for building a student's background knowledge. Suggestions for building this component into your instruction are provided in chapter 1.

• Students may also need to rely on connections that show a lack of direct experience with the topic or are opposite or somehow different from those featured in their reading passages (several examples of this are shown in the What to Look For: Key Indicators of Successful Student Performance section for nonfiction works in this strategy). These connections are also often overlooked by students, yet they provide a framework upon which to add new information. Teachers may want to watch that this approach doesn't become overused.

Text Suggestions

Beginning with realistic fiction is an easy way to introduce this strategy. Selecting a humorous intermediate-grade chapter book, especially one partially based in a school setting, guarantees that most students will successfully identify numerous connections. For works of fiction, students will often be able to make numerous and varied connections. Popular authors are often masterful at creating authentic school events. However, while introducing this strategy, teachers might want to avoid fiction that features figurative language, such as poetry and tall tales, which often include personification, idioms, and similes. Although wonderful techniques to save for instruction in other strategies, they may be confusing to students who are initially trying to make connections.

However, most intermediate-grade students will struggle much more with works of nonfiction. Here, students typically want to rely on their personal experience, yet their experiences with these topics may not be vast. As a result, they may not feel the same level of success working through this strategy for texts of different genres. Teacher assistance and encouragement will help them meet with success. Transferring this skill to works of nonfiction is a strategic way to help students strengthen their ability to work with content and informational text. Small-format guided reading texts are good choices for this. The subject matter can be selected to coincide with units of study in the social studies or science curriculums, or high-interest texts on any subject will be suitable.

In addition, works of historical fiction, as well as historical or multicultural biographies, provide great opportunities to challenge students once they become skilled with this strategy. They offer students of various backgrounds an opportunity to share new ideas.

Student-Friendly Chat on the Importance of the Strategy

When providing instruction on using the making connections to aid understanding strategy with fiction, you can use the following dialogue as a way to explain the importance of this strategy to your students:

> Good readers use prior knowledge and experiences to better understand what they're reading. Sometimes it's helpful to think about how you "know" or "connect with" a character, event, or some part of the book you're reading. Your connection could be any of these three:
>
> 1. Text-to-Self Connection (T–S). These include experiences you share from your background. For example, you might be a really good soccer or football player and share experiences with a character from a book who plays the same sport. Also, you might share a feeling with a character, such as being frightened or excited.
>
> 2. Text-to-Text Connection (T–T). These include experiences you read about in other writings. For example, you may be familiar with fairy tale characters from reading books about them. Likewise, you may enjoy reading books that are in a series where you need to know what happened in earlier volumes. Also, you might have a favorite author who may write about similar things.
>
> 3. Text-to-World Connection (T–W). These include experiences you know and share with others simply because of your common worldly experiences. These might be things you seem to know to do without being told, like your automatic reflexes, such as blinking. Or it might be things that everyone just seems to know, like that the President's job is pretty important.
>
> These types of connections may overlap, but it's fun to think about how you know or "connect with" something.

Practice With Prompts Using the Read-Along Guide—Fiction

This strategy is typically introduced and covered only in the Introductory Read-Along Guide, although you may feature it in a nonfiction Guide as well (see chapter 4 for more detailed discussion on the Read-Along Guide). After this initial instruction, we often furthered our instruction using teachable moments. Here, we began by referring back to our experience with the strategy in our Introductory Guide and then encouraged students to simply transfer the skill as they worked with new texts. Determining how often to formally cover this strategy in a Read-Along Guide is a decision best left to the teacher.

You can use the following dialogue as a way to explain to students how they should begin their practice in the use of the strategy specifically with fiction texts:

> Let's practice thinking about connections we make during our reading. Use the prompt below to record your connection and label it T–S, T–T, or T–W to identify what type of connection you've made. To work with this strategy, you'll be asked to pay close attention to your thoughts as you're reading. Often, we automatically make connections as we read, so when that happens you'll simply record your

connection. Other times, we may need to search our minds a bit and s-t-r-e-t-c-h an experience we've had that might help us better understand what we're reading. We'll practice this, too.

Figure 15 illustrates how students will respond in the Guide to prompts about their reading as a way to monitor their use of Strategy 5 with fiction. In this example, a fourth-grade student responded to prompts about making connections to aid understanding while reading *Skinnybones* (Park, 1997). Featured excerpts from the book provide insights on how the student applied the strategy while reading.

What to Look For: Key Indicators of Successful Student Performance—Fiction

- *Student connections are believable and logical.* In the first entry of Figure 15, the student has made a text-to-world connection, recognizing that a reference made in her book was to a character connected to a breakfast cereal that most everyone is familiar with and that has appeared in television advertising.

- *Connections may be indirect or transferred to similar situations.* The second entry shows that the connection might be considered all or any one of the three.

FIGURE 15
Fourth-Grade Student's Responses to Read-Along Guide Prompts for Strategy 5 (Fiction)

A. Excerpts From *Skinnybones*

Most of the boys in my class brought in pictures of baseball or football players. A few others brought in pictures of policemen.

    I brought in a picture of the Lucky Charms guy. I cut it off the front of the cereal box.

    My teacher was pretty worried about it, too. She called me right up to her desk. (p. 24)

At first, I thought this was some weird new punishment she'd read about in one of those parenting magazines. But instead, she got a pencil and made a mark on the wall at the very top of my head. (p. 25)

The coach just shook his head. "Alex, I ordered you a small. A large would eat you up and spit you out."

    Then he gave my uniform to Randy and handed me the eensy-weensy, itsy-bitsy, practically-the-size-a-baby-would-wear...small. (pp. 29–30)

From SKINNYBONES by Barbara Park, copyright © 1982, 1997 by Barbara Park. Used by permission of Alfred A. Knopf, an imprint of Random House Children's Books, a division of Random House, Inc.

B. Student Response

When I Read (Page #)	I Thought About...	Type of Connection
p. 24	The Lucky Charms guy I've seen on the cereal boxes and TV ads.	T–W
p. 25	The parents' magazines I've seen at the doctor's office.	T–S, T–T, T–W
p. 30	How Alex and I wear the same size clothing.	T–S

Interestingly, although she does not read magazines geared for parents, she certainly understood the type of magazine that was discussed in her book. This response demonstrates that the student is able to substitute an actual experience for one that is similar. This response is a good indicator that this student can apply similar or indirect experiences to help her understand events that she might not have experienced firsthand. This skill is one that may be absent or limited in some readers, but it is one that will help build comprehension.

- *Inconsequential differences do not interfere with a student's ability to make connections.* The last example in Figure 15 shows that the student has made a strong connection to the main character, Alex. Here, the reader (a female) demonstrates that her shared experiences are not detracted from by issues of gender. Some students may not be able to get beyond the fact that they are a different gender than the main character(s) in the book. Still, working to replace these mental barriers and instead focusing on identifying shared experiences is one that will help build comprehension.

- *Students can accurately recognize all types of connections.* Although the student has demonstrated use of all types of connections, the distinction among them isn't necessarily important.

Practice With Prompts Using the Read-Along Guide—Nonfiction
Although this strategy is often introduced and covered only in the Introductory Read-Along Guide for works of fiction, the same is not necessarily true for works of nonfiction. While working with this genre, teachers may choose to offer repeated practice with it, as it may enable students to grasp valuable background information more quickly if they can establish a connection to it. This is often needed for instruction in the content areas.

You can use the following dialogue as a way to explain to students how they should begin their practice in the use of the strategy specifically with nonfiction texts:

Sometimes it's hard to make connections when you're reading nonfiction, especially if your book is about a person who is very different from you, or if it's about a place you've never been, or if it's about an event you're learning about for the first time. But it's important to try your best! Think of similar experiences you may have had, or perhaps you know someone who has shared an experience with someone in your book. There are even other approaches you could take we'll learn about as we practice this strategy with nonfiction. Get ready to stretch your thinking! Use the prompt below to record your connection and label it T–S, T–T, or T–W.

Figure 16 illustrates how students will respond in the Guide to prompts about their reading as a way to monitor their use of Strategy 5 with nonfiction. In this example, a fourth-grade student responded to prompts about making connections to aid understanding while reading *Floating and Paddling* (Strebor, 2000). Featured excerpts from the book provide insights on how the student applied the strategy while reading.

What to Look For: Key Indicators of Successful Student Performance—Nonfiction

- *Students are able to consider connections outside of their immediate experiences.* The first entry in Figure 16 shows the student making a connection to his immediate experience of having birch trees in his yard. After some prompting from his teacher, he also realized that in a recent social studies class, he learned about birch-bark canoes used by the Native Americans.

- *Students may make connections based on differences.* The second type of connection is one in which the student has made based on differences rather than similarities to something he knows. At first, students may not think these are connections. However, they also enable students to grasp new meaning and build comprehension.

• *Students are able to grasp glimmers of a connection.* The last connection in Figure 16 was a stretch. Here, the teacher encouraged the student to tell everything he knew about China. Although he initially claimed to know nothing about China, he eventually provided this response. Somewhat similar to the example above it, the student used a lack of experience as part of his response ("I've never been to China"), yet he was further encouraged to add to this ("I have some toys from China"). This response provided enough of a framework upon which to attach his new information—bamboo rafts were made and used in China.

Strategy Connections

This strategy is closely related to Strategy 6, Visualizing to Support the Text. For example, students may first make a connection to something and then create a visual image to accompany that connection. As teachers may want to feature both strategies in an Introductory Read-Along Guide, letting students know that these two strategies may work together assures them that their response is perfectly appropriate.

In contrast, teachers may not want to feature this strategy together with Strategy 9, Finding the Important or Main Idea, as students may place an exaggerated significance on a detail to which they can connect and become sidetracked if they are trying to identify the main idea of a passage. It might also be helpful to caution students who may be at risk of having this difficulty (based on teacher observations of students' practice in their Guides).

Test-Taking Tips

• Unlike many of the other strategies where test questions can be directly linked to assessing a student's ability with a skill such as identifying the main idea or sequencing events, making connections is one that is indirectly tested through other question formats. The primary purpose of this strategy is to help students comprehend what they're reading.

• Some test questions that could indirectly rely on use of this strategy might be those in which students must empathize with a character or place themselves in a circumstance in which they have no or little experience in order to answer a question. For example, questions that rely on predicting or inferring how a character might feel or act could rely on a student's ability to put themselves in that character's place.

For instance, if asked, "How do you suppose Thomas Alva Edison felt when he could not figure out how to get a light bulb to light?" students can probably relate to Thomas Edison even though they have no experience inventing a light bulb—this is because they *have* met challenges which have proved difficult. Making connections to either works of fiction or nonfiction gives students practice considering experiences they may not have actually had, especially as teachers work to extend their skills in this area.

• Another test-taking benefit students may get from this strategy is they may be able to consider other avenues for answering questions. At times, especially with inferential or prediction questions, students may quickly become stumped because they have no experience with matters relating to the question. However, considering their practice with text-to-world and text-to-text connections, they could extend their resources to those outside of their own experience, which would be helpful with some test questions.

Visualizing to Support the Text

DIFFICULTY RATING 2

When readers are able to make pictures in their minds of the people, places, or events they're reading about, they're better able to support and develop their comprehension. We often refer to this as making movies in our minds. Giving students the opportunity to illustrate the cover of their Read-Along Guide (see chapter 4) supports their ability to visualize.

Teacher Tips for Strategy Instruction

• The amount of background knowledge students bring to their reading experiences affects their ability to comprehend. Some readers may have more trouble than others visualizing episodes from their reading. Teachers may need to assist students in creating images by suggesting relationships among ideas or by suggesting experiences that will help students create an appropriate visual. Modeling may also be a helpful device for students struggling with this.

• Some students have a great deal of trouble visualizing. This appears to be true no matter if their attempts are in connection to their reading or to activities in other content areas. Through continued practice, most students demonstrate improvement. Teachers may consider pairing visual learners with those who find this activity challenging. This method of providing additional support also helps develop this skill.

• Most intermediate-grade students will struggle with creating images for works of nonfiction. Here, students typically want to rely on their personal experiences, yet their experiences may not be vast. As a result, they may not feel the same level of success when using this strategy for works of nonfiction. Teacher assistance and encouragement will help them meet with success.

• Teachers might want to assist struggling readers by providing supplementary materials for building a student's background knowledge. Suggestions for building this component into your instruction are provided in chapter 1.

• In addition to helping students build their comprehension, working with this strategy also enables teachers to gain invaluable insight on a student's background knowledge. As shown in the sample prompt that appears later in this section, common ideas or shared experiences that we might assume or take for granted as present in every child, such as the story of Humpty Dumpty, may be absent. Providing students with this information not only fills long-standing gaps but also reduces the risk that it may lead to even further misunderstanding.

- Many of the sample Read-Along Guides included in Appendix A have a front cover that includes space for a student's illustration. Typically students color their cover at the close of an instructional unit. Displaying student work may further help those students who have trouble visualizing.

Text Suggestions

Texts that contain descriptive passages—fiction, nonfiction, historical fiction, and numerous others—make good choices for instruction in this strategy. Many students feel that this strategy is only useful with works of fiction. However, it clearly is one that will also help build comprehension as students engage in works of nonfiction. Readers Theatre and other dramatic passages might also be good choices as student may visualize action or expression and then perform it as well.

Teachers may want to initially avoid working with illustrated picture books or chapter books so that students can explore their own skill in visualizing. Likewise, graphic novels and comic books might not enable students to develop this skill.

Student-Friendly Chat on the Importance of the Strategy

When providing instruction on visualizing to support the text, you can use the following dialogue as a way to explain the importance of this strategy to your students:

> Good readers use this strategy to help them fully understand the words, actions, characters, setting, and other elements of the text they're reading. It's like having a movie playing in your head. Sometimes you can create a movie from some descriptive words the author has written. Other times, simply sharing an experience (such as through a connection) makes it easy to create a picture in your mind. Sometimes you get short, little movie pictures, while other times your movie might follow along with several pages of text.

Practice With Prompts Using the Read-Along Guide

This strategy is typically introduced and covered only in the Introductory Read-Along Guide. After this initial instruction, we often furthered our instruction using teachable moments. Here, we began by referring back to our experience with the strategy in our Introductory Guide and then encouraged students to simply transfer the skill as they worked with new texts. Determining how often to formally cover this strategy in a Read-Along Guide is a decision best left to the teacher. Like some of the other strategies featured in the Introductory Read-Along Guide, this one also provides an opportunity to encourage students to reflect on their experiences as they read. Helping students recognize the power of this skill will enable them to call it into action should they need it to help support comprehension.

You can use the following dialogue as a way to explain to students how they should begin their practice in the use of the strategy:

Let's practice visualizing (creating pictures in our mind). To practice this strategy, you'll be asked to pay close attention to your thoughts as you're reading. Whenever you get pictures in your mind, simply record what you see. Try to describe what you see clearly so anyone reading your Guide will be able to see exactly the same picture as you. Use the prompt to record the times when you visualized.

Figure 17 illustrates how students will respond in the Guide to prompts about their reading as a way to monitor their use of Strategy 6. In this example, a fourth-grade student responded to prompts about visualizing to support the text while read-

---

FIGURE 17
Fourth-Grade Student's Responses to Read-Along Guide Prompts for Strategy 6

A. Excerpts From *Skinnybones*

Once—just to prove my theory—I did a baseball cap experiment with my grandmother. My grandmother's about eighty years old, but she doesn't look it. She doesn't need a cane or anything, and she only wears glasses when she reads. (pp. 49–50)

I couldn't stand to look anymore, so I covered my eyes with my hands and waited until he was finished. After circling my head with the clippers about twenty more times, he finally shut them off.
    Slowly I opened my eyes. No! It couldn't be! My hair was gone! *Totally* gone, I mean! I looked like a hard-boiled egg with a face! (p. 54)

That's when I remembered it! My baseball cap! I had to find my baseball cap!
    I flew down the hall to my room. *Please! Please! Just let it be where I can find it*, I prayed. (p. 56)

"...Geez, it's a good thing they keep hitting you in the skull. Otherwise, you could get hurt."
    For the millionth time in my life, T.J. shoved me to the ground again and sat on top of me. (p. 59)

B. Student Response

When I Read (Page #)	I Could Picture...
p. 49	bug eyes, a crooked smile, and skinny legs and socks. A freaky-looking person. He looks like a hard-boiled egg, like Humpty Dumpty.
p. 50	My grandma wearing a baseball hat sort of slumped down on one side.
p. 54	shaving off clumps of Alex's hair, which fall to the floor. A barber ~~making a mistake with Alex's hair~~. Alex ~~looks worried~~. frowns.
p. 56	Alex is praying on one knee with his head bent down. He pictures his cap in a think bubble.
p. 59	T.J. shoving Alex and then sitting on him. Alex laughs like it always happens to him. ~~T.J. on Alex. Alex is mad but it's funny.~~

ing *Skinnybones* (Park, 1997). Featured excerpts from the book provide insights on how the student applied the strategy while reading.

What to Look For: Key Indicators of Successful Student Performance

- *Students' pictures are well developed and appropriate.* For many of these practice responses in Figure 17, the student was encouraged to add more description to his entries, which he did by rereading the passage. Although the added description doesn't affect the content of the entries for pages 49 and 54, there are significant changes made to those for pages 56 and 59. Regarding page 56, the reader became aware that Alex wanted his baseball cap, which he pictured only during his rereading of that passage. Here, he added to his understanding of the event. For page 59, the reader changes his mind and pictures Alex laughing based on text clues that suggest this regularly happens to Alex. Here, the reader reshaped his understanding of the event.

- *Pictures often capture experiences from a student's background.* The entry for page 50 clearly demonstrates that the reader connects to this humorous book by easily picturing his own grandmother in place of Alex's grandmother.

- *Student responses demonstrate ideas typically shared by most students.* The last sentence of the entry for page 49 was only added after the students began sharing their responses. Without the addition of the last sentence, this student's entry suspiciously lacked any clues suggesting he was aware of the egg-shaped nursery tale character Humpty Dumpty who is mentioned in the text. However, the student added this information based on the recurring "egg images" offered by other members of his group as they shared responses. Clearly, this reader was able to refine his understanding of Humpty Dumpty. Although originally missing what might be considered typical background knowledge of most intermediate-level students growing up in the United States, the end result is that this student now shares the same knowledge as his classmates.

- *Descriptions allow others to "see" what the reader has seen.* Encouraging students to describe the images they picture sets the stage for a time when they will encounter more complicated texts, such as nonfiction or informational content-based passages. Such works, which may cover material that is little known or new to students, may be more challenging to understand. Developing this skill of gleaning key pieces of information and making sense of them through visual representations is one way that may make this task less daunting.

Strategy Connections

This strategy can easily be grouped with numerous others. First, this strategy is closely related to Strategy 5, Making Connections to Aid Understanding. For example, students may first make a connection to something and then create visual images to accompany that connection. As teachers may want to feature both of these strategies in an Introductory Read-Along Guide, letting students know that these two strategies may work together assures them that their response is perfectly appropriate. This strategy may also assist readers as they develop their skill with Strategy

16, Drawing Conclusions and Making Inferences. By picturing episodes from their reading, students may gain a more insightful understanding of a character's actions or motives that is not directly expressed in the text. In addition, this strategy may also assist readers as they develop their skill with Strategy 14, Interpreting Figurative Language. As students struggle to understand idioms, personification, metaphors, and other creative language techniques, visualizing may help them see relationships between ideas and how they are presented through colorful language techniques that might otherwise be confusing.

On the other hand, teachers may not want to feature this strategy together with Strategy 9, Finding the Important or Main Idea, as students may place an exaggerated significance on a detail or event to which they're able to conjure up fantastic visual images and become sidetracked if they are trying to identify the main idea of a passage. It might also be helpful to caution students who may be at risk of having this difficulty (based on teacher observations of student's practice in their Guide).

Test-Taking Tips

- Unlike many of the other strategies where test questions can be directly linked to assessing a student's ability with a skill such as identifying the main idea, sequencing events, and so on, visualizing is one that is indirectly tested through other question formats. The primary purpose of this strategy is to help students comprehend what they're reading.

- Some test questions that could indirectly rely on use of this strategy might be ones involving predictions or inferential questions. Here, hypothetical situations or events not explicitly stated but implied may be better tackled by students if they are able to visualize possible outcomes through the aid of mental pictures to make appropriate inferences. As in other strategies that are not directly tested, students nonetheless could benefit from this skill by understanding and having a comfort level with the process of visualizing.

- Another test-taking benefit students may get from this strategy is their ability to empathize with individuals or characters, more fully understand complex issues, and experience things in which they have no firsthand experience if they are able to recall mental images. These mental images could be from things they've seen in textbooks, movies, or while researching on their computers. They could also be observations of things they've witnessed. Here, too, the process of being able to conjure mental images could be one that might prove helpful with test questions.

STRATEGY	
7	

Making Predictions

Engaged readers become involved in the material they are reading. Good readers make logical predictions about what will happen next in a story. Making predictions not only maintains readers' interest in the text but also assists them with comprehension as they test predictions.

Teacher Tips for Strategy Instruction

• During initial instruction a teacher may pause at a predetermined part of a passage and ask students to make a prediction in order to monitor their ability to authentically apply the strategy. Monitoring students when they are engaged in authentic reading activities may be necessary to determine if students are challenged by this strategy.

• A student's level of engagement with the text he or she is reading varies and will affect the student's ability to make predictions. If students struggle to make predictions, it may be because they simply don't like the story or characters, they are unable to comprehend and become disengaged with the text, or they are unable to creatively anticipate an outcome when given a set of circumstances. Determining which obstacle is causing the interference—through methods such as teacher observation and student assessment—will be important.

• Some students may need a longer period of time to develop and articulate (verbally or in writing) a prediction. Allowing them this added time is one way teachers can help students develop this ability. They may also benefit from listening to other students' predictions during group instruction. In addition to these suggestions, encouraging students to draw pictures of what they think might happen next in the story may be another approach to take.

• At times, students may become sidetracked by their personal experiences, which will interfere with their ability to make a logic-based prediction. As a result, students may lose track of events in the story, lose meaning, and become disengaged. Students can also become sidetracked if they place an exaggerated significance on a minor event. Here, too, the result is that the students lose track of meaning and may eventually disengage from the text.

• During group instruction, it may be necessary for teachers to remind students that predictions are thoughtful ideas, not wild guesses. In addition, reminders that it's OK for students' predictions to be wrong may also be needed. At times, students may choose to turn this into a competitive event. Clarifying events in the story or helping to steer students who might have been sidetracked may be a more effective way of working with all students.

Text Suggestions

Beginning with realistic fiction is an easy way to introduce this strategy. Selecting a humorous intermediate-grade chapter book that is partially based in a school setting guarantees that most students will be successful making predictions. Texts that contain action-based plots and that lead to reliable and believable outcomes are well suited to instruction in this strategy. Also, works of historical fiction that blend elements of mystery often have strong plots and provide a great opportunity to challenge students once they become skilled with this strategy.

   Although students may be more comfortable making predictions for works of fiction or realistic fiction (especially if they contain elements of mystery), they can also make predictions while reading nonfiction. Encouraging students to make predictions based on personal experience (if the work is narrative fiction) or on text clues such as subheadings or photo captions (if the work is informational) is a worthwhile approach to extend this strategy and skill development. Transferring this skill to works of nonfiction is a strategic way to help students strengthen their ability to work with different genres and also to practice their skills with content and informational text. Narrative nonfiction written by peers in the intermediate grades is a good source to explore, and small-format guided-reading works are ideal choices for content and information works. The subject matter can be selected to coincide with units of study in the social studies or science curriculums, or high-interest texts on any subject will be suitable.

Student-Friendly Chat on the Importance of the Strategy

When providing instruction on using this strategy, you can use the following dialogue as a way to explain its importance to your students:

> Readers are always guessing about what's going to happen next in their story. Guessing (or making predictions) about what's going to happen and then discovering whether the prediction is right or wrong is something that good readers do without thinking about it. It's like a game they play while they're reading. What's nice about the game is that you don't lose points if your prediction is wrong. When our predictions are wrong and we're surprised by something in a story, it often makes us enjoy the story that much more!
>
> Readers' predictions are based on other events that might have happened in the story. They could also come from what readers know about a character. Readers' own experiences might also help them make predictions. Making predictions and testing them helps us understand a story.

Practice With Prompts Using the Read-Along Guide

This strategy is typically introduced and covered only in our Introductory Read-Along Guide. After this initial instruction, we often furthered our instruction using teachable moments. Here, we began by referring back to our experience with the strategy in our Introductory Guide and then encouraged students to simply transfer the skill as they worked with new texts. Determining how often to formally cover this strategy in a Read-Along Guide is a decision best left to the teacher. Like some of the other strategies featured in the Introductory Read-Along Guide, this one also provides an opportunity to encourage students to reflect on their experiences as they read and keep their comprehension in check.

You can use the following dialogue as a way to explain to students how they should begin their practice in the use of the strategy:

> Let's practice making some predictions. To practice this strategy, you'll be asked to pay close attention to your thoughts as you're reading. Whenever you start to make a prediction by thinking about what might happen next in the story, just write down your idea. Your prediction could be about an event, a character's reaction, or an

outcome. Please keep in mind that your prediction should be thoughtful, not a wild guess. Use the prompt and write down your prediction.

Figure 18 illustrates how students will respond in the Guide to prompts about their reading as a way to monitor their use of Strategy 7. In this example, a fourth-grade student responded to prompts about making predictions while reading *Skinnybones* (Park, 1997). Featured excerpts from the book provide insights on how the student applied the strategy while reading.

FIGURE 18
Fourth-Grade Student's Responses to Read-Along Guide Prompts for Strategy 7

A. Excerpts From *Skinnybones*

It wasn't surprising that I couldn't eat any dinner that night. And I didn't sleep at all. Mostly, I just lay in bed trying to think of a way to get out of playing. I must have gone through a hundred plans before I finally came up with one that I thought might work.

It was pretty extreme. But it was my only chance.

The next morning, I made sure my parents were at the breakfast table. Then I dragged myself into the kitchen on my stomach and slowly pulled myself over to the table.

"Morning," I said weakly. (pp. 64–65)

As soon as he stepped up to the plate, I could tell he was really nervous. He kept trying to spit, but nothing would come out. Instead, he just kept making this funny sound with his lips...like *puh...puh...puh.* It was pretty awful....

T.J. went into his windup for the second pitch. This time he threw it a little slower. Just as the ball got to the plate, it curved.

Kevin swung with all his might.

"Steeerrriiikkke two!" yelled the umpire again. (p. 75)

I called them into a huddle for a pep talk.

"Okay, you guys," I said. "All we need to do is hold 'em. What do you say? Let's get them out one-two-three! Three up. Three down!"

Densel Johnson, the first baseman, laughed right in my face.... (p. 76–77)

From SKINNYBONES by Barbara Park, copyright © 1982, 1997 by Barbara Park. Used by permission of Alfred A. Knopf, an imprint of Random House Children's Books, a division of Random House, Inc.

B. Student Response

When I Read (Page #)	I Predicted That...
p. 65	Alex is going to pretend to be sick so he can get out of the game.
p. 74	Alex is going to hit a home run and help his team win the game.
p. 75	T.J. was going to throw a perfect pitch right over the plate but Kevin would be expecting some sort of fancy pitch and not be able to hit it. This happened to me.
p. 76	Alex's teammates won't listen to Alex during his pep talk because Alex isn't the kind of person to cheer people up when things are bad.

What to Look For: Key Indicators of Successful Student Performance

- *Predictions should be based on logical happenings in the story.* In the entry for page 65 in Figure 18, the reader predicts Alex will feign illness to avoid playing a baseball game. This is a logical assumption as Alex has played similar pranks in the story. Additionally, on page 74, the reader predicts Alex will help win the baseball game by hitting a home run. Although this may be considered unlikely based on earlier evidence in the text, it is nonetheless possible as Alex begins the game by catching a pop-up fly and a ground ball.

- *If students introduce their background into the prediction, there should be a clear connection to events in the story.* In the entry for page 75 in Figure 18, the reader clearly makes a prediction based on his own experience of having miscalculated a pitch. Although this prediction may be unique to this student, it is connected to the events in the story; the pitcher, T.J., has already thrown two tricky pitches that Kevin has missed, and it is likely that Kevin will be anticipating a third tricky pitch. Here the reader even imagines a surprise conclusion (that the pitch won't be tricky, and because of this, Kevin will miss it).

- *All students typically make predictions at climactic points in the story, though predictions may differ.* On page 74, the reader predicts Alex will help win the baseball game by hitting a home run. Like this student, most intermediate students are fond of Alex and will make encouraging predictions that he will be successful (for example, Alex hitting a home run), but others believe he will foil T.J.'s perfect pitching record in other ways.

- *Students should progress in making inference-based predictions as well as routine-based predictions.* The entry for page 76 shows that the reader believes he knows a great deal about Alex's character. This knowledge is based on the reader's ability to make inferences about Alex throughout the story. Meanwhile, the entries for pages 65, 74, and 75 are routine-based predictions, meaning similar events or circumstances have occurred earlier in the story.

- *Predictions should demonstrate an understanding of sequential events in the story.* All of these entries show that the reader appears aware of events up to the page where a new prediction began. This reader appears to have correctly interpreted the story and there are no misunderstandings evident in his entries.

Strategy Connections

This strategy can easily be grouped with numerous others. It is closely related to Strategy 5, Making Connections to Aid Understanding, and Strategy 6, Visualizing to Support the Text. For example, students might make a connection to something in the text or create a visual image as they read, and their prediction might then be linked to the connections or visual. If teachers want to feature all of these strategies in one Read-Along Guide, they may want to provide initial instruction separately and then have students discover the connection among the three as they practice independently.

In addition, students may be introduced to making predictions for works of non-fiction during instruction in Strategy 3, Using Visual Text Clues to Figure Out Meaning. This strategy may also be related to Strategy 15, Recognizing Cause-and-Effect Relationships. Here, the effect (what happens) could be represented through a prediction, and the cause (why something happened) would provide the insights leading readers to project a likely outcome.

Test-Taking Tips

- A student's ability to make logical predictions is one that is assessed not only through multiple-choice format questions but also through short- and extended-response questions as well. Often, multiple-choice questions designed to assess a student's ability to make predictions may appear in several formats and may rely on the use of other strategies, as in the following examples:

    What would *most likely* happen next in the story?

This sample prediction question seeks to assess a student's ability to understand sequential events.

    What will *most likely* happen after the main character...?

This type of prediction question asks students to consider an event by projecting farther into the future and is based on cumulative cause-and-effect relationships.

    The main character has *most likely* learned that...?

This sample prediction question is based on inferential clues, yet it will also rely on cause-and-effect relationships.

Despite the many versions of asking prediction-based questions, correct answers for all versions rely on logical responses that can be supported. Clues within the passage must lead students to select or generate the most believable outcome. Encouraging students to look for proof to support the selection they feel best answers the questions is a good way to help students evaluate multiple responses.

- Teachers may want to practice having students evaluate responses during instructional reading time by asking them to support their own predictions using text-based examples. Having the students evaluate their own responses is a first step in helping them successfully evaluate multiple responses so they can determine why one prediction may be better than another. This process is an extension of this strategy that may be difficult for some readers to grasp. The following example represents another way these questions may be asked:

    Why do you think...?

Here, too, correct answers rely on logical responses that can be supported through text clues.

- For short- and extended-response questions, a typical prompt used that call for predictions may begin with the word *predict* and often requires that students use skills to determine cause-and-effect relationships similar to those used when answering multiple-choice questions. For example, in a short-response question in one of our end-of-unit assessments, we asked the following:

  > Predict what Abigail might do to celebrate her 16th birthday. Use information from the passage to support your answer.

  If readers are unable to understand cause-and-effect relationships or if they struggle to transfer these understandings to similar experiences, they will have trouble making predictions and thus comprehending the text. Practicing these types of responses has proven worthwhile in helping struggling students with this skill.

- In addition to using informational and other nonfiction works, consider using other genres as well. State and other high-stakes assessments may ask prediction-based questions about passages in multiple genres, such as realistic fiction, informational nonfiction, and poetry. Building student proficiency across the genres is beneficial.

Synthesizing to Gain New Meaning

DIFFICULTY
5
RATING

When students are able to construct new meaning and build onto their ever-growing body of knowledge, they are synthesizing—or creating new understandings. To this end, students use many of the comprehension strategies described in this text, selecting those that seem most appropriate for any given set of circumstances. Demonstrating an ability to synthesize information is like a finale where a student's new knowledge is internalized and becomes a workable tool for them to call upon and use as needed. Suggested methods of providing instruction in this strategy for fiction and for nonfiction are discussed separately in the sections that follow.

Teacher Tips for Strategy Instruction

- There are many ways teachers might choose to provide instruction in this strategy. For example, if working with a fiction text, determining how a character changes from the beginning to the end of a story is one way. Identifying a problem and its solution in the story is another. Likewise, teachers may decide to incorporate the use of graphic organizers, such as story maps, story webs, or others, to work with this strategy (see the sample prompt on page 92). However, working with ideas and concepts after reading the *entire* text may be best suited for this strategy, as the outcome of all events and a character's involvement in the outcome will be known (as illustrated in Figure 19 on page 92).

- When working with fiction texts, students may have trouble grasping the scope of a character or breadth of an event and may instead focus on smaller components of each. In essence, these students may still be progressing in their ability to step back from a situation so that they can evaluate it in its entirety. Modeling this skill and demonstrating consideration for whole events is one way to guide students as they begin to develop this difficult skill.

- Students may have trouble remembering and retrieving events that took place earlier in the story. Key episodes may be identified during group instruction by other classmates, or teacher reminders may be necessary. Encouraging students to return to earlier passages in the story (an approach that—although used in Strategy 2, Finding Word Meaning and Building Vocabulary Using Context Clues, to clear up misunderstandings—may not be perceived by students to apply here) to review these key episodes may be necessary.

- When working with a fiction text, students may have trouble describing character traits, especially if this is one of the first times they are exposed to this concept and activity. Some suggestions to help with this are to provide students with a list of character traits while working through this strategy or to include a minilesson during small-group instruction and create a list of students' and their siblings' personality traits.

  Related to this, students may have trouble linking behaviors and traits. Although relationships between behaviors and traits are often evident to students, other times they may not. This is particularly true if students must rely on their ability to infer a character's behavior or motive or if cause-and-effect relationships between behaviors and traits are not well defined. Close teacher monitoring may be necessary during instruction with this strategy.

- Typically, students approach this activity using two strategies, both completely appropriate and engaging. Students may begin working from the top down, first identifying a trait and then seeking support. Alternatively, they may begin to list support from the text and then arrive at a trait that best identifies the character's similar pattern of behavior. In both cases, students may adjust their ideas through checks and balances during the activity. For example, if students are unable to locate three action-based pieces of evidence to support a trait they've listed (as the Guide prompt asks them to do), they may abandon the trait in favor of another they can support with three examples.

- With nonfiction texts, this strategy is best used when aligned with the content curriculum so students can pull from existing knowledge. Although students may not understand an issue in its entirety as they are developing their knowledge in content areas, they will have some existing knowledge upon which to build new information. Students also may be unsure about their existing knowledge. Still, encouraging them to complete the "I already knew that..." section in the prompt for using the strategy with nonfiction texts (see page 93), can readily help them to recall nuggets of knowledge that, no matter how small or seemingly irrelevant, can serve as the foundation point from which to build. This method of applying the strategy to nonfiction is, in our experience, an exciting way for students to grasp the mechanics of building their own knowledge.

Text Suggestions

Beginning with realistic fiction is an easy way to introduce this strategy. Selecting a humorous intermediate-grade chapter book, partially based in a school setting, guarantees that most students will find the main character likeable and may connect to that character's positive character traits (and possibly the less desirable traits as well).

Working with small or moderate-sized chapter books as opposed to lengthier texts may be better suited for initial instruction with this strategy, as students must be able to recall information taking place in the beginning of the text so that they can use this information to construct new ideas based on what may happen in the end of the story. Selecting texts that will enable students to keep information fresh and easily retrievable are important considerations for teachers.

Transferring this strategy to works of nonfiction can help students strengthen their ability to work with content and informational text. Small-format guided reading works are good choices for this. The subject matter can be selected to coincide with units of study in the social studies or science curricula, or high-interest texts on any subject will be suitable. Teachers may wish to work with manageable chunks of information while providing instruction with nonfiction. Students may need time to digest information in small doses rather than in its entirety, as would be typical for using the strategy with smaller fiction texts.

Student-Friendly Chat on the Importance of the Strategy

When providing instruction on using the synthesizing to gain new meaning strategy, you can use the following dialogue as a way to explain its importance to your students:

> Good readers take stock of meaning while reading. This means they stop and think about what they've read; they add new, important ideas to their knowledge base; and they continuously add new thoughts to an ever-growing body of knowledge. It's as if their knowledge is "morphing." This also means that they are able to separate out important information from less important details and get the gist of the meaning. Synthesizing means that you actively collect and organize information you've learned from your reading. It's like filing information into folders you've stored in your mind. As you do this, you begin to discover ideas and even reshape your understanding to create new ideas. As you read, this process occurs continuously—you expand and reshape your ever-growing body of knowledge. It's like your knowledge is "morphing" into something new and exciting!

Practice With Prompts Using the Read-Along Guide—Fiction

While reading works of fiction, one method to provide instruction in synthesizing is through identifying and providing text-based evidence to support character traits of the main characters from the story. This activity encourages students to reflect on a character's behaviors, actions, and motives throughout the entire story. As readers get to know a character, their opinions and insights change, and they go through a process of building, shaping, and reshaping their views as they progress through a text.

As such, working with character traits is a good way to introduce the complex idea of synthesizing. It is also an activity best presented at the end of a text. This strategy is typically introduced and covered in our Introductory Read-Along Guide, yet it is also featured in numerous other Guides. Further practice with this strategy, especially in multiple genres, encourages students to reflect on ways their own knowledge changes and develops. Supporting students as autonomous learners is a clear benefit of working with this strategy.

You can use the following dialogue as a way to explain to students how they should begin their practice in the use of the strategy:

> After we complete our reading of the text, we will practice synthesizing by thinking about the main character using information from all of the chapters. As you complete your book, you'll be asked to consider everything you learned about a main character and think of some traits that best describe what that character is like. You'll also be asked to support the traits you've chosen with evidence from the story. Using a graphic organizer, we'll identify some of the character's character traits and support our thinking with details from the chapters. This exercise will call on our synthesizing skills. As this is an ongoing strategy, we'll practice it a little differently than with the other strategies we've learned.

Figure 19 illustrates how students will respond in the Guide to prompts about their reading as a way to monitor their use of Strategy 8 with fiction. In this example, a fourth-grade student responded to prompts about synthesizing to gain new meaning while reading the entirety of *Skinnybones* (Park, 1997). Excerpts have not been included with the example, as students are synthesizing from the book as a whole.

What to Look For: Key Indicators of Successful Student Performance—Fiction

- *Students are able to recognize multiple traits.* Often, lengthier works of fiction geared for students in the middle and upper elementary levels include characters who may be more complex than those appearing in works geared for lower levels. Characters' actions often demonstrate many traits that can be recognized and described by readers.

- *Students are able to consider that a character may have less desirable or negative traits as well as positive traits.* At times, a character's behaviors may reflect personality traits that most students might consider negative. For example, some consider that Alex lies because he has low self-esteem. Because of this, students may react differently toward a character, some disliking him while others tolerate and even appreciate his mildly negative trait. Recognizing both the good and bad that coexist in a character demonstrates a student's insightful ability to reconcile conflicting information.

- *An assortment of action-based details are used by the student to support the traits.* Students are able to recognize multiple actions that may support a single trait. For

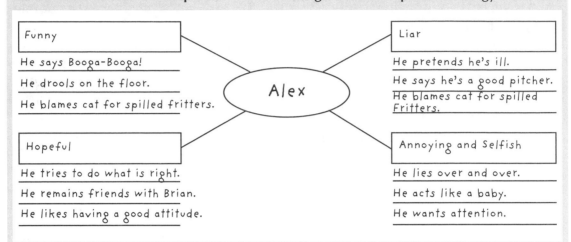

FIGURE 19
Fourth-Grade Student's Responses to Read-Along Guide Prompts for Strategy 8 (Fiction)

Funny
He says Booga-Booga!
He drools on the floor.
He blames cat for spilled fritters.

Liar
He pretends he's ill.
He says he's a good pitcher.
He blames cat for spilled Fritters.

Alex

Hopeful
He tries to do what is right.
He remains friends with Brian.
He likes having a good attitude.

Annoying and Selfish
He lies over and over.
He acts like a baby.
He wants attention.

example, the student responses show three pieces of different evidence to support each trait listed for Alex. As is evident, the support represents different events appearing in several areas throughout the text—and still they support a single behavioral trait.

- *As students progress with this skill, they often begin to discriminate between traits that are similar; for example, "nice" and "friendly."* Through their evidence-based support, they are able to select a more specific trait based on the character's actions or other criteria. Clearly, this process reflects a student's ability (and desire) to carefully and thoughtfully consider how a character's behavior is best described.

Practice With Prompts Using the Read-Along Guide—Nonfiction

While reading works of nonfiction, one method to provide instruction in synthesizing is by asking students to consider how new information has helped them build their understanding. This prompt asks students to explore their thinking and how it has changed with the addition of new information. In essence, it asks them to think about the mental processes that happen naturally as they construct new knowledge. As is clear from the directions that follow, students are asked to consider several new ideas they've learned and bring them to their small-group instruction for discussion where the teacher may help (if needed) shape their new ideas. Although the fiction version of this strategy is introduced in the Introductory Read-Along Guide, we waited to provide instruction in the nonfiction version until later in the year.

You can use the following dialogue as a way to explain to students how they should begin their practice in the use of the strategy:

As you read your book, you'll be asked to share the new information you've learned about something and explain how the new information helped you reshape and build your knowledge. Using your sticky notes, identify three to five new, significant facts that you learned from your reading. Think about how these facts added to your understanding.

Figure 20 illustrates how students will respond in the Guide to prompts about their reading as a way to monitor their use of Strategy 8 with nonfiction. In this example, a fourth-grade student responded to prompts about synthesizing to gain new meaning while reading *If You Were There When They Signed the Constitution* (Levy, 1992). Featured excerpts from the book provide insights on how the student applied the strategy while reading.

What to Look For: Key Indicators of Successful Student Performance—Nonfiction

• *Students identify new information that is pertinent to the content of the nonfiction passage.* As students begin to build their knowledge (especially while working with nonfiction), teachers may need to help students distinguish noteworthy information that will help build their understanding. In the example in Figure 20, the student has identified a noteworthy fact relevant to his study of government, and he has also demonstrated a solid understanding of this new information as he further explains its meaning in the "What I didn't know was" section of the prompt.

FIGURE 20
Fourth-Grade Student's Responses to Read-Along Guide Prompts for Strategy 8 (Nonfiction)

A. Excerpt From *If You Were There When They Signed the Constitution*
Then the President gets the bill. If he or she doesn't like it, the President can say no, or veto it. (*Veto* comes from the Latin word for "forbid.")
   But the President's veto doesn't have to be the end of a bill. Congress can pass a bill over the President's veto if two thirds of both the House and the Senate think the bill should be a law. (p. 65)

From IF YOU WERE THERE WHEN THEY SIGNED THE CONSTITUTION by Elizabeth Levy. Copyright © 1992 by Elizabeth Levy. Reprinted by permission of Scholastic Inc.

B. Student Response

On page __65__ the significant fact I found was _the president doesn't have the final say on_ _passing a bill into law._

I already knew that _the president helped to make laws._

What I didn't know was _even if the president vetoes a bill and doesn't want it to become law_ _it can still become one if two thirds of Congress thinks it should be law._

This new fact is important because _it helps me understand how our system of government_ _works. I get that it's a system of checks and balances._

- *Information students select seems congruent to some aspect of a student's prior knowledge.* In this example, there could be a variety of ways the student might incorporate the information and existing knowledge, such as information about the President (his or her role or decision-making ability), how bills are passed, or even how laws are made. In essence, the information is not only pertinent but also seems easily integrated into some aspect of the student's prior knowledge.
- *Students are able to express the significance of their new information.* As shown in Figure 20, the student has expanded his understanding of the government in terms of its checks-and-balances system. Teachers may need to assist students in linking their identified fact to a broader concept and help them express their ideas.

Strategy Connections

This strategy can be grouped with others, but you may wish to provide a generous amount of time for it, as students benefit from much discussion and think-aloud time. In addition, this strategy relies on many others. As such, teachers may need to provide careful monitoring during instruction and adjust the degree of direct instruction depending on when this strategy is introduced. Early in the year, many students may not have developed proficiency with support strategies needed to successfully work with synthesizing. Recognizing that this strategy is one that will be revisited often—whether through guided reading or other forms of instruction—reassures students that it is a skill that develops over time.

For example, we often feature Strategy 11, Telling Fact From Opinion, with this synthesizing strategy so that students begin to develop a keen awareness of the differences between fact and opinion as they build their understanding through synthesizing, especially as they read informational material. In addition, Strategy 15, Recognizing Cause-and-Effect Relationships, and Strategy 16, Drawing Conclusions and Making Inferences, will most directly help students complete the character-trait graphic organizer. The degree of assistance students need with these strategies and the manner in which this assistance is provided is best determined by the teacher.

Test-Taking Tips

- In addition to using nonfiction and informational works, consider using other genres, such as folk tales, tall tales, and poetry. State and other high-stakes assessments ask questions that rely on a student's synthesizing skills about passages within many different genres, which suggests that building student proficiency across the genres is beneficial.
- Although this strategy is generally used to evaluate broad events and arrive at new understandings, it may by assessed through multiple-choice questions as well as short- and extended-response questions. Practice in both types will better prepare students to use their synthesizing skills no matter which format is used.
- In multiple-choice questions, students might be asked to select a word from among several choices that best describes a character, as in the following example:

    The main character is best described as _____.

Here students have to evaluate a character's behavior through the entire story to determine the best response. Students will benefit by being reminded to consider the entirety of their knowledge about a character when responding to these questions.

- In short- or extended-response questions, students might be asked to do the following:

> Explain how a character changes from the beginning to the end of the story.
>
> Explain how a certain *event* or *component* changed from the beginning to the end of the story. For example, how did a character's luck change from the beginning to the end, or how did the character's view about a situation change from the beginning to the end?

Certainly, these types of questions rely on a student's ability to assess changing situations and arrive at deeper insights. With these types of questions, students may benefit if they compare a character or event from the beginning to the end without considering how changes came about, which are details that may distract them from noting the most obvious changes.

- For short- and extended-response questions, a typical prompt used in conjunction with the above mentioned questions is to "Use details from the passage(s) to support your answer." If struggling readers are unable to recall events over time, view episodes or events as they contribute to larger idea, and recognize relationships between ideas (whether linked through cause and effect, inferential, or otherwise), they will have difficulty supporting this type of change-over-time question in their writing. In our experience, practicing these types of response questions has proven worthwhile in helping struggling students with this skill.

CHAPTER 3

Instruction in Key Comprehension Strategies: The Skill-Building Nine

"I learned how to find a significant fact and also how to tell why it's important. I know this helps me build my knowledge."

—Justin C., fourth-grade student

"I think I understand things better now because I know many of the strategies. I can use a lot of them to help me understand, or I can use one of them. I might not even really know I'm using them."

—Ameilee S., fifth-grade student

L ike chapter 2, this chapter is devoted to the first component of the Quality Comprehension Model: instruction of key comprehension strategies. However, while chapter 2 offered guidelines and recommendations for providing instruction on the foundational eight comprehension strategies, this chapter is devoted to the following skill-building nine strategies:

Strategy 9: Finding the Important or Main Idea

Strategy 10: Identifying Facts and Details

Strategy 11: Telling Fact From Opinion

Strategy 12: Understanding Sequence

Strategy 13: Comparing and Contrasting

Strategy 14: Interpreting Figurative Language

Strategy 15: Recognizing Cause-and-Effect Relationships

Strategy 16: Drawing Conclusions and Making Inferences

Strategy 17: Summarizing

We often refer to these skill-building nine strategies as outcome skills because they represent skills proficient readers are capable of successfully demonstrating. When the strategies are taught through direct instruction in a small-group environment using leveled materials and a specific degree of teacher assistance that is tailored to meet the needs of each reader in the group, they become strategic devices for building comprehension. While the foundational eight comprehension strategies discussed in chapter 2 will be featured in the Introductory Read-Along Guide (see chapter 4 for more detailed discussion on the Read-Along Guide), the skill-building nine strategies will be featured in smaller Read-Along Guides that work specifically with three or four strategies from this set. The frequency of formal instruction in each strategy is determined by the teacher and is based on teacher observations and student assessments. Following this formal instruction, teachers often use informal instruction—through teachable moments, during content-based lessons, or by other avenues—for additional practice. The frequency of informal instruction is also determined by the teacher.

As in chapter 2, for each comprehension strategy we have provided a wealth of helpful information that is intended to be used by teachers in a variety of ways. First, each comprehension strategy is given a difficulty rating on a scale of 1–5 (with 5 being the most difficult). An explanation of each strategy and the skills used when the strategy is used opens the discussion, and then each comprehension strategy includes instructional recommendations for exploration of the strategy in the following categories (see pages 46–47 in chapter 2 for details on the type of information covered in these categories):

• Teacher Tips for Strategy Instruction

• Text Suggestions

• Student-Friendly Chat on the Importance of the Strategy

• Practice With Prompts for the Read-Along Guide

- What to Look For: Key Indicators of Successful Student Performance
- Strategy Connections
- Test-Taking Tips

Finding the Important or Main Idea

The main idea of a reading passage is best described as the most important idea that is conveyed in that passage, or what the passage is mostly about. Answering the questions, "What is this passage mostly about?" and "What important overall idea does the author express?" are two ways to identify the main idea. The main idea of a passage or text can also be constructed by first determining key details or facts and then blending this key information to form a complete main idea.

Teacher Tips for Strategy Instruction

- This strategy is very difficult for students to initially grasp with lengthier passages. Therefore, to help students develop a comfortable level of basic skill, consider beginning with smaller units such as paragraphs. Identifying the main idea of each paragraph in a multiple-paragraph passage will then enable students to connect the ideas together to form a main idea of the entire reading passage.

- Until a basic skill level in this strategy is developed, students may benefit from an emphasis on direct instruction and group participation during instructional time rather than on independent practice. However, during this initial stage, students can be encouraged to use sticky notes to mark key details during their independent activities (perhaps noting the three to five most significant details). Then during small-group time, student's sticky notes can be discussed, a consensus among all students can be reached, and finally students can collectively construct the main idea as the teacher facilitates this entire process.

- Teachers may wish to instruct students to think of the important or main idea by having them answer the questions posed in the strategy description: "What is this passage mostly about?" "What important overall idea does the author express?" Thinking in terms of the answers to these questions could be a viable way for students to grasp the concept of main idea.

- If students' thinking becomes entangled in small details, have them ask themselves the question, "Would the overall meaning of the passage change if I left out this idea?" Using this approach, students might better distinguish a small detail from the main idea.

- Some struggling readers may not be able to separate their own experiences from those they are reading about and unknowingly assign greater significance (than the author intended) to the shared experience. These students may benefit by going back to the passage and underlining or assigning a "weight" (by counting lines of text) to the space where the shared "significant" experience appeared. Once done, the student may grasp the true importance of the experience by comparing its size or weight to that of the overall passage. For example, if an idea is expressed in one sentence in a multipage reading passage and is not discussed further, chances are it will not express a main idea. Students quickly grasp the ability to weigh ideas using this method.

Text Suggestions

Short informational texts lend themselves well to practicing this strategy. The subject matter can be selected to coincide with units of study in social studies, science, or other content areas. Today, there are many publishers producing short books on just about every subject imaginable. Likewise, there are online services available where you can search for content-specific or thematic books and print them as needed.

Passages from textbooks, as well as from supplementary student newspapers or student newsmagazines, may also include good passages to work with. You might find that a textbook used for social studies, for example, does a great job of developing a student's ability to scan an informational passage and answer factual questions, but keep in mind it may not challenge students to construct a statement about the main idea. Practicing a new skill with a familiar source is great practice. Practicing this skill with other types of works of nonfiction, such as biographies, is also recommended.

Texts that have some clear organizational structure, such as chapter titles and further levels of subtitles, can provide additional support for struggling readers. Here students can benefit not only from clues about the subject but also from clues signaling that a subject is about to change.

Student-Friendly Chat on the Importance of the Strategy

When providing instruction on finding the important or main idea, you can use the following dialogue as a way to explain the importance of this strategy to your students:

> The main idea is a pretty big idea that tells what a paragraph or an entire reading passage is mainly about. It's important to understand the main idea so that you're clear about the meaning of the passage and so that you've understood the passage just as the author wants you to. The main idea is not a small detail, although all of the small details together make up the main idea. Sometimes a main idea is stated in a topic sentence, a closing sentence, or somewhere else within the passage. Other times it's not stated, and you have to construct it by piecing together the important details.

Practice With Prompts Using the Read-Along Guide—Finding the Main Idea Using Support Details

The skill students will practice when using this prompt is determining the importance of ideas by distinguishing between whether something is a supporting detail or if it is critical in expressing the main idea of the passage or text. You can use the following dialogue as a way to explain to students how they should begin their practice in the use of the strategy:

> Let's practice identifying important support details within the passage. To learn and practice this strategy, you'll be asked to identify the main idea of paragraphs within a reading passage. Then you'll blend them together to summarize the main idea of the entire passage. Sometimes it's best to first identify details in your reading passage that seem important. These details will support your main idea. As you begin to list these key details of support, you'll actually be building your understanding of the main idea of the whole reading passage.

Figure 21 illustrates how students will respond in the Guide about their reading as a way to monitor their use of Strategy 9. In this example, a fourth-grade student responded to the prompt in order to find the main idea using support details while reading *Native Americans in New York* (George, 2003). Featured excerpts from the book provide insights on how the student applied the strategy while reading.

FIGURE 21
Fourth-Grade Student's Responses to Read-Along Guide Prompts for Strategy 9 (Using Support Details)

A. Excerpts From *Native Americans in New York*
New York's first people were **nomads** who arrived from the north 11,000 years ago. They hunted and gathered wild vegetables in the pine forests that covered the area.

    Their **descendants**, the Algonquian, learned to plant corn, beans, and squash so they would not have to move around in search of food. They began to establish **permanent** settlements in the Hudson River valley and on Long Island around 700 B.C.

    Around the year 1300, the Iroquois moved onto the land west of the Algonquian. They were soon fighting with the Algonquian and with each other for food and land, and to win honor in battle. (p. 5)

B. Student Response

The main idea in pages ____4____ to ____5____ is
    New York's first people were thought to be nomads, and they were then
    followed by the Algonquian and the Iroquois.

Support/p. ___5___	Support/p. ___5___	Support/p. ___5___
The first people were nomads who arrived from the North. (topic sentence)	Their descendants, the Algonquians, learned to plant.	The Iroquois moved onto the land west of the Algonquians.

What to Look For: Key Indicators of Successful Student Performance—Finding the Main Idea Using Support Details

• *Students make thoughtful selections from among several ideas.* In Figure 21, the student notes that he chose a topic sentence to use as support for a paragraph on page 5. Students may use topic or closing sentences from paragraphs, or they may rewrite ideas in their own words. Deciding when one method may be preferable over another usually gets students talking about what's important in the text and also how information is presented in the text. This kind of analysis contributes to students' grasp of the main idea and also shows their progress at identifying what is and what is not critical to the main idea.

• *Students demonstrate critical thinking as they select highlights to include in a main idea.* As students work to capture important support ideas, they often struggle with trying to create parallel ideas that simply may not be present in the text. For example, the text the students read states that the Algonquian planted but did not provide a similar discussion for the Iroquois. As a result, the student chose to omit mention of planting as he constructed the main idea for the passage. Student responses should reflect this ongoing progressive refinement of their thinking.

• *Students refine their thoughts and capture a well-articulated central idea.* Learning to write a carefully articulated sentence that captures the main idea takes practice. Although building a consensus about what should be included in the main idea may be difficult during initial skill practice, students generally progress to a point where only inconsequential differences are present. Students will need to understand that their views may be uniquely expressed but that the gist of the main idea is similar.

Practice With Prompts Using the Read-Along Guide—Finding the Main Idea Using Facts
Using this prompt, students first locate key facts and then combine these understandings into one overall main idea. Although similar to using support details, this prompt allows students to explore a passage in terms of key facts, which could be numbers, dates, or other important data. This approach may be easier for some students to grasp.

You can use the following dialogue as a way to explain to students how they should begin their practice in the use of the strategy:

> To learn and practice this strategy, you'll be asked to locate or summarize the main idea of a reading passage in your Read-Along Guide. One way to do this is to locate facts in your reading passage. You will need to identify 5–7 key facts within the passage. Once you have these facts, you can use them to construct your main idea. As you begin to list these key facts, you'll actually be building your understanding of the main idea of the whole reading passage.

Figure 22 illustrates how students will respond in the Guide about their reading as a way to monitor their use of Strategy 9. In this example, a fourth-grade student used the prompt in order to find the main idea by using facts while reading

Native Americans in New York. Featured excerpts from the book provide insights on how the student applied the strategy while reading.

What to Look For: Key Indicators of Successful Student Performance—Finding the Main Idea Using Facts

- *Students select key facts that serve to support a larger idea.* Using this method, students often begin by looking for key names, dates, and places. The student whose response is featured in Figure 22 has listed main events sequentially by time so that the ideas are easy to follow. This is not always the case. For example, some students may select only names, while others focus on dates or places. Although students may be successful at listing key facts using one of these strategies, they may neither understand key connections nor grasp the main idea of the passage. This will become obvious if they are unable to use their facts to write a main idea. Deciding how to locate and list key facts from the text is a good topic to discuss and model while using this method.

- *Students can manipulate information.* For this prompt, students typically list in sequential order all key facts from the passage. As students begin to construct the main idea by weighing the importance of the facts, they will find it necessary to not only eliminate some facts but also to shuffle the order of some facts. In Figure

---

FIGURE 22
Fourth-Grade Student's Responses to Read-Along Guide Prompts for Strategy 9 (Using Facts)

A. Excerpts From *Native Americans in New York*

New York's first people were **nomads** who arrived from the north 11,000 years ago. They hunted and gathered wild vegetables in the pine forests that covered the area.

Their **descendants**, the Algonquian, learned to plant corn, beans, and squash so they would not have to move around in search of food. They began to establish **permanent** settlements in the Hudson River valley and on Long Island around 700 B.C.

Around the year 1300, the Iroquois moved onto the land west of the Algonquian. They were soon fighting with the Algonquian and with each other for food and land, and to win honor in battle. (p. 5)

From *Native Americans in New York* by Lynn George. © 2003 by The Rosen Publishing Group. Reprinted with permission.

B. Student Response

Key Facts	Main Idea
1. The first people in New York arrived many years ago and were called nomads. (p. 5) 2. They were hunters and gatherers. (p. 5) 3. Algonquian were their descendents. (p. 5) 4. They made settlements. (p. 5) 5. They planted corn, beans, and squash. (p. 5) 6. The Iroquois arrived in 1300. (p. 5)	The Algonquian and the Iroquois were descendents of the nomads, who were the first people who lived in New York many years ago.

22, the student writes a main idea by flip-flopping the order of events and further eliminating all but the most essential fact. For example, the student's sixth key fact is more critical to the main idea than the second, fourth, and fifth key facts (all of which were eliminated from the main idea).

• *Students can retrace their thinking and further refine it as they wish.* By reviewing the key facts from the passage, students can analyze their own reasons for recording them yet also step back from that process to further consider varying levels of importance. During their group instruction, the students decided that a main idea for this two-page reading passage did not need to mimic their step-by-step learning process. Instead, they lead with what they learned—how these two Native American groups arrived in New York.

• *Students select key ideas from among many.* In the preceding example, the student listed no more than six ideas. Limiting the number of facts students can list causes them to reflect on those they are considering and imposes thoughtful criteria for their inclusion.

Strategy Connections

This strategy is closely connected to Strategy 10, Identifying Facts and Details, and featuring these two strategies together in a Read-Along Guide will help students grasp how facts and details contribute to identifying the main idea.

Often, struggling readers will get sidetracked by one or more specific details and mistakenly identify the detail as the main idea. This is especially true if the struggling reader is incorrectly using Strategy 5, Making Connections to Aid Understanding, and Strategy 6, Visualizing to Support the Text, by making connections to the detail but being unable to step back from his or her personal experiences. To prevent this, avoid featuring either Strategy 5 or Strategy 6 with Strategy 9 in a single Read-Along Guide, and also caution students who demonstrate this difficulty.

Test-Taking Tips

• In addition to using informational and other nonfiction works, consider using other genres such as poetry and fiction as well. State and other high-stakes assessments ask main idea questions about passages within many different genres, which suggests that building student proficiency in identifying main idea across the genres is beneficial.

• Some common forms of questions about main idea on assessments or other state tests include the following:

> What is the main idea of this paragraph or passage?
> What is this paragraph or passage mostly about?
> Why did the author write this passage?
> What is a good title for this passage?

• Incorrect answers usually include specific details that, although true, don't represent the entire selection. Students can usually eliminate "false" or "far-out" (in that they have nothing to do with the passage) selections. Yet students may mistake a "true" fact for a main idea.

Identifying Facts and Details

Facts and details provide substance within a reading passage. Typically, they support a main idea or topic sentence (see Strategy 9, Finding the Important or Main Idea). Another view on facts and details is that they provide evidence for general claims made in topic sentences. By identifying facts and details (and recognizing how they connect to main or big ideas), students gain an in-depth level of understanding of a text.

Teacher Tips for Strategy Instruction

- Although it may be surprising, this strategy is often very troublesome for students. Proficient readers are usually able to make connections between the facts and details and the main idea. Because of this connection, not only are they able to successfully comprehend what they're reading but also they're able to go back into a passage and locate specific facts or details if they need to. On the other hand, struggling readers seem to have trouble making this connection. As a result, their ability to comprehend is challenged, as is their ability to go back to a passage and readily locate facts and details. Providing instruction on where main ideas and key facts and details are linked is thus a critical approach to support comprehension for struggling readers. Likewise, providing these struggling readers with further scanning techniques, such as using keywords or reviewing subheadings and titles, will be helpful.

- Often, students show a strength identifying certain types of facts. For example, locating who, when, and where seem easier for readers, as these pieces of information are often proper nouns or dates and are thus easy to detect. However, locating facts that will explain why or what may be more complicated for students. Recommending certain prompts for certain passages may encourage students to explore all types of questions.

- At times, students may swiftly pass over names and places, hardly paying any attention to them as they read, merely recognizing that a word is a proper noun such as an individual's name or the name of a place, and then moving on. This is a reading strategy some teachers encourage, especially at the lower elementary levels when students are learning to read. Teachers can best determine how they wish their intermediate-grade students to approach difficult proper nouns in terms of strategy instruction. Perhaps the aforementioned approach may be useful for struggling readers, and even for ELLs. Working with difficult proper nouns is a skill that develops with practice. Your approach to this matter may affect your instruction of this strategy, as students may or may not be skilled in working with some facts and details.

Text Suggestions

Providing instruction in this strategy using a variety of texts that span the genres will be useful. Fiction, nonfiction, informational books, poetry, and biographies all pose their own challenges for students in recognizing facts and details and their relationship to main ideas.

Small-format, informational guided reading texts lend themselves well to introducing this strategy. The subject matter can be selected to coincide with units of study in the social studies or science curriculum. For subsequent instruction in this strategy, consider using passages from textbooks and supplementary student newspapers or newsmagazines.

Texts that have some clear organizational structure, such as chapter titles and further levels of subtitles, can provide additional support for struggling readers. Here students can benefit not only from clues about the subject but also from clues signaling that a subject is about to change.

Student-Friendly Chat on the Importance of the Strategy

When providing instruction on identifying facts and details, you can use the following dialogue as a way to explain the importance of this strategy to your students:

> Writers use facts and details for many reasons. Facts and details support a main idea and, in so doing, provide more information about the main idea. Facts and details may
>
> - Describe a person, place, or thing
> - Explain how to do something
> - Tell the order in which things happen
> - Share an experience, idea, or opinion
>
> An easy way to find facts and details is to look for sentences that tell about the who, what, where, when, why, and how of the main idea.

Practice With Prompts Using the Read-Along Guide

Enabling students to recognize the relationship between the facts and details and the main idea is one way to provide instruction in this strategy. Also, by using the prompts (who, what, where, when, why, and how), students can begin to develop an understanding of the many different ways facts and details can be presented. You can use the following dialogue as a way to explain to students how they should begin their practice in the use of the strategy:

> Let's practice identifying facts and details within our reading passages. One way to do this is to create questions that your classmates can answer by scanning for information within the reading passage. As you read your book, you'll be asked to create some questions using who, what, where, when, why, and how. Answers to the questions should highlight the facts and details that appear within the passage. You'll get the chance to ask your questions to classmates during small-group instruction time. See if your classmates can recall the facts and details!

Figure 23 illustrates how students will respond in the Guide about their reading as a way to monitor their use of Strategy 10. In this example, a fourth-grade student responded to prompts about identifying facts and details while reading *If You*

FIGURE 23
Fourth-Grade Student's Responses to Read-Along Guide Prompts for Strategy 10

A. Excerpts From *If You Lived With the Iroquois*

Which nations made up the Iroquois League?
In the beginning, five nations made up the League: the Mohawk, Oneida, Onondaga, Cayuga, and Seneca....
In the early 1700s, the Tuscarora nation...asked to join the League. They were accepted, and the British then called the League the Six Nations. (pp. 8–9)

What kind of work did people do?
...Work also depended on the season:
• In the spring, you would peel elm bark for longhouses and canoes, tap trees for maple syrup,...
• When the ground was ready for planting, you'd sow seeds for all the vegetables.
• In the late summer and fall, you'd harvest the crops and prepare them for storage.
• In the fall, you'd begin hunting and continue through part of the winter.
• During the winter, you'd spend a good deal of time indoors, making and repairing clothing, tools, bowls, baskets, and instruments of all kinds. (p. 49)

Girls and women, and boys and men often did different kinds of work. Men made tools for hunting and weapons for war.... Women made clay pots and baskets, cradleboards for carrying babies, clothing and moccasins.... (p. 50)

Were there special holiday festivals?
...For some ceremonies, tobacco was thrown on the fire.... Tobacco was a sacred plant and was used only for religious purposes. (p. 60)

The Midwinter or New Year's Festival...was the longest.... The festival began when two elders visited every house in the village to announce the new year. (p. 63)

From IF YOU LIVED WITH THE IROQUOIS by Ellen Levine. Copyright © 1998 by Ellen Levine. Reprinted by permission of Scholastic Inc.

B. Student Response

For this passage ___8–9___ , create two who, what, when, where, or why questions to test your classmate's ability to recall facts and details.
1.   Who were the five nations who made up the Iroquois League?
2.   When did the Tuscarora nation join the Iroquois League?

For this passage 48–50, create two who, what, when, where, or why questions to test your classmate's ability to recall facts and details.
1.   ~~Why were jobs~~ What jobs were done during different seasons?
2.   How did the men's jobs differ from the women's jobs?

For this passage 60–63, create two who, what, when, where, or why questions to test your classmate's ability to recall facts and details.
1.   ~~Were festivals held throughout the year?~~ Why was tobacco important?
2.   Where did the elders visit to begin the celebration of the Midwinter Festival?

Lived With the Iroquois (Levine, 1998). Featured excerpts from the book provide insights on how the student applied the strategy while reading.

What to Look For: Key Indicators of Successful Student Performance

- *Students have used key information as the basis for questions.* In Figure 23, it is evident by comparing this student's questions to the text that he successfully identified important information upon which to base his questions. Teachers will want to be sure that students have relied on information from the text to construct their questions.

- *Students have aligned their questions with text-based information.* In Figure 23, in the student's first entry for pages 48–50, he realized his initial question, "Why were jobs done during different seasons?," was not going to be answered using substantial facts or details from the passage. As such he was encouraged to alter it to "What jobs were done during different seasons?" so that it would better reflect the facts and details in the passage and thus be a more significant question. Teachers may need to help students modify questions if they are not aligned with information in the text. Also, encouraging others to share appropriate responses during small-group instruction is another useful method of assisting students in this matter.

- *Questions rely on more than a "yes" or "no" response.* In the first entry in Figure 23, the student's original question for pages 60–63 was "Were festivals held throughout the year?" When he asked a classmate this question, he realized that he mistakenly asked a question that didn't rely on fact or detail from the passage and instead could be answered by a simple "yes" or "no." Although his first attempt to alter the question (not evident in the sample) was to add the word *why* in front of the original ("Why were festivals held throughout the year?"), he was also displeased with this question, as the answer was not easily represented through concise facts or details in the passage. (If his classmate had responded with an insightful response in which he synthesized the close connection between Native American festivals and their respect for the natural environment, this would have been perfectly fine.) Still, the student decided to alter his question to the one shown, for which there were clear and concise facts to support a response. Encouraging students to ask open-ended questions that rely on information from the text may help students who struggle with this skill.

- *Students demonstrate an ability to ask all types of questions.* If a student is able to use all prompts effectively, it should be evident that he was able to first identify important facts and details and then create questions for them using varied formats, as illustrated by the student's varied questions in Figure 23.

Strategy Connections

Practice in this strategy in several Read-Along Guides will further help intermediate-level readers. This strategy is closely connected to Strategy 9, Finding the Important or Main Idea. Having the two strategies together in one Read-Along Guide helps students grasp the relationship between the facts and details and the main idea. Another strategy that will nicely blend with this one is Strategy 15, Recognizing

Cause-and-Effect Relationships. In this strategy, students are guided to recognize relationships between ideas.

On the other hand, because the use of who, what, when, where, how, and why questions is very different from Strategy 4, Asking Questions to Engage in the Text (where readers question events, character's actions, or an author's intention), you might not want to feature Strategies 10 and 4 together in one Guide. Likewise, the idea of making "connections" between the facts and details and the main ideas is an instructional device used here that is very different from the type of "connections" students are asked to make in Strategy 5, Making Connections (where students draw relationships between their experiences and what they're reading). As such, you might not want to feature Strategies 5 and 10 together either. Additionally, you may want to avoid grouping this strategy with Strategy 11, Telling Fact From Opinion, at least during initial instruction so that students do not get confused.

Test-Taking Tips

- A student's ability to use facts and details is one that is assessed not only through multiple-choice format questions but also through short- and extended-response questions.

- Often, multiple-choice questions designed to assess a student's ability to recognize facts and details rely on the use of the following words: *who, what, when, where, why,* or *how.* At times, these words are used at the beginning of the questions, such as in the following example:

  Who was responsible for bringing water to the race?

  At other times, they may be located elsewhere, especially if the passage is nonfiction and there is some historical debate about a correct answer, such as in the following example:

  According to the article, why did George Washington want a new flag?

  Answers to these types of questions are usually clearly stated somewhere in the passage. Students may not need to use higher-level thinking skills, such as inferring, to arrive at answers. However, ensuring that they have selected a correct answer by reviewing the appropriate section in the passage is necessary. Tricky answers that may be very similar to a correct response or that represent common errors made by students often comprise the group of responses. Suggesting that students underline the correct response in the passage is one method to encourage students to carefully review their choice.

- As discussed above, the ease with which students are able to respond to both multiple-choice and short- and extended-response questions on facts and details depends largely on their ability to recognize relationships as well as to locate information in the passage. For struggling readers, both tasks may be challenging.

While responding to multiple-choice questions, struggling readers may attempt to reread the entire passage to locate or figure out the answer. Sadly, they quickly realize that this method is too time-consuming—or worse still, they get frustrated and simply guess. Providing keyword scanning techniques, such as using keywords from the question, is one way these students might be able to better narrow down their searches.

- For short- and extended-response questions, a typical prompt used when information must be pulled from the passage is the following:

    Use details from the passage(s) to support your answer.

If struggling readers are unable to make connections between details and main ideas as they read, they will have trouble supporting a point through this type of connection in their writing. Practicing and modeling these types of responses has proven worthwhile in helping struggling students with this skill.

- In addition to questions that require students to search out specific answers, there are also questions about facts and details that ask students to determine which facts or details seem more important than others to support a main idea. Typical prompts used in this type of situation include the following:

    Which detail tells more about the main idea?
    Which detail about the main idea is most important in the story?

Here, students must compare and evaluate facts or details in terms of the main idea of an entire passage. Students will obviously have to read the responses provided in the test question and determine which one seems to fit best.

Telling Fact From Opinion

Being able to tell if something is fact or opinion helps students better understand what they are reading. Can ideas be proven through facts? Is the author expressing personal views? Knowing this distinction gives students a deeper understanding of the text.

Teacher Tips for Strategy Instruction

- Some students may not clearly understand the concept of opinion, so you may need to help them with this prior to instruction in this strategy. One way to start is by selecting issues about which students have pretty strong feelings, such as whether or not school should be extended through the summer. Allowing students to create their own fact and opinion statements and then to quiz their peers on whether they are fact or opinion is a great way to practice and refine this skill (see the Practice With Prompts section for Strategy 11).

- Students who are beginning to shape their own opinions often struggle with this concept. At times, their opinion might not be relevant to the topic, it might not align with the facts provided, or it might not be expressed well. Modeling how others form opinions—by basing them on facts they read—is a good way to start. Students will also benefit from listening to their classmates during small-group instruction.

- Once students have grasped the meaning of opinion, the next stumbling block is their inability to tell fact from opinion. Here, too, you may find it necessary to support the instruction by providing additional examples from everyday school experiences. Then, progress to reading passages where keywords provide clues. As students develop an understanding, try tackling more challenging passages, such as those in which keywords are absent. Finally, identifying fact from opinion in nonfiction or informational texts may be very difficult. Allowing time to discuss and clarify the differences in these cases will be helpful.

- Often, students welcome a challenging debate as to whether or not something is a fact or an opinion. Typically, these types of debates can't be resolved with information provided in your text. Further researching the issue is a great extension activity or keeping the question open may be all that time permits.

Text Suggestions

Introducing students to political cartoons is great way to launch this lesson. Though it may require some research to locate appropriate cartoons, there may be acceptable substitutes within graphic novels, comic books, and illustrated stories—all of which are gaining in appeal. In addition, many works of fiction and nonfiction can be used with this strategy. It will be necessary to carefully review fiction and nonfiction texts to be sure they contain opinions, as some texts are very careful to present just facts. If necessary, supplement the text you select with articles or other materials if you're unable to find both fact and opinion readily expressed in a single source. Passages from student newspapers or even student newsmagazines may include good passages to work with. Practicing this skill with other types of nonfiction, such as biographies, is also recommended.

Short informational texts might not lend themselves well to practicing this strategy, as many do not purposefully contain opinions.

Student-Friendly Chat on the Importance of the Strategy

When providing instruction on telling fact from fiction, you can use the following dialogue as a way to explain the importance of this strategy to students:

Telling fact from opinion is sometimes harder then we imagine. Facts express ideas that can be proven, whereas an opinion tells what someone thinks or feels. Often, there are keywords that help us determine if something is a fact or an opinion. For example, using words like *greatest* and phrases like *I believe...*, *I think...*, and *I feel...* often signal that an opinion is coming.

Practice With Prompts Using the Read-Along Guide

Comparing the difference between facts and opinions that appear in a reading passage is a good way to begin introducing this strategy for practice. Encouraging students to develop their own opinions based on the facts they've learned is another way to extend this practice. When students develop their own opinions, they are better able to recognize opinions expressed by others.

You can use the following dialogue as a way to explain to students how they should begin their practice in the use of the strategy:

> As we learn about the events that unfold in our books, we'll discuss whether or not something is fact or opinion. We'll even play a challenging game to help us practice telling fact from opinion and then we'll create our own opinions using new facts we've learned. In each reading passage, try to identify one fact and one opinion. Look for keywords that might help you. Then try to write an opinion of your own about what you've read. To play our fact versus opinion game, challenge your friends in two ways: See if they can tell which idea is a fact and which one is an opinion (mix up their order sometimes). Then ask them if they agree or disagree with your opinion and ask them to explain why or why not.

Figure 24 illustrates how students will respond in the Guide about their reading as a way to monitor their use of Strategy 11. In this example, a fourth-grade student responded to prompts about telling fact from opinion while reading *If You Were*

FIGURE 24
Fourth-Grade Student's Responses to Read-Along Guide Prompts for Strategy 11

A. Excerpt From *If You Were There When They Signed the Constitution*
Who was Alexander Hamilton, and what was he like?
Alexander Hamilton was a delegate from New York State. He was born in the West Indies. He was probably one of the smartest young men at the Convention. Some people at the Convention said he was too smart for his own good. He would go on to become our first secretary of the treasury. (p. 34)

From IF YOU WERE THERE WHEN THEY SIGNED THE CONSTITUTION by Elizabeth Levy. Copyright © 1992 by Elizabeth Levy. Reprinted by permission of Scholastic Inc.

B. Student Response

Pages: ____32–35____

Fact: _Alexander Hamilton became our first secretary of the treasury._

Opinion: _Alexander Hamilton was probably one of the smartest young men at the Convention._

My Opinion: _Alexander Hamilton was one of the greatest contributors to our nation. He was at the Convention and also became secretary of the treasury._

There When They Signed the Constitution (Levy, 1992). Featured excerpts from the book provide insights on how the student applied the strategy while reading.

What to Look For: Key Indicators of Successful Student Performance

- *Students correctly recognize facts.* As shown in the sample response in Figure 24, the student was able to recognize a fact from the reading passage. As this was a nonfiction text (and was carefully edited to avoid any unintentional bias from the author), the student did not have trouble recognizing facts throughout this unit. Reminding students that facts can be proven and that they should pause and question themselves may be helpful.

- *Students are able to identify opinions that may or may not contain word clues.* Although there were few opinions in the passage in Figure 24, the student was able to rely on clue words to identify them. In this case, the use of the word *smartest* tipped her off. Modeling aloud the thinking process to identify opinions is a technique teachers can use to aid students.

- *Students successfully distinguish fact from opinion when no keywords are used (and especially if tricky examples appear in the text).* Sentences such as "Some people at the Convention said he was too smart for his own good" may be confusing. The student in the preceding example struggled over whether this was a fact or an opinion. That Hamilton may have been too smart for his own good was an opinion. But that some people at the Convention may have said this could possibly be a proven fact. In this case, the teacher explained the difference to the student and encouraged her to keep this as an open question to answer as her knowledge of Hamilton and the Convention continued to grow.

- *Students demonstrate an ability to form an opinion that they can support.* As evidenced by the final section of the sample response, the student has been able to use the information gathered from the reading passage to begin to shape her own opinion about Alexander Hamilton.

Strategy Connections

This strategy may be linked closely to Strategy 8, Synthesizing to Gain New Meaning, and Strategy 16, Drawing Conclusions and Making Inferences. While working with facts and opinions, it may be necessary for students to evaluate many ideas and try to understand the underlying message before determining if something is fact or opinion. This strategy is also related to Strategy 10, Identifying Facts and Details. Although related, teachers might want to avoid placing Strategy 10 and Strategy 11 together in a Guide until students have had initial instruction in each. However, the connection between the two would certainly make them compatible to feature together in future Guides after initial instruction has taken place.

Test-Taking Tips

- In addition to using informational and other nonfiction works, consider using realistic fiction and mysteries. State and other high-stakes assessments ask fact or opinion questions about passages within different genres, which suggests that building student proficiency with this skill across the genres may be beneficial.

- Multiple-choice questions on fact and opinion may be asked in several ways. A student's ability to tell fact from opinion regarding a character or an event from a passage is one way the questions may be posed, as illustrated in the following examples:

> According to the article, what does everyone know for sure about [famous person]?
>
> According to the article, no one knows for sure if [famous person] _____.

Another way these types of questions might be asked is through very straightforward questions like the following:

> According to the article, which sentence is a fact?

- Reminding students to ask themselves if something can be proven or not is a good way to help them distinguish between fact and opinion. The process of pausing to question their own thinking is a skill that may need strengthening and developing and is key in helping students to monitor their own comprehension.

- For short- and extended-response questions, students might be asked to express an opinion in a letter or article and support it with details from the reading passages. As this skill is a tricky one for many students, practicing and allowing students time to develop it may be beneficial.

Understanding Sequence

Making sense of the order in which ideas are presented is useful to students as they try to understand situations or events they read about or if they are trying to learn new skills or follow procedures. Recognizing the sequential order of events helps students understand story plots as well as complex ideas in informational texts.

Teacher Tips for Strategy Instruction

- There are many ways to initiate instruction in this strategy. In addition to using the Read-Along Guide prompt described on page 116, a timeline or organizer listing ideas is one approach you could use. Here a student could organize events on a timeline using dates to sequence the entries. If, however, dates or other "time-based" details aren't used, entries can be listed by page number, order, or other method determined by the teacher.

- You could also begin by providing students with four out-of-order events to put in chronological order. This might be especially helpful for students who struggle to distinguish important ideas from less important ones. Additionally, having students locate page numbers for events could provide further clues to help if events in the text progress sequentially through time.

- At times, students may be unable to distinguish significant ideas and may include irrelevant or very minor ideas to include during practice. Therefore, this skill needs to be practiced so that students are able to distinguish important events or actions from those that are subordinate. In turn, this will aid them in completing timelines and organizers accurately. Teachers will need to model this skill and monitor students' progress.

- Although wanting to allow a good amount of flexibility in students' written practice examples, teachers can delicately balance a concern that students identify significant ideas by giving them a guideline in the form of a question: "Did the event or idea make a difference in the story?" If students can answer yes, then most likely they've identified a significant idea.

- Some students may not be highly motivated to go back to the text to search out key information they will need to sequence multiple events. It may be necessary for you to determine if a student's lack of progress stems more from comprehension difficulties or motivational issues.

Text Suggestions

Working with short or chapter books of moderate length as opposed to lengthier texts may be better suited for initial instruction with this strategy, especially with works of fiction. Transferring this strategy to works of nonfiction is a strategic way to help students strengthen their ability to work with informational text and content area–related texts. Recognizing different uses of the same strategy will be an insightful discovery made by students as they move from one genre to another.

For initial instruction, teachers may want to avoid fantasy and science fiction, as both genres may feature unpredictable events and use nonlinear literary devices. This could cause confusion among some students. On the other hand, for students who demonstrate proficiency with this strategy, the challenges posed by fantasy or science fiction might be welcome.

Students may also have difficulty with this strategy if the text they are reading doesn't present events in a predictable order. Working with a text that presents time sequentially may be the easiest to initiate instruction. For example, informational texts or content area–based works may include dates to provide additional sequential clues.

Student-Friendly Chat on the Importance of the Strategy

When providing instruction on understanding sequence, you can use the following dialogue as a way to explain the importance of this strategy to your students:

The order in which things happen in a passage is called sequence. Sometimes clue words such as *first*, *next*, *last*, or others clearly signal an order. Other times, there are no signals and you must carefully retrace actions, steps, or events to check their order. This can be tricky, especially if you are asked to place multiple events in the correct order. That's because you must always check what came before the event as well as what came after it. Yikes, that's a lot of information to juggle! Still, knowing the order of events is important because it is a valuable tool for comprehension. It allows you to follow the plot of a story or to understand the order of a series of steps or actions in a process or event.

Practice With Prompts Using the Read-Along Guide

The Read-Along Guide prompt in Figure 25 provides students with some events and asks them to fill in events, episodes, or ideas around those provided. The sample prompt relies on a student's ability to interpret and evaluate multiple ideas or events simultaneously.

You can use the following dialogue as a way to explain to students how they should begin their practice in the use of the strategy:

> As you read your book, you'll practice sequencing by completing a chart. At times you might be working around events or ideas I provide. Other times, you might be asked to sequence events entirely on your own. Remember that you might need to think about several events and determine the order in which they occurred in relation to one another. For example, if I've completed the first and third box, you'll have to determine what event happened between them and write it in the second box.

Figure 25 illustrates how students will respond in the Guide about their reading as a way to monitor their use of Strategy 12. In this example, a fourth-grade student responded to prompts about understanding sequence while reading *The Courage of Sarah Noble* (Dalgliesh, 1954). Featured excerpts from the book provide insights on how the student applied the strategy while reading.

What to Look For: Key Indicators of Successful Student Performance

- *Students can successfully identify events or ideas in correct sequential order.* During initial instruction, the teacher may want to provide prompts and ask students to fill in significant events around them, as in Figure 25. As students progress with this strategy, they should demonstrate an ability to do this independently. Once they progress to this level, teachers can give students a prompt page where all of the boxes are blank and they have to determine sequence on their own.

- *Events or ideas expressed by students should be concise and developed.* Although some students may be tempted to quickly pull short fragments of information directly from the text, they should be encouraged to consider their selection carefully and develop and express the idea clearly, as in Figure 25.

- *Events or ideas should be significant and important to the story.* Students may need some practice separating out significant ideas from less significant ones as they practice sequencing. Juggling ideas and events while trying to evaluate the merit of each is difficult. Often, other strategies, such as identifying the main idea, may be called upon to help with this process.

A. Excerpts From *The Courage of Sarah Noble*

The spring night was cold, and Sarah drew her warm cloak close. That was comfortable, too. She thought of how her mother had put it around her the day she and father had started on this hard journey... (p. 1)

"Wooo—oooh!" Such a strange sound from a nearby tree.
"Father?"
"An owl, Sarah. He is telling you goodnight." (p. 2)

"FATHER!"
"Yes, Sarah, it is a wold. But I have my musket, and I am awake."
"I can't sleep, Father. Tell me about home?" (p. 3)

"I said, 'I will go and cook for you, Father.'"
"It was a blessing the Lord gave me daughters, as well as sons," said John Noble.
"And of them all of eight years old and a born cook. For Mary would not come, nor Hannah." (p. 4)

Reprinted with the permission of Atheneum Books for Young Readers, an imprint of Simon & Schuster Children's Publishing Division from THE COURAGE OF SARAH NOBLE by Alice Dalgliesh. Copyright 1954 Alice Dalgliesh and Leonard Weisgard; copyright renewed © 1982 Margaret B. Evans and Leonard Weisgard.

B. Student Response

Pages Chapter 1, pages 1–5

Directions: Let's practice Sequencing Events. Complete the chart.

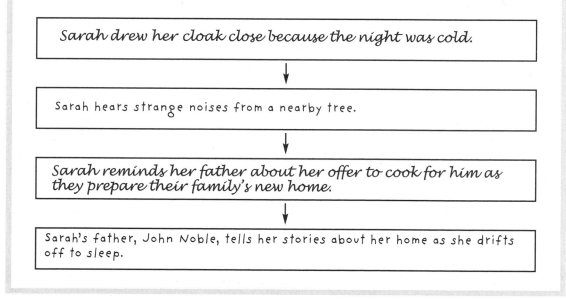

Sarah drew her cloak close because the night was cold.

↓

Sarah hears strange noises from a nearby tree.

↓

Sarah reminds her father about her offer to cook for him as they prepare their family's new home.

↓

Sarah's father, John Noble, tells her stories about her home as she drifts off to sleep.

- *Students' skill at sequencing should be evident whether or not keyword clues appear in the text.* The chapter responded to in the sample response in Figure 25 has a simple plot, with few challenging episodes. As a result, the student was able to successfully identify key events and correctly sequence them around teacher prompts. There may be times, however, when students have difficulty sequencing events. Relying on the use of clues through keyword prompts is a skill teachers might want students to practice. Also, students can demonstrate proficiency with this strategy if they are able to successfully sequence complex materials that either do not contain prompts or that make use of creative literary devices, such as flashback or forward time travel.

Strategy Connections

This strategy is closely connected to Strategy 9, Finding the Important or Main Idea, and Strategy 10, Identifying Facts and Details. Both strategies will enable students to delineate significant events and ideas from subordinate ones. Extra teacher support with this strategy may be necessary.

Test-Taking Tips

- In addition to using nonfiction and informational works, consider using other genres such as folk tales, tall tales, and poetry. State and other high-stakes assessments ask questions that rely on a student's sequencing skills about passages within many different genres, which suggests that building student proficiency across the genres is beneficial.

- Although best used to help students create a cohesive understanding of multiple events and ideas that may or may not be sequentially presented in text, this strategy may nonetheless be assessed using small sections of reading passages. Also, the format used may be multiple-choice questions or short- and extended-response questions.

- Typical multiple-choice questions that assess sequencing are usually straightforward. They may be asked in several different ways, such as the following examples:

    Which event happened first in the story?

    In the article, what happened right after the president signed the bill?

  There can also be other strategies, such as Strategy 10, Identifying Facts and Details, or Strategy 7, Making Predictions, linked to some of the sequencing questions, as in the following example:

    During the 1700s, the boundaries for the original colonies _____.

  Here the date signifies that multiple time frames are given in the passage. Students will have to pay attention to the date clue to select the correct answer. The obvious error will be for students to select the answer linked to another time frame provided in the passage.

      Another common sequencing question, "What will happen next?" asks students to consider events throughout the story and predict a logical outcome that could follow from them. A student's ability to make predictions as well as sequence will be needed.

- Multiple-choice questions on sequencing also might rely on the use of graphic organizers where some events are provided and students must select the best response that fills in the gap. These graphic organizers may be horizontal or vertical.

Sequencing may also be assessed using timelines where students are required to enter an event between others provided in the questions.

Comparing and Contrasting

Considering ways in which information or ideas may relate to something else—either through similarities or differences—is a strategy students may use to help them with comprehension. Authors may present information or ideas through relationships to other concepts that highlight ways in which they are similar or different. Understanding these relationships enables students to grasp meaning. Students will use a Venn diagram to consider these similarities and differences in their texts.

Teacher Tips for Strategy Instruction

- Modeling and sharing varying responses from student Venn diagrams will aid those who might struggle with this strategy.

- At times, students may select insignificant or minor topics for their comparisons. For example, comparisons made on the basis of appearance may be generally incidental to the meaning of the story. Encouraging students to find ideas that are key within the teacher-provided topics (and which would seem out of place in other topics) might help guide students during their selection process. Including a comparison where the student's life and experiences can be used is another good way to help students who have trouble with this strategy.

- Identifying similarities may be harder than identifying differences—or vice versa. If teachers recognize this, they may choose to recommend a lesser quantity of one or the other so that students are not tempted to include insignificant details in their comparisons.

- Depending on the topics selected by the teacher for comparison, a student's background knowledge may be called upon. Through careful monitoring, teachers can vary the level of their assistance based on the individual needs of the students.

- Often, students compare ideas that are not parallel. For example, in the student sample on page 121, students might provide an idea about a character's family life for one side of the Venn but speak about work life on the other side. Generally, students who make this type of error do not understand the use of the Venn diagram for comparative purposes. If their misunderstanding persists, teachers can provide broad topic areas for the students to compare.

- Sometimes, students may only identify two key ideas and not challenge themselves to consider other possibilities. Therefore, you may want to specify a named quantity of ideas; for example, four or five comparisons. Likewise, providing a maximum number of ideas will curb some students who might be tempted to list every detail, no matter how insignificant.

Text Suggestions

As there are many different ways this strategy can be used, text selection will largely be based on a teacher's objective. Is it to support content information? Will it be to discover the depth of a character? Will it be to review characteristics of genres? Comparisons can be made between just about anything: genres, characters, ideas, themes, and so on. The possibilities are limitless.

Providing instruction in this strategy using a variety of texts that span the genres will be useful. Fiction, nonfiction, informational books, poetry, and biographies each pose their own challenges for students in terms of either recognizing comparisons or developing their understanding by drawing their own comparisons. Progressing to more complex comparisons within content areas can be made using works of historical fiction or informational texts.

As previously mentioned, when introducing this strategy, some students might benefit from making comparisons in which their background information may be helpful. As such, selecting realistic fiction texts featuring characters who are in some ways similar to students may be beneficial.

Student-Friendly Chat on the Importance of the Strategy

When providing instruction on using this strategy, you can use the following dialogue as a way to explain the importance of this strategy to your students:

> Comparing and contrasting is a fancy way for seeing how things are alike and how they're different. When you compare two or more things, you're seeing how they're alike. When you contrast two or more things, you're seeing how they're different. You can compare and contrast just about anything—people, places, things, and events! Knowing ways in which people, places, things, and events are similar and different helps you gain deeper understandings. One tool that we've all worked with before to compare and contrast items is a Venn diagram.

Practice With Prompts Using the Read-Along Guide

Most intermediate-level students are familiar with Venn diagrams, a common graphic organizer used to compare ideas, having used them in earlier grades. However, you can use the following dialogue as a way to explain to students how they should begin their practice in the use of this strategy with a Venn diagram:

> As you read your book, you'll be asked to compare and contrast certain items using a Venn diagram. We'll work on these together and build our understanding of the character as well as the events that take place. I will provide labels for the two concepts you're going to compare. Then you can complete the diagram.

Figure 26 illustrates how students will respond in the Guide about their reading as a way to monitor their use of Strategy 13. In this example, a fourth-grade student used a Venn diagram to compare and contrast ideas after reading *Samuel's*

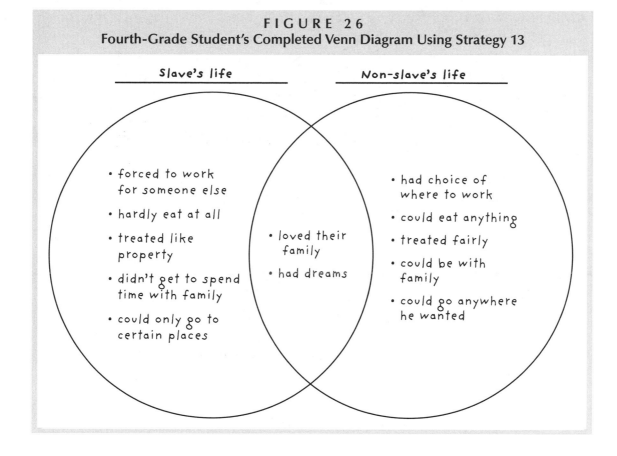

FIGURE 26
Fourth-Grade Student's Completed Venn Diagram Using Strategy 13

Slave's life

Non-slave's life

- forced to work for someone else
- hardly eat at all
- treated like property
- didn't get to spend time with family
- could only go to certain places

- loved their family
- had dreams

- had choice of where to work
- could eat anything
- treated fairly
- could be with family
- could go anywhere he wanted

Choice (Berleth, 1990); in the diagram, the life of a slave was compared to the life of a non-slave.

What to Look For: Key Indicators of Successful Student Performance

- *Students identify significant ideas.* In Figure 26, the student has selected key ideas that are relevant to the concepts provided by the teacher. This is true for her expression of the differences as well as the similarities. Some students may need help clarifying the concepts the teacher has selected for comparison. As such, teachers may wish to use some time within the small-group instruction to monitor this activity.

- *Differences are expressed in parallel ideas.* In Figure 26, the student was careful to express comparisons that covered the same topic across the two sides of the Venn diagram. For example, the first idea expresses one of work environment, the second idea expresses one of basic needs, and the third covers ownership. Assisting students in grasping this concept of parallelism may take some time, especially with works of nonfiction or historical fiction where terms and concepts may be new to students. Continuing to build background knowledge will help with this skill.

• *Differences are developed and equitable.* In Figure 26, the student has not over-simplified her ideas by stating that a slave's life was one way and the free person's life was "not" that way. Instead she expressed her ideas after giving consideration to the ways in which the two lifestyles were unique. Students may initially want to make oversimplified comparisons, but modeling how to instead describe the more intricate differences typically resolves this problem.

Strategy Connections

This strategy might rely on a student's ability to apply Strategy 8, Synthesizing to Gain New Meaning. This is largely because students may need to synthesize their understanding of facts and details into broad categories that can be used for comparisons, therefore allowing students to make parallel comparisons that are accurate.

Another useful strategy that will assist students with their ability to make logical and appropriate comparisons is Strategy 9, Finding the Important or Main Idea. Encouraging students to focus on comparisons that are substantial will help them to avoid ones that are both obvious and inconsequential. For example, some categories of comparisons may not lead the student to a deeper understanding of what they've read. A guiding question teachers might want to have students consider as they make their comparisons is, "Why is this an important comparison?" If students cannot arrive at a reasonable answer, chances are they might want to try another. Another idea is to have students list all comparisons they can make and then order them in terms of their importance.

Strategy 15, Recognizing Cause-and-Effect Relationships, would also assist students as they construct comparisons, especially those that may include historical events. For example a comparison of the Revolutionary War and the Civil War would seem incomplete if details on the causes and effects of each were not compared.

Test-Taking Tips

• A student's ability to make valid comparisons is one that is assessed not only through multiple-choice questions but also through short- and extended-response questions. Often, multiple-choice questions designed to assess a student's ability to recognize comparisons may rely on the use of the following words: *like*, *alike*, or *similar*, such as in the following test question:

    According to the passage, how are baby raccoons and baby squirrels alike?

  Text passages may or may not make direct comparisons. At times, students may find the correct response directly stated in the passage, while other times the comparison may be inferred.

• Another form of multiple-choice question used here is one that might feature a graphic organizer that makes multiple comparisons, as illustrated in the following example:

An otter is like a...	Because...
Seal	Its babies are called pups.
Platypus	Its babies drink milk.
Frog	It lives mainly in the water.
1	It has fur.
Duck	2

1. To best complete the chart, which creature belongs in the space marked '1'?
   a. fish
   b. beaver
   c. shark
   d. human

2. To best complete the chart, which group of words belongs in the space marked '2'?
   a. It uses body parts to glide in water.
   b. Its bill is rubbery.
   c. It has sharp teeth.
   d. It has whiskers.

- Some students may have trouble transferring their ability to easily compare ideas from a graphic organizer like a Venn diagram to a comparison question. Have students practice recognizing comparisons both graphically and through context may be beneficial.

- Some extended-response questions may ask for comparisons. Practice with using a graphic organizer as a quick planning device for this type of writing prompt is one way to prepare students for this type of activity.

Interpreting Figurative Language

Authors express ideas using many literary techniques, some of which may be grouped beneath a general heading of figurative language. Colorful descriptions and vibrant comparisons are some of the benefits readers enjoy through similes, metaphors, personification, idioms, and other forms of figurative language. Recognizing these common techniques and developing an ability to interpret their meaning in a variety of literary settings is a skill students will need to grasp. To help students understand and practice this strategy, we will work with two different prompts: one for identifying, describing, and interpreting figurative language and one for responding to poetic features and techniques.

Teacher Tips for Strategy Instruction

• Students experience varying degrees of difficulty with this strategy. While most students have some difficulty initially using this strategy, teachers may also find that those students who may have consistently struggled with other strategies are quick to interpret figurative language with relative ease. Careful monitoring will help teachers determine how best to provide individual assistance.

• Often, acting out some of the common figurative language techniques enables students to better grasp comparisons, especially if they have trouble visualizing to support the text (a strategy that also works together with this one). Likewise, encouraging students to write poetry in which they can explore poetic features and techniques better enables them to identify the techniques.

• Students generally seem quick to grasp similes and personification. Metaphors and idioms are more complex and may take much practice. Likewise, teachers may need to provide more support as students work with idioms, especially for ELLs who may have trouble with the nonliteral vocabulary. Unless students are familiar with some of these sayings, they have few strategies available to them to help, especially for those that are nonsensical.

• It may become difficult to distinguish between historic figures of speech, historic slang, and idioms during this instruction (especially during instruction with tall tales and folk tales). We generally do not make a distinction. However, providing instruction in commonly used idioms often provides students with a more refined grasp of idioms.

• We encourage you to include in your discussions and the Read-Along Guide any other examples of figurative language that may appear in books or reading passages with which you're working. For example, books you select to use may include many similes or examples of personification—poetry often includes a great variety of these features. Scanning the book in advance will let you know you have a good representation of a variety of figurative language forms. Once students begin to recognize and understand a few of these figurative language techniques, they are better able to quickly grasp others.

• Many of the techniques rely on a student's ability to hear repeated sounds, such as rhyme, assonance, and alliteration. For these techniques, read-alouds might be useful.

• You may wish to keep a running list where students can post figurative language they have found in their reading. Often students will point out cases where they have spied idioms, similes, metaphors, and other creative uses of language. Enabling students to keep track of this is a sure way to provide ongoing instruction in this strategy.

Text Suggestions

This strategy is one that works well with poetry, tall tales, and folklore where language is often used creatively. Introducing the strategy with a particular genre guarantees that unique features will be present. For example, genres that have a strong oral tradition, such as tall tales and other folk literature, often feature colorful language that may be distinct to a location or a group of people. Also, carefully selecting authors, such as Roald Dahl, who use much figurative language is another option.

Picture books or illustrated stories may also provide students with a good introduction as students are able to explore how others interpret figurative language prior to tackling this challenge independently.

Student-Friendly Chat on the Importance of the Strategy

When providing instruction on interpreting figurative language, you can use the following dialogue as a way to explain the importance of this strategy to your students:

> Figurative language is a kind of colorful or playful language that authors use so that readers can make great pictures in their mind, chuckle out loud, or just enjoy creative ways in which ideas are expressed. There are many tools authors use to craft their figurative language: Some techniques you're probably familiar with are similes, metaphors, personification, and idioms. Still there are others—lots of others! You'll want to be able to identify these other techniques so you can better understand what you're reading or simply to take pleasure in the creative way an author has expressed his or her ideas.
>
> - Simile—phrase that compares things using the words *like* or *as*
>
> - Metaphor—phrase that compares things without using special words (like similes do)
>
> - Idiom—saying that has another meaning and is not literal
>
> - Personification—phrase with human-like traits given to nonhumans
>
> Before we begin working in our Guide, we'll find some examples to share. This will help you better understand what they are.

Practice With Prompts Using the Read-Along Guide—Identifying, Describing, and Interpreting Figurative Language

When using this prompt, you can use the following dialogue as a way to explain to students how they should begin their practice in the use of the strategy:

> To work with this strategy, we'll try to find some examples of personification, simile, metaphor, and idioms in our reading. Then we'll get to the fun part of playing "figurative language detective" where we'll try to figure out or interpret their meaning. When you find an example, you will record it in your Guide.

Figure 27 illustrates how students will respond in the Guide about their reading as a way to monitor their use of Strategy 14. In this example, a fourth-grade student responded to a prompt by identifying, describing, and interpreting figurative language while reading *Mike Fink* (Kellogg, 1992) and the section on Davy Crockett in *Teaching Tall Tales* (West, 1998). Featured excerpts from the books provide insights on how the student applied the strategy while reading.

What to Look For: Key Indicators of Successful Student Performance—Identifying, Describing, and Interpreting Figurative Language

• *Students correctly identify the type of figurative language.* The student whose response is featured in Figure 27 has correctly identified the use of a simile, personification, and idiom in one tall tale, as well as the use of a metaphor in another. He has also provided clear and complete examples of their use in the reading passage. As an extension, students may be asked to practice using figurative language in their own writing.

- *Students can demonstrate an ability to interpret the meaning of the passage that includes the figurative language.* In Figure 27, the student has accurately described the meaning of the language and clearly states how the form of figurative language was used. This reader has a well-developed sense of these forms of figurative language. Teachers may find that some forms of figurative language are more difficult for some students to grasp. Developing proficiency with all forms may require that teachers monitor student success and adjust their instructional time accordingly.

- *Students can distinguish the different kinds of figurative language.* Encouraging students to try and identify all types will better help them distinguish one from another. Though the complete Guide is not shown here, the teacher provided instruction with several tall tales and guided students who were unable to identify all four examples of figurative language through repeated practice.

Practice With Prompts Using the Read-Along Guide—Responding to Poetic Features and Techniques

Once students have gained some experience working with this initial set of figurative language techniques, you may wish to provide them with other experiences. Poetry or narrative verse are good genres for furthering students' skills with figurative language. A second prompt on responding to poetic features and techniques might encourage students to identify and list new techniques and to readily identify the techniques they have already learned as they come upon them in new materials they are reading. For example, as students read from an anthology of poetry or a work written in narrative verse, they could be responsible for identifying techniques and listing the page numbers on which they are found. Following their reading and after they have listed the techniques, they might be asked to include a discussion of two or three techniques in a written response (see chapter 5 for more on the written-response section of the Read-Along Guide).

You can use the following dialogue as a way to explain to students how they should begin their practice in the use of the strategy:

As we work through this unit, we'll try to find examples of many of these other forms of figurative language and poetic techniques, too. In the chart, we can note the page numbers where we find them. Additionally, we will also record our ideas about events in the passages, describe our reaction to the events, and explain the meaning of some of the poetic language we've found.

Figure 28 illustrates how students will respond in the Guide about their reading as a way to monitor their use of Strategy 14. In this example, a fourth-grade student responded to a prompt about poetic features and techniques while reading *Love That Dog* (Creech, 2001) and the poem "Street Music" from *Street Music: City Poems*

Fourth-Grade Student's Responses to Read-Along Guide Prompts for Strategy 14
(Responding to Poetic Features and Techniques)

A. Excerpts From *Love That Dog* and "Street Music"

February 15

I like that poem
we read today
about street music
in the city. (p. 31)

From *Love That Dog* by Sharon Creech. Text copyright © 1998 by Sharon Creech. Reprinted with permission from HarperCollins Publishers.

Street Music
By Arnold Adoff

This city:	v o c a b u l a r i e s	a n
t h e	of	o r c h e s t r a
a l w a y s	clash	of rolling drums
n o i s e	flash	and battle blasts
g r i n d i n g	screeching	assaulting
up from the	hot metal l a n g u a g e	my ears
s u b w a y s	c o m b i n a t i o n s:	with
u n d e r	as p l a n e s	t h e
g r o u n d:	o v e r h e a d	a l w a y s
slamming from bus tires	r o a r	n o i s e of
and taxi horns and engines		t h i s c i t y:
of cars and trucks in all		
		street music. (n.p.)

From *Street Music: City Poems* by Arnold Adoff. Text copyright © 1995 by Arnold Adoff. Used by permission of HarperCollins Publishers.

B. Student Response
Write the page numbers for as many techniques and features as you can find:

Simile—phrase that compares things using the words <u>like</u> or <u>as</u>
Example: _pages 8, 9_

Metaphor—phrase that compares things without using special words (like similes do)
Example: _pages 1, 6_

Idiom—saying that has another meanings and is not literal
Example: _____

Personification—phrase with human-like traits given to non-humans
Example: _pages 6, 8_

I found a big number of poetic features today. Some were repetition, a simile, and looking different because of space. There was a lot of repetition in the poems "My Yellow Dog" and "The Apple". Words just kept on repeating themselves until you just couldn't say the word any longer. I found a simile in "Street Music" when it said, "Hot, metal language combinations as plains overhead roar." In that same poem I found space features between the text. It looked fairly different from a poem with stanzas. In conclusion, these are some of the poetic features I found.

(Adoff, 1995). Featured excerpts from the two works provide insights on how the student applied the strategy while reading. The first part of the prompt page demonstrates a student's ability to identify figurative language—here, the student lists page numbers where she finds the features. The second part of the prompt page shows the third paragraph from the student's written response section (also see Figure 46 on page 175)—here, she demonstrates an understanding of the use of figurative language in the poem "Street Music" by Arnold Adoff.

What to Look For: Key Indicators of Successful Student Performance—Responding to Poetic Features and Techniques

- *Being able to recognize and distinguish the different techniques from a more complex listing is a sign of a very proficient reader.* Though correctly interpreting figurative language may be considered more important than recognizing what type it is, the two skills are linked.

- *As students progress with this skill, they become more comfortable expressing their interpretation.* In the example, the student has fully developed her explanation of the techniques she has found and is able to clearly interpret their meaning.

- *Students identify multiple techniques and demonstrate variety in their selection.* This student was able to select significant strategies from among many. At times, students may wish to select end rhyme or list spacing or punctuation features consistently. Encouraging students to take risks identifying some of the more complex techniques may be necessary.

- *Students demonstrate some type of engagement with the poem.* Certainly students will benefit by being able to identify these techniques. However, unless there is some form of engagement expressed, this could become a chore to some students. Balancing the two may become necessary for some students. This student states she is able to picture an activity based on the poet's selection of words. She is drawn into and enjoying the poem.

Strategy Connections

Interpreting figurative language is a strategy that relies on many other strategies. As such, teachers may have to provide careful monitoring and adjust the degree of direct instruction depending on when this strategy is taught. Many students may not have developed the background knowledge or understanding of phonemic concepts needed to successfully interpret some ideas expressed through figurative language. For example, students unfamiliar with city sounds may have difficulty understanding Adoff's poem. Likewise, students who have difficulty recognizing vowel or consonant sounds may have trouble identifying poetic forms such as assonance, alliteration, or even repetition. Strategy 1, Using Fix-Up Methods When Meaning Is Challenged, and Strategy 2, Finding Word Meaning and Building Vocabulary Using Context Clues, may be adjusted to accommodate figurative phrases or ideas. For example, if slang is used within an idiom, the aforementioned strategies may be useful to help students interpret meaning. This strategy is also closely connected to Strategy 6, Visualizing to Support the Text. Here students may use pictures they create in their minds to help them interpret meaning. Likewise, students may need to rely on skills most closely related to Strategy 2, Finding Word Meaning and Building Vocabulary Using Context Clues, and Strategy 16, Drawing Conclusions and Making Inferences.

Test-Taking Tips

- Include a broad range of genres while working with this strategy, even those that may not typically include figurative language. State and other high-stakes assessments often ask questions about figurative language using passages within many different genres, which suggests that building student proficiency across the genres is beneficial.

- Topics that are often linked to figurative language that may appear on tests include separating real from make-believe and variations of this, such as identifying truths from exaggerations. The following are examples of these types of questions:

  Which of these lines from the poem shows something imaginary and not real?

  Which event from the passage shows something that could really happen?

- Questions that rely on a student's ability to interpret figurative language are often asked using the multiple-choice format. There are many ways these could be asked. For example, the following questions are examples that assess a student's ability to interpret similes or metaphors:

  What does the poet compare to a Bengal tiger?

  Which line in the poem shows a letter is like a song?

  Personification is another feature tested through multiple-choice questions, such as in the following examples:

  The speaker in the poem knows that plants are kind because they _____.

  When the poet says "the half moon is shy," what does she mean?

  Other questions seeking to assess a student's ability interpreting the use of figurative language techniques may be about tone, author's purpose, or the action taking place in the passage, such as in the following:

  What word best describes the tone of the poem?

  From this poem, we can tell that the speaker _____.

  What are the birds doing in the poem?

- In addition to multiple-choice questions, short- and extended-response questions may also rely on a student's skill at interpreting figurative language. For example, students may be asked to construct a persuasive essay using information from a poem or creative passage that includes figurative language. Additionally, multiple-choice questions assessing figurative comparisons can be presented in story webs or through other graphic organizers.

Recognizing Cause-and-Effect Relationships

Understanding relationships between ideas helps students grasp meaning by enabling them to link outcomes to causes. Gaining a cohesive understanding of not only what is happening in a passage but also why it is happening provides students with a greater depth of understanding.

Teacher Tips for Strategy Instruction

- Students may have difficulty distinguishing between causes and effects. Students may initially confuse them and simply repeat the cause for the effect or vice versa. Noting that one expresses why something happened and the other expresses what happened (as in the student practice samples) may be helpful.

- Students may find it easier to identify effects first and then determine the causes. This approach may be helpful not only when first introducing this strategy but also as a reminder throughout the duration of instruction, especially if the strategy is used with works in multiple genres.

- Teachers may wish to cluster pages in the text students are reading while providing initial instruction in this strategy. For example, in the student samples on page 133, students were instructed to identify two cause-and-effect relationships in one chapter. This may be a more manageable chunk of text to work with than anything either larger or smaller. (This decision will also depend on the text used.)

- A student's background knowledge will affect his or her ability to identify cause-and-effect relationships that are not directly stated in the text. This is true with works of fiction as well as other genres. Teachers may provide students with other materials to help build background knowledge.

- At times, students may get lost in details and feel overwhelmed trying to single out any one cause of some event that took place. Encouraging them to categorize like ideas together, if possible, and to simply narrow their list (instead of trying to use only one event) may be helpful.

- While working with curriculum-related historical fiction or nonfiction and informational texts, students may not recognize cause-and-effect relationships, especially if they are being exposed to concepts and ideas for the first time. For example, intermediate-level students may not be aware of difficult ideas such as those they might encounter in social studies—war, slavery, and others. Close teacher monitoring of students' progress with this strategy will enable teachers to provide assistance with content-based issues when necessary.

Text Suggestions

Working with small or moderate-sized chapter books as opposed to lengthier texts may be better suited for initial instruction with this strategy, especially with works of fiction. Transferring this strategy to works of nonfiction is a strategic way to help students strengthen their ability to work with informational text and content area–related texts. Content area–based texts may also be good choices to work with for instruction in this strategy. Recognizing the cause-and-effect relationships for some topics, such as those within social studies, is critical in developing a student's understanding of historical events.

Historical fiction is another good genre for instruction in this strategy, as events may easily be linked to causes. Moving from fiction to historical fiction (before addressing informational texts) might make for a smoother transition for some students. Likewise, it will give teachers an opportunity to build students' understanding of complex historical issues.

Student-Friendly Chat on the Importance of the Strategy

When providing instruction on recognizing cause-and-effect relationships, you can use the following dialogue as a way to explain the importance of this strategy to your students:

> Often events or ideas in a passage are somehow linked together, such as in a cause-and-effect relationship. Here, what happens is called the effect. Also, why it happens is called the cause. Sometimes clue words such as *since, because, as a result*, or others clearly show that connection between what happened and why. Other times, you can easily find the cause and the effect by asking yourself two questions:
> 1. *What* happened? (This will tell you the *effect*.)
> 2. *Why* did it happen? (This will tell you the *cause*.)

Practice With Prompts Using the Read-Along Guide

The Read-Along Guide prompt asks students to identify episodes that represent linked cause-and-effect relationships. You can use the following dialogue to explain to students how they should begin their practice in the strategy:

> As you read your book, I am going to give you an event, and you are going to have to identify the cause-and-effect connections. Using the prompt in your Read-Along Guide, let's practice recognizing both causes and effects by completing the chart. At times you might be asked to find one or the other—or both.

Figure 29 illustrates how students will respond in the Guide about their reading as a way to monitor their use of Strategy 15. In this example, a fourth-grade student responded to prompts about recognizing cause-and-effect relationships while reading *The Courage of Sarah Noble* (Dalgliesh, 1954). Featured excerpts from the book provide insights on how the student applied the strategy while reading.

What to Look For: Key Indicators of Successful Student Performance

- *Students demonstrate an ability to link related causes and effects.* As is shown in the first example of Figure 29 (the student's response to pages 23–28), the teacher provided prompts and asked students to identify the linked effect, as in the first example, or the linked cause, as in the second example. Showing an ability to identify

FIGURE 29
FIGURE 29

Fourth-Grade Student's Responses to Read-Along Guide Prompts for Strategy 15

A. Excerpts From *The Courage of Sarah Noble*

But after it was done, he said to her, "I must begin the work on the house. It should be finished before winter. You will not mind staying here, Sarah, while Thomas and I work?" (p. 23)

She did not want her father to go, but the house must be built. So she looked at him steadily and said, "I will stay here, Father." But to herself she was saying, "Keep up your courage, Sarah Noble. Keep up your courage!" (pp. 23–24)

INDIANS!
They were all around her, some of them crowded in the opening of the palisade. But they were young Indians, not any older than she was. Still, there were many of them.... Sarah kept as still as a rabbit in danger. (p. 25)

There were many things to do. Tall John's wife taught Sarah how to weave a basket. And because Sarah's clothes were stiff and heavy, the Indian woman made her clothes of deerskin such as the Indians wore when the days grew colder. (p. 42)

"...I think it would be well to put on your own clothes, or your mother will surely not know you!" So Sarah put on her clothes, piece by stiff piece. She now thought of buttons as tiresome, and as for petticoats.... (p. 46)

B. Student Response
Pages Chapter 6, pp. 23–28

Cause (Why)	Effect (What)
John Noble tells Sarah he and Thomas must work on the house. He asks Sarah if she minds staying alone at the cave.	Sarah didn't want her dad to go, but she tells him it's OK. Then she tells herself she must keep up her courage.
Young Indian children crept closer and closer to Sarah. They surrounded her.	Sarah kept as still as a rabbit in danger.

Pages Chapter 9, pp. 42–46

Cause (Why)	Effect (What)
Because Sarah's clothes were stiff and heavy...	The Indian women made Sarah new clothes out of deerskin.
Sarah wanted to be sure her mother could recognize her.	Sarah put her old clothes back on.

effects when given the causes and vice versa is an indication that students are gaining proficiency in distinguishing the difference between these two concepts.

- *Examples of linked causes and effects can be identified independently and are clear.* Although the teacher provided either the cause or the effect in the first set of examples, she allowed the student to provide this information in the third and fourth examples so that the student would identify examples of cause and effect independently. Clearly the student whose work is featured in Figure 29 can identify and establish clear connections between cause-and-effect relationships from within a group of pages independently.

- *Inferred or implied relationships that may not be directly stated in the text are used by the students.* In the second example of Figure 29, the student establishes that Sarah's behavior of remaining perfectly still is a response to her concern that Native American children are surrounding her. Though remaining still is a common response to being fearful or uncertain, this action may not suggest it is a response to fear to all students. Teachers may need to monitor a student's understanding of these types of emotion-based inferences.

- *Students are able to categorize multiple events that may be components of cause-and-effect relationships.* Students may get tangled up in this strategy if they are not able to cluster multiple events that have to do with the same cause or the same effect. In the first example in Figure 29, the response shows multiple events used within both the cause and the effect.

- *Students' practice demonstrates insightfulness.* By showing capabilities with several of the indicators described previously (inferring and working with multiple events), students clearly show insightfulness in identifying, linking, and expressing these cause-and-effect relationships.

Strategy Connections

This strategy is closely connected to Strategy 16, Drawing Conclusions and Making Inferences. Being able to interpret the reasons for character actions or motives will be critical for recognizing links within cause-and-effect relationships. The degree of assistance students may need with this strategy (particularly in content areas) and the manner in which this assistance is provided are best determined by the teacher.

Test-Taking Tips

- In addition to using nonfiction and informational works, consider using other genres such as folk tales, tall tales, and poetry. State and other high-stakes assessments ask questions that rely on a student's ability to identify cause-and-effect relationships in passages that span a range of genres, which suggests that building student proficiency across the genres may be beneficial.

- This strategy may be assessed using methods and question formats similar to those used for assessing a student's skill with facts and details. Obviously, facts and details can comprise the parts of cause-and-effect relationships. As such, many of the same test-taking issues apply. For example, multiple-choice questions designed to assess a student's ability to recognize cause-and-effect relationships may rely on the use of the following words: *who, what, when, where, why,* or *how.*

However, they may also be asked a question that leads with a cause and the selection of responses represent the effects, as in the following example:

Because the boy wanted to calm the frightened dog...

This type of question would be followed by a selection of choices from which the student must select the best answer. Typically, these types of questions are open-ended and thus are not asked using a standard question-and-answer format.

Answers to this type of cause-and-effect question may or may not be clearly stated somewhere in the passage. Students may need to use higher-level thinking skills, such as inferring, to arrive at answers. Still, encouraging students to hunt clues upon which to base their selection may help them at least narrow down correct answers in the list or even omit wrong answers.

- Like the test-taking tips for Strategy 10, Identifying Facts and Details, questions that are used to assess this strategy may also be short- or extended-response questions. Here, too, they may be open-ended questions that lead with *who, what, when, where, why,* or *how.* Typically, responses to these questions are more involved than similar questions asked in the multiple-choice format.

- For short- and extended-response questions, students will often be asked to "Use details from the passage(s) to support your answer." If struggling readers are unable to make connections between causes and effects, they will have trouble supporting their ideas through this type of connection in their writing. Practicing these types of responses proves worthwhile in helping struggling students with this skill.

- The ease with which students are able to respond to both multiple-choice and short- and extended-response questions on cause and effect depends largely on their ability to recognize relationships as well as to locate information in the passage. For struggling readers, both tasks may be challenging. Reminding students to question themselves while reading (why and what) to monitor their own understanding is a means for teachers to support instruction in this strategy.

Drawing Conclusions and Making Inferences

At times, students need almost a "sixth sense" to interpret what they're reading so that they can understand action, events, or a character's motives or feelings that are not directly stated in the passage. As most readers become engaged in their reading, this "sense" helps them follow the plot, explain events or actions, and piece together ideas without having to be explicitly told. It makes the reader an active participant in the unfolding story.

Teacher Tips for Strategy Instruction

- Suggesting that students write "Who, What, and Why" on the top of their practice sheet might help guide some students and give them a plan of action to begin, as illustrated in the sample provided for this strategy.

- Students may have trouble linking behaviors and traits. Although relationships between behaviors and traits are often evident to students, other times they may not be. Close teacher monitoring may be necessary during instruction with this skill.

- Even while working with smaller sections of text or chapters, teachers might wish to carefully model the process of linking ideas and piecing together clues to draw inferences and conclusions through a think-aloud. Also, modeling the process of finding clues from the text, background knowledge, or predictions, provides students with avenues to search out meaning in ways they might not have considered.

Text Suggestions

Nonfiction, historical fiction, mysteries, and other types of texts that engage and challenge students are good selections for this strategy. As this strategy is so closely linked to Strategy 14, Interpreting Figurative Language, working with genres such as poetry is also a good way encourage students to infer. Picture books or illustrated stories may also provide students with a good introduction to making inferences as students are able to explore how illustrators may help to interpret characters' reactions or responses. Although this may be a good way to launch instruction in the strategy, some students may begin to rely on illustrations and not take risks drawing inferences independently. Alternating your use of picture books with short chapter books that do not contain illustrations is one way to avoid this potential problem.

On the other hand, working with informational and content area–based texts, which tend to present factual information in a more straightforward manner, may not provide students with the opportunity to make inferences and draw conclusions.

Student-Friendly Chat on the Importance of the Strategy

When providing instruction on drawing conclusions and making inferences, you can use the following dialogue as a way to explain the importance of this strategy to your students:

> Drawing conclusions and making inferences means that you "read between the lines" to gain an understanding of something in the story—or ask yourself, "What is the author trying to tell me?" Rather than being told exactly what's happening, you must figure out what's happening. For example, you might have to figure out what a character means by reading between the lines of his or her words or dialogue. Or you might have to read between the lines to figure out why a character is acting a certain way. Instead of being told, you grasp your understanding of why something in the story is happening by piecing together clues and information. This is what it means to make inferences. When you make inferences, you might be using text clues, your background knowledge, new knowledge you gained while reading the book, and/or your predictions.

Practice With Prompts Using the Read-Along Guide

Selecting passages from a text that do not directly express an idea or a feeling is one way of working with this strategy. As shown in the student practice example that follows, the Guide will include selected passages from the text, and the student will then have to draw conclusions or make inferences in order to determine meaning.

You can use the following dialogue as a way to explain to students how they should begin their practice in the use of the strategy:

> As you read your book, you'll be asked to infer something about a character or an event based on quotations pulled from the text. We'll practice one together, and then you'll be given specific passages from the text where inferring is needed to grasp and understand the meaning of the story.

Figure 30 illustrates how students will respond in the Guide about their reading as a way to monitor their use of Strategy 16. In this example, a fourth-grade student responded to prompts about drawing conclusions and making inferences while reading *Toliver's Secret* (Brady, 1976). Featured excerpts from the book provide insights on how the student applied the strategy while reading.

FIGURE 30
Fourth-Grade Student's Responses to Read-Along Guide Prompts for Strategy 16

A. Excerpt From *Toliver's Secret*

Everyone knew the brave Patriots could drive the British out. Washington had driven them out of Boston last year, hadn't he?

But the British had three times as many men as Washington had – and all of them well trained in war. They defeated him at Brooklyn Heights and they captured New York City. They drove his army north and in November captured Fort Washington, where they took three thousand prisoners. People heard the news in stunned surprise.

Then the British took Fort Lee across Hudson's River with all of Washington's cannon. And finally they sent what was left of his army scurrying across New Jersey. The colonists could hardly believe such news. They had felt so sure that courage and the will to win would be enough to beat back the British. (p. 18)

From TOLIVER'S SECRET by Esther Wood Brady, illustrated by Richard Cuffari, copyright © 1976 by Esther Wood Brady. Illustrations copyright © Richard Cuffari. Used by permission of Crown Publishers, an imprint of Random House Children's Books, a division of Random House, Inc.

B. Student Response

Text Quote: " "They had felt so sure that courage and the will to win would be enough to beat back the British." (chapter 2, p. 18)

Meaning:
(I think... because...)
I think this means that the Patriots thought they could win every battle against the British just because they were brave and determined and they wanted to win really, really badly. I think this because they were stunned when the British defeated them in some major battles.

What to Look For: Key Indicators of Successful Student Performance

• *Students successfully identify key ideas suggested in the passage.* In Figure 30, the reader has identified "who" was involved—the Patriots and the British. Also, he correctly established "what" was implied—the Patriots assumed they would win battles. Finally, the reader pulls the pieces together to interpret "why" this happened—they were determined and wanted to win badly. The student had placed these key ideas—who, what, and why—on the top of his practice pages to help guide his thinking.

• *Inferences have been supported.* Supporting conclusions and inferences with ideas expressed in the text further indicates that the student is pulling clues from other areas to piece together information. For example, in the sample response, the reader pulls into his response (and thinking) that the Patriots had been losing many battles. Linking that idea to the new information suggests he's able to associate related ideas independently, without an author having to make this connection for him.

• *Figurative language, vocabulary, and other literary devices have been interpreted correctly.* In this passage, the reader had to interpret an idiom—"beat back" the British. He also had to interpret a figurative use of the idea of using courage and will as implements to win battles. Although students may not be asked to interpret these types of devices while making inferences, being able to call upon the skill is helpful.

Strategy Connections

This strategy relies on many others. As such, teachers may have to provide careful monitoring during instruction and adjust their degree of direct instruction. Also, the skill involves complex judgment calls that may be intimidating to students. Recognizing that this strategy is one that will be revisited often—whether through guided reading or other forms of instruction—reassures students that it is a skill that develops over time. Teachers may wish to introduce instruction in this strategy after numerous others have been introduced, such as Strategy 2, Finding Word Meaning and Building Vocabulary Using Context Clues; Strategy 8, Synthesizing to Gain New Meaning; and Strategy 14, Interpreting Figurative Language.

Test-Taking Tips

• State and other high-stakes assessments ask inferential questions about passages within different genres, which suggests that building student proficiency with this skill across the genres may be beneficial.

• A student's ability to make logical inferences and reach conclusions is one that is assessed not only through multiple-choice questions but also through short- and extended-response questions as well. Practicing and sharing in their group responses to both types of questions should be beneficial.

• Multiple-choice questions related to this strategy may be asked in several ways. A student's ability to "read between the lines" is one way, as in the following examples:

> The information in the articles suggests that....

Why does the article recommend that hikers' food supplies be wrapped carefully at night time?

Another way these types of questions might be asked is through questions relating to an author's purpose, as in the following examples:

The author probably wrote this article to _____.

How does the author make the article interesting to the reader?

- Reviewing the Test-Taking Tips for Strategy 14, Interpreting Figurative Language, may also be helpful, as inferential questions may rely on interpreting figurative literary devices or even genre-specific concepts, as in the following example:

Which word best describes the tone of the poem?

- In addition to multiple-choice questions, short- and extended-response questions may also rely on a student's ability to make inferences. For example, students may be asked to identify, explain, and support a character's actions, motives, or feelings using information from a reading passage. Some short-response questions might appear as follows:

Write three examples that show a character is excited.

Why did the characters become annoyed with one another?

What three things show that a dog is intelligent?

Certainly, any variation of asking students to show the relationship between a character's action and emotional state is an inferential question.

- Extended-response questions often rely on a student's ability to make numerous inferences throughout the duration of the reading passage. These types of questions span an entire reading passage, as illustrated in the following examples:

How does a character feel at the beginning of the story?

Why does the character change at the end?

What caused a character to change?

Inferential skills might also be called into action to explain why characters' views are different, as in the following example:

Explain why two characters find a situation confusing while a third doesn't.

- Questions that rely on a student's ability to read between the lines and interpret events in a passage often suggest the understated theme of a passage. As such, they tend to cover broad ideas that may prove difficult for students to grasp, as in the following example.

What do people get from being helpful or considerate toward one another? Support your answer with details from the reading passages.

• Although students might perform well on multiple-choice questions that rely on inferential skills, working with the short- and extended-response questions tends to pose many more challenges.

Summarizing

DIFFICULTY
5
RATING

A summary is a brief description containing critical information about a passage. To prepare a concise summary, students must evaluate ideas, selecting which among them should be included, omitted, or possibly combined with others. Developing a skill to determine which ideas are integral to the meaning of a passage is complex, as it relies on the use of many other comprehension skills.

Teacher Tips for Strategy Instruction

• Students often have trouble understanding how lengthy a summary should be. Teachers may wish to clarify that there is no correct answer to this but that students might use the space provided in their Guide as a criterion to determine length. Students can also practice adjusting the length of their summaries and refining their selection process. Not only is this good practice, but also students often welcome the challenge of writing a one-sentence summary about an entire book.

• Teachers may wish to have students write summaries based on chapters or page clusters instead of having them write one summary at the end of an entire text. Practicing with shorter, more manageable sections enables students to grow comfortable with the complex process of selecting what should be included, omitted, or combined prior to tackling (and juggling) a vast amount of information.

• Even while working with shorter sections or chapters, teachers might wish to carefully model the process of selecting, omitting, and combining ideas to prepare a concise summary through a think-aloud.

• Teachers might wish to allow for a greater amount of discussion time for the instruction of this strategy, as students will benefit from the process of working together to prepare a summary. Often, teachers will have students write ideas to go into summaries on sticky notes to bring to discussion.

• Students may try to locate a summary directly in the passage, which they will not find. Unlike locating facts and details and unlike locating a main idea that could be expressed in a topic or closing sentence, the summary will not be featured so succinctly in a passage. Students may need further help understanding this. Samples from book reviews, catalog blurbs, and other similar prompts could help students better understand the difference between a summary and these other elements.

- After students have had the opportunity to learn from teacher modeling and work with classmates in group activities, they should also be encouraged to practice this skill independently. This will also enable teachers to monitor student progress.

- Students may have trouble selecting key ideas for their summaries. Providing them with some guidelines, such as identifying story elements at the beginning of a story (setting, characters, problem) and then keeping in mind the question "Does this seem critical?" may be helpful. Students might also benefit from answering who, what, when, where, and why questions.

- As students sometimes get off track and begin to include predictions or their feelings about an event or character, teachers might not want to include a written response section with this Read-Along Guide. Certainly, many students are able to separate the two types of writing. However, others may find it difficult.

- Because this strategy requires students to evaluate ideas, introducing the concept of theme during this instruction may be considered a welcome challenge for teachers and students to tackle.

Text Suggestions

This strategy might be best introduced with engaging and shorter works of fiction or historical fiction that do not have an overly complex plot. Mysteries are also good choices, as they are written to intentionally pique readers' interest. Also, readers often pay careful attention to details in this genre that will be helpful as they prepare summaries. Nonfiction and informational texts also present good challenges for students to organize different types of information in a usable format. Additionally, as students progress through school, they will find that the ability to summarize content-based information will be necessary for many genres.

Student-Friendly Chat on the Importance of the Strategy

When providing instruction on summarizing, you can use the following dialogue as a way to explain the importance of this strategy to your students:

> A summary is a brief recounting or description of the main ideas and events that took place in a reading passage. Instead of telling everything that happened, select only the really, really important parts to include in your summary. Deciding what should be left in and what can be taken out of a summary is how you get to practice using your skills at finding the main idea, identifying key facts and details, sequencing, and other strategies.

Practice With Prompts Using the Read-Along Guide

Asking students to practice the skill by working with smaller sections or chapters prior to writing a summary of the entire passage or text is one way of working with this strategy. As such, you can use the following dialogue as a way to explain to students how they should begin their practice of the strategy in the Guide:

As we read our book together, we'll create a summary for the cluster of pages we cover each day using our skills at finding the main idea, identifying key facts and details, sequencing, and others. Then, we'll see how to blend those ideas together to make one summary for the whole book.

Figure 31 illustrates how students will respond in the Guide about their daily reading as a way to monitor their use of Strategy 17. In this example, a fourth-grade

---

FIGURE 31
Fourth-Grade Student's Responses to Read-Along Guide Prompts for Strategy 17

A. Excerpts From *Phoebe the Spy*

In 1776, the year Phoebe Fraunces was thirteen years old, her father gave her a very dangerous job. Phoebe was going to be a spy.

At that time most black people in New York were slaves. But Phoebe and her family had always been free. Phoebe's father, Samuel Fraunces, owned the Queen's Head Tavern. The Queen's Head was a popular eating and meeting place. George Washington (who was now General George Washington, commander in chief of the American Army).... (p. 7)

"...General Washington is in dread, dread danger. It is he who is keeping the colonies together. But there are those who'd like to see the colonies separated and so ruled more easily by the king." (p. 11)

"...I want you to live there and be his housekeeper, Phoebe. I know you will be a good one. But your real job will be to watch—to listen— to spy out every bit of information you can. I want you to find out if there is someone planning to kill him and how he plans to do it. Your real job will be to save General Washington's life." (p. 12)

At the thought of her father Phoebe rocked back and forth on the cot in despair, still clutching her bundle. How could she take care of this big, quiet, unfriendly house, with its gleaming floors and stiff furniture? And take care of General Washington, too? She could not do it. Her father had asked too much. (p. 20)

B. Student Response

Pages ___7–11___ Date ___April 22___

In these pages,

We learn the story happens in 1776. A thirteen year old girl named Phoebe is given a dangerous job by her father, Samuel Fraunces. The two are working in their family tavern which is a known meeting place for Patriots when Samuel tells Phoebe about a dangerous mission.

Pages ___12–20___ Date ___April 22___

In these pages,

Phoebe learns her mission is to save General Washington because someone with a name that starts with the letter T is trying to kill him. She is also made aware this person may be a bodyguard. Phoebe will pretend to be a housekeeper at Mortier House where Washington will be staying. As Phoebe arrives at M. House, she grows sad and discouraged.

---

student responded to prompts about summarizing while reading *Phoebe the Spy* (Griffin, 1977). Featured excerpts from the book provide insights on how the student applied the strategy while reading.

What to Look For: Key Indicators of Successful Student Performance

- *Students express key ideas of setting, characters, and plot that have been introduced in the reading section.* Though these typical story concepts are often presented in the beginning of a passage, they might either be missed by students or trivialized and omitted from the summary. For example, in the summary covering pages 7–11 in the sample student response in Figure 31, the teacher prompted students to include the year the story took place, 1776. This was omitted by many students but might later be important if the students were to prepare an overall summary of the book.

- *The problem or conflict has been identified (providing it appeared in the passage).* Although many students are able to identify a problem in a story, others may have trouble for different reasons. For example, it may have been brewing or is present over a lengthy period of time in the story and thus seems routine rather than troublesome. Also, they might not be able to distinguish which of several problems might be more critical. From these two passages, it is clear that the major problem (an attempt will be made on Washington's life) unfolds quickly and most readers are able to identify it. However, some claim that the problem is that Phoebe is feeling sad (in the second passage). Although this student included this detail in the summary for pages 12–20, the teacher clarified the main problem with all students during small-group instruction.

- *Details that are included significantly support or develop ideas that are integral to the meaning of the passage.* Although this reader has included what might be considered extraneous detail, such as Phoebe's age in the first example, he felt this was important, as it made him think about the notion of danger from a child's point of view, which he shared during small-group instruction. According to the student, had Phoebe been as old as his dad, the danger might seem different.

- *Students place correct emphasis or weight on ideas.* Although this is tricky for several reasons, the value that students place on an idea or event should be based on circumstances that can be reasonably supported in the text. For example, although not evident in the example in Figure 31, it's not hard to imagine that many students begin guessing the culprit whose name begins with *T*. As such they often express lengthy ideas that support their feelings rather than provide key ideas to capture what happened in the story.

- *Students express the solution to the problem.* Although not shown in the example, the student included a solution to the problem in the final clustered summary he prepared, which is a critical component to include in a summary.

Strategy Connections

This strategy relies on a student's ability to use several strategies, such as Strategy 5, Making Connections to Aid Understanding, and Strategy 9, Finding the Important or Main Idea, among others. As such, teachers may have to provide careful monitoring during instruction and adjust their degree of direct instruction. Also, the skill involves complex judgment calls that may be intimidating to students. Recognizing that this strategy is one that will be revisited often—whether through guided reading or other forms of instruction—reassures students that it is a skill that develops over time.

Teachers might not want to provide initial instruction in this strategy together with Strategy 7, Making Predictions, as summaries tend to rely on information found in the text.

Test-Taking Tips

- Unlike many of the other strategies where test questions can be directly linked to assessing a student's ability at identifying the main idea, sequencing events, and so on, summarizing is one that may be indirectly tested in a written response question. Also, reviewing the test-taking tips for Strategy 9, Finding the Important or Main Idea, will be helpful.

- You might also wish to remind students that summaries are not retellings. Should a written response question ask for an answer that requires support using details, students should be cautioned to summarize main ideas—not retell an entire passage.

CHAPTER 4

Understanding, Creating, and Using the Read-Along Guide

"I like using the Read-Along Guides and writing things down in them. The practice helps me a lot, and the responses are fun. We worked on a ton of different techniques and we practiced a ton of skills."

—Page S., fourth-grade student

"I liked using the Read-Along Guides, and I liked how they helped me understand more about the book. Some skills were really helpful for me."

—Emily Z., third-grade student

As mentioned in chapter 1, the Read-Along Guide is a multipage writing component used by students and teachers to support reading instruction and student skill-building in the key comprehension strategies taught primarily through small-group instruction. In chapters 2 and 3, you saw pieces of the Read-Along Guide in the Practice With Prompts Using the Read-Along Guide section for each strategy. In this chapter you will discover how those components all fit together to form complete Read-Along Guides. An Introductory Read-Along Guide will help students better understand and practice using the foundational eight strategies discussed in chapter 2, while other Guides typically feature three to four comprehension strategies and space for students to practice using the strategies, as well as a written response section (which will be discussed in greater detail in chapter 5).

To provide a visual conception of what a Read-Along Guide looks like, Figure 32 shows a reduced-sized example of a full Read-Along Guide completed by a fourth-grade student based on his comprehension strategy use while reading *The Courage of Sarah Noble* (Dalgliesh, 1954). In this Guide, the student practiced his use of Strategy 12, Understanding Sequence; Strategy 15, Recognizing Cause-and-Effect Relationships; Strategy 7, Making Predictions; and Strategy 2, Finding Word Meaning and Building Vocabulary Using Context Clues. This chapter discusses the steps to create a Read-Along Guide, beginning with your text selection (further information on materials to use during your instruction is included in chapter 6) through tailoring your Guide to specific books and strategies (as shown in Figure 32). Within these steps we will provide guidelines for many issues such as format, inclusion of the written response section, and others to help you with this process.

The Read-Along Guide component of the Quality Comprehension Model meets the needs of intermediate-level learners in several ways. First, it helps them stay focused. The Guide is a single point of reference for the objective of the instructional lesson. In their Guide, students will find blurbs reminding them what they will be looking for as they read. Examples and prompts also guide the students as they practice working with a comprehension strategy. For example, if the comprehension strategy was Strategy 16, Drawing Conclusions and Making Inferences, students would be reminded that they will be "reading between the lines."

In addition, the Read-Along Guide helps students stay organized. As students practice the strategies by writing responses directly in their Guide, everything they need is there for them. There are no workbook pages or separate sheets of paper. The students bring the Guide with their book back and forth as their group meets. Further, the Guide encourages intermediate-level students to demonstrate in multiple ways their ability to grasp the content of their reading. In their Guide, students are being asked to demonstrate in writing ways in which they have used the strategies to understand what they have read. In addition to these practice areas, the written response area allows students to express views, share insights, and connect with the literature in ways that the earlier practice might not enable them to demonstrate.

The Read-Along Guide will not only meet the needs of your intermediate-level learners but also addresses your needs as a teacher. First, the Guide enables you to

FIGURE 32
Student's Reduced-Size Read-Along Guide for *The Courage of Sarah Noble*

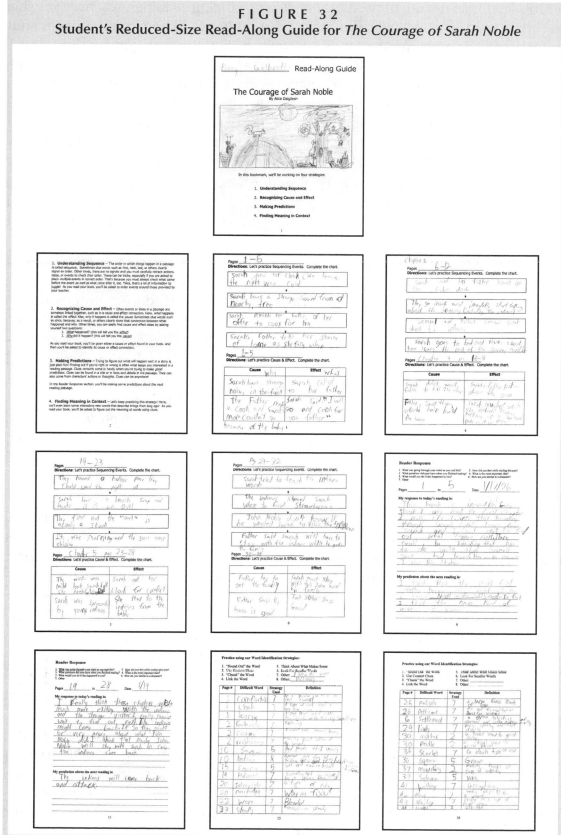

address individual student needs. By reviewing students' Guides, teachers are able to both examine and evaluate whether or not a student is having trouble understanding a concept or grasping the use of a comprehension strategy. Without this insight, little can be done to help correct a misunderstanding or develop a necessary skill. In addition, Guides make it easy for you to tailor instruction according to the skills and abilities of each student. The Guide can easily be adjusted to meet specific needs of students in the class. For example, one group of students may be asked to pull new or unusual vocabulary from the text, while another group may be given the vocabulary and directed to find the meaning. ELLs may be given new vocabulary or phrases in their native language and in English. Further, the Guide provides you with a format that works well with multiple leveled books. Students are typically provided instruction in the same three to four comprehension strategies—no matter what level reader they are. The flexible format of the Guide enables teachers to select appropriately leveled texts for each student and provide instruction in clustered groups.

Additionally, the Guide allows you to acknowledge and address any emotionally or socially charged issues that may stem from content instruction. As students are exposed to texts and ideas that might cover sensitive topics, such as war, or socially charged issues that stem from historical study, such as injustice, teachers can intervene and determine an appropriate course of action. Though teacher guidance may help some students maneuver around tricky issues aligned to the content curriculum, it may also help scaffold instructional practices in critical literacy, which is an emerging literacy that encourages the exploration of social issues (Heffernan, 2004; McLaughlin & DeVoogd, 2004). Though we may have unknowingly started down the path of this developing literary focus, we were often thrilled by the direction in which our students wished to go on many social issues and thoughtfully guided them on this journey as necessary. Likewise, teachers can guide students by helping them make connections that might otherwise be complex or vague, such as the Fourth of July holiday and the Revolutionary War. The Read-Along Guide provides the impetus for this type of assistance and guidance, which often brings more meaning to what students are reading. Finally, the Guide minimizes the need for lengthy daily planning with other paraprofessionals providing instructional assistance. The Guide already reflects what will be taught (strategies on which instruction will be provided have been determined earlier) and also provides the structure for how they will be taught through predetermined prompts. In essence, the framework of the Guide gives teachers an easy-to-follow routine so their time can be spent on instruction with students.

This chapter provides a basic and easy-to-use five-step process for creating Read-Along Guides, while also providing guidance on adapting the Guides to meet your classroom's unique needs and on finding time for the Guides in busy classroom schedules. As it will become clear in this chapter, the Guide is not a workbook, there is not one set of correct answers, and there is not one expectation for how it will be completed by all students.

Creating the Read-Along Guide

Although you might be building your text collections and inventorying your available resources, you have made a decision that there is no better time than the present to begin. Perhaps you are nearing completion of a unit and want to try out this strategy-based instruction in your next unit. Or maybe you (and a colleague) have located some leveled texts and want to launch an entirely new unit using them. These could be some of the scenarios that have led you to the point at which you now are in need of a Read-Along Guide. As discussed in the Introduction, our first Guides looked very different from how they do today. We started slow and progressed over time.

Similarly, although we have provided a collection of our Guides ready for you to use, you will probably want to adjust them or create your own at some point, possibly using your own prompts and devising your own formats. Tailoring the Guides to reflect your own instructional needs is one of the greatest benefits of working with them, and we strongly encourage you to do this. The guidelines we present here will help streamline the learning curve you encounter as you adjust the samples included here or as you create your first few Guides. We want to assure you that both processes become routine and quick. This is the same advice we offer to workshop participants—mostly teachers—who express a common concern that they have precious little free time to create materials.

Whether you use the Guides included in this book or wish to start by creating your own, the discussions below will be helpful. The steps we recommend for creating a Read-Along Guide are as follows:

Step 1: Select Your Texts

Step 2: Select Your Strategies

Step 3: Review and Further Organize Your Instructional Unit Plan

Step 4: Create a Master Read-Along Guide

Step 5: Tailor Your Guide to Specific Books and Uses

Step 1: Select Your Texts

Let's assume you have selected and leveled some books from your existing collections (discussed in chapter 6). They may align with or support your curriculum instruction, and you will have double-checked that your selection spans the appropriate reading ranges for the number of reading groups you wish to have. You have also checked that you have sufficient quantities or have planned to have students share. As briefly discussed in the Introduction, your groups will be composed of students who fall within a close range of reading levels (prior to grouping your students you will have to determine each student's reading level through some form of assessment). For example, at the fourth-grade level, many of us have tried to work with three reading groups. One group might contain students reading at levels L–N, another at levels O–Q, and the third at levels R–T. Though it might be ideal to have sufficient quantities of three different levels of theme-based books so that you could have all students within each small group reading at an instructional level (Fountas

& Pinnell, 1996), this may not be possible, especially when you are starting. Don't let this jeopardize or stall your plans. Instead, alter your instruction to compensate. For example, you might have to provide a little more direct instruction and careful monitoring when using a work that might be leveled a bit too high for a particular group, while also minimizing the independent seat work required from students in that group. Obviously, the opposite is true should you have to work with a leveled book that is mildly too low for a particular group. There have been times where we have used one book, leveled comfortably in a midrange position, for all three groups of students. Rather than consider this a problem, we consider it to be part of the flexibility of this approach.

Step 2: Select Your Strategies

As we discussed in chapters 2 and 3, we recommend first providing instruction in the foundational eight strategies and then selecting strategies from the skill-building nine based on your text selections, student needs, and the difficulty level of the strategies. Initially, this process is relatively easy, and determining which strategies will work well with your books may be your only concern. As discussed earlier, there are some books better suited for instruction in particular strategies. For example, if you have selected a nonfiction informational book, you may not wish to provide instruction on Strategy 14, Interpreting Figurative Language. Although matching strategies to texts will soon become routine, a quick review of chapters 2 and 3 will offer some guidance.

When providing instruction in the foundational eight strategies, you will likely use the Introductory Read-Along Guide (see Appendix A for a reproducible version of the Introductory Read-Along Guide). Following this instruction, you may then feature three to four strategies at a time (selecting any combination from either the foundational eight or the skill-building nine) in more focused Read-Along Guides. This seems to be a manageable and comfortable number of strategies for students to work with at one time and will prevent your Read-Along Guides from becoming too bulky and cumbersome. Appendix A offers reproducible samples of two different Guides we have created that cluster similar strategies together. Read-Along Guide A—Nonfiction, which is specifically created for use with nonfiction texts, features the following strategies together:

Strategy 9: Finding the Important or Main Idea

Strategy 10: Identifying Facts and Details

Strategy 2: Finding Word Meaning and Building Vocabulary Using Context Clues

Read-Along Guide B—Generic, which is appropriate for use with texts of multiple genres, features the following strategies together:

Strategy 12: Understanding Sequence

Strategy 15: Recognizing Cause-and-Effect Relationships

Strategy 7: Making Predictions

Strategy 2: Finding Word Meaning and Building Vocabulary Using Context Clues

Appendix A also offers individual strategy pages for the following strategies:

Strategy 11: Telling Fact From Opinion

Strategy 13: Comparing and Contrasting

Strategy 14: Interpreting Figurative Language

Strategy 16: Drawing Conclusions and Making Inferences

Strategy 17: Summarizing

These strategies can be clustered together any way that you see fit in order to align with your instruction.

Additionally, you may want to repeat the use of a strategy in multiple Guides. For example, once we introduced Strategy 2, Finding Word Meaning and Building Vocabulary Using Context Clues, we often repeated this in many Guides, believing it not only helped to build background knowledge but represented a critical skill for students to master (you may notice that this strategy is repeated not only in the Introductory Read-Along Guide but also in Guides A and B in Appendix A). Although we may have counted this as the fourth strategy, we knew we did not need to provide instruction in its use (which was required of the other three strategies) but would instead simply allow the students to practice. As you make your decisions about which strategies to use together in the focused Guides, you might want to consider selecting three or four to begin with, knowing that you can alter this number if you have reason to do so.

If you plan to cover specific strategies within a certain amount of time, you might find that this selection process could require a little more finesse once you begin completing instructional units. For example, if you have already provided instruction in a strategy, such as Strategy 15, Recognizing Cause-and-Effect Relationships, and it has been grasped moderately well by the students, you might not want to repeat instruction on that strategy again until you get through others you haven't yet covered. You might even find that strategies for which you wish to provide instruction may determine which books you select, which is a reversal of steps 1 and 2. Although this happened at times, we never had significant trouble with the strategy selection process, and we managed to provide instruction in all strategies (some more often than others), while maintaining a strong and balanced language arts reading program.

Once you have selected your strategies, you will need to determine how you would like students to practice them. This is where the strategy pages featuring prompts will come in handy. We have provided prompts for each of the 17 strategies featured in this text. You can use the ones we have provided, alter them to suit your needs, or design your own. There may be times when two strategies are featured together and other times when the strategies are practiced separately. We tried to create practice prompts that would represent authentic use of the strategies. If strategies seemed connected, we tried to authenticate that as well. Use your judgment as to which strategy prompts you might like to feature together and pick and choose accordingly.

Step 3: Review and Further Organize Your Instructional Unit Plan

As was discussed in chapter 1, the instructional unit plan helps you to organize your small-group instruction (see Figure 5 in chapter 1 for an example of a completed instructional unit plan, and see Appendix B for a reproducible version). By now, you have selected some texts and some strategies, and you can start to fill in sections of this plan. In addition to helping you organize your small-group instruction, it also helps you to coordinate, track, and pace what could be multiple reading groups, each group reading a different text (samples are provided for different configurations in chapter 1). We have found that most instructional units averaged five to seven days (meeting with all three groups every day), which seems an adequate and comfortable amount of time for instruction. Often this involved coordinating reading as well as pre- and postreading activities so that the three reading groups were paced equally and would complete an instructional unit around the same time. Synchronizing the start and finish times of our multiple groups was important to us because we generally provided all groups with the same end-of-unit assessment and wanted to administer this at one time, and we also wanted optimum flexibility in beginning our next reading lesson, whether it was whole-class read-aloud or another strategy-based unit.

To begin organizing, segment the amount of reading for each text into manageable and logical chunks, keeping in mind the level of the text, the students' skills, and the difficulty of the strategy practice (a difficulty rating is provided for each strategy in chapters 2 and 3). For example, a group composed of readers at levels R–T might have to read a 20-page chapter independently (and even possibly complete some activities for homework), while another group of readers at levels O–Q might be assigned 9 pages of text to read (with 2 additional pages to be read aloud together during that group's instruction time), and the third group of readers at levels L–N might have to complete a designated number of pages together with the teacher during their instructional time. It is important to note that the volume of reading assigned to a specific group did not always align with a particular reading level. For example, one year while providing instruction in a unit on Native Americans, some teachers assigned their highest level readers only 4 pages of text to read as the strategies they were working on were difficult. In addition to this, the teachers were continuing to build student background knowledge on the topic, and as this was one of our early instructional units, students were still adjusting to their return to school and exposure to ideas and concepts with which they may be very unfamiliar. Though you might be tempted to associate volume with reading level and chunk your reading this way, this may not at all be the case when working with leveled readers. Nonetheless, with some practice, segmenting the texts for each of three groups will become routine and any mistakes you make can be remedied as you work with a group.

Determining pre- or postactivities for each of the groups is the next step to record on your instructional unit plan. Preactivities might include minilessons to introduce the topic or theme, the Read-Along Guide, or otherwise. Instruction for the prereading activity might be with the whole class for a portion of the time, with brief small-group meetings to follow. Another example might be that all three groups have a different prereading activity and meet in groups from the start. Postreading activities, which might include additional reading activities, more practice with strategies, or other activities, are handled very much the same way—with great flexibility. One group might have only a portion of a class session for a postactivity, while another group might have two days for theirs. Adjusting both the pre- and postreading activities will enable you to pace and synchronize the instructional units.

Step 4: Create a Master Read-Along Guide

Once these components of the instructional unit plan are in place, you have a good idea of the amount of time your instructional unit will take. Now the plan can help you in terms of creating your Read-Along Guide. The first step is to determine how many days' worth of practice prompts you want to include in the Read-Along Guide. Although chapters 2 and 3 typically feature an example of one day's activity with a prompt, you will need to include enough in the Guide for the length of time in your instructional unit (reproducible versions of the prompt pages for all strategies appear in Appendix A). In other words, these prompts need to be duplicated multiple times in your Guide in order to provide repeated practice. For example, the prompt for sequencing may appear five times in the Guide to coincide with five days of instruction.

To determine how many times to repeat a prompt in one Guide, we often work with the greatest number of days needed for any of the groups to complete the assigned reading, knowing some groups will not completely fill their Guide (unless they do so during postreading activities). Although we could have tailored the Guides so that an ideal amount of practice space was created per reading group, we purposefully tried to minimize the number of "masters" we needed so our copying procedures could be streamlined. As an example of how to determine the number of practice prompts to include, suppose you want students to practice Strategy 9, Finding the Important or Main Idea, across eight brief segments of reading (averaging two segments per each of four days of instruction); you would then group two of these per page and include four pages of prompts in your Guide. Including this maximum number of pages helps make the Guide accessible for multiple reading groups with students of varying ability; in this case some groups would be able to practice the strategy daily and therefore make use of all eight prompts, while others might have required more teacher assistance and use the prompt only six times out of the eight.

You may also cluster different prompts together on individual pages of the Guides. For example, samples featuring two practice prompts for Strategy 9, clustered together with two prompts for Strategy 10, Identifying Facts and Details—as these two strategies are closely linked together, we often feature them together (see Figure 33 and Read-Along Guide A—Nonfiction in Appendix A for one version). We also often feature Strategy 12, Understanding Sequence, with Strategy 15, Recognizing Cause-and-Effect Relationships, on one prompt page, as illustrated in Figure 34 (see also Read-Along Guide B—Generic in Appendix A).

FIGURE 33
View of Prompt Page Combining Strategies 9 and 10

Strategy 9 and 10: Finding the Important or Main Idea and Identifying Facts and Details

Directions: Summarize or locate the main idea for your reading passage and then find three examples from the passage that support the main idea.

The main idea in pages _____ to _____ is

_____

_____

_____

Support/p. _____	Support/p. _____	Support/p. _____

For this passage, create two who, what, when, where, or why questions to test your classmate's ability to recall facts and details

1. _____
2. _____

Directions: As you read through the text, look for important details (names, dates, events) and record them in the Key Facts section of the chart. Decide which key facts seem most important and write a brief statement describing the main idea of this passage. This statement should explain the overall idea the author is trying to express.

Key Facts	Main Idea

Other times, you may want to keep separate strategy prompts in separate locations in the Guides. For example, for Strategy 2, Finding Word Meaning and Building Vocabulary Using Context Clues, we use a prompt page we like to draw attention to and keep separate. Typically, we allotted one page for this and placed it on the back cover (after initial instruction) so students had quick access to it and could work with the Strategy 2 prompt often as they encountered difficult words (see Figure 35 for a view of the prompt page for Strategy 2).

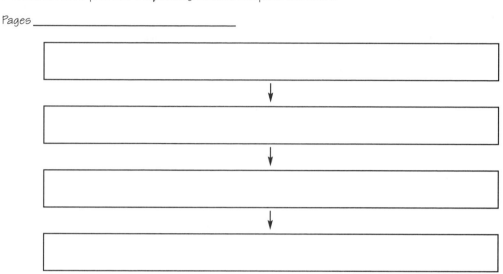

FIGURE 34
View of Prompt Page Combining Strategies 12 and 15

Strategy 12: Understanding Sequence

Directions: Let's practice Sequencing Events. Complete the chart.

Pages _____

Strategy 15: Recognizing Cause-and-Effect Relationships

Directions: Let's practice Cause and Effect. Complete the chart.

Pages _____

Cause (Why)	Effect (What)

In addition to including your strategy practice pages, you might wish to include space for student written response (see Figure 36). As was mentioned in chapter 1 and will be discussed further in chapter 5, this section is very important and, among other things, serves to provide teachers with a check on student comprehension. Most teachers want students to write a journal response daily in conjunction with the daily assigned reading. Some teachers rely on the maximum number of days used to determine how many response sections should be included in their

---

FIGURE 35

View of Separate Prompt Page for Strategy 2

Strategy 2: Finding Word Meaning and Building Vocabulary Using Context Clues

Practice Using Our Word Identification Strategies:

1. Sound Out the Word
2. "Chunk" the Word Use Context Clues
3. Link the Word to a Known Word
4. Look For Smaller Words That You Recognize

5. Use Context Clues
6. Think About What Makes Sense
7. Other: _____
8. Other: _____

Page #	New or Unfamiliar Word	Method(s) Used	Definition

Guide (as discussed previously regarding Strategy 9). For example, if you planned that the reading will take six sessions, you should place six response sections in the Guide. The amount of independent work time each group has may affect the number of sessions they complete. Likewise, despite using the same sized written response section for all groups, many teachers often vary their requirements for the length of the response depending upon the needs and skills of students within the groups. At other times, teachers may create another "master" and use different-sized spaces for the written response section.

Last, the cover and the inside front cover should be included. We tried to make the cover of the Guides attractive and informative, while also realizing the importance of keeping them electronically reusable so teachers can use them for a variety of books. There is usually space for students to fill in the title, author, and their own names (for example, see Figure 37a for a cover of a Read-Along Guide created for a

FIGURE 36
View of Response Section

Reader Response
1. What was going through your mind as you read this?
2. What questions did your have when you finished reading?
3. What would you do if this happened to you?
4. How did you feel while reading this part?
5. What was the most important idea?
6. How are you similar to a character?
7. Other

Pages _____ to _____   Date _____

My response to today's reading is _____
_____
_____
_____
_____
_____
_____
_____
_____
_____
_____

unit on immigration). There is also usually a box for the student to illustrate a favorite scene, sometimes completed as a postreading activity (see Figure 37b for a cover of a Read-Along Guide created for the book *Samuel's Choice*; Berleth, 1990). Similarly, we have also featured questions or illustrations that may have been a prompt for prereading activities and linked to the instructional unit. We often liked to list on the cover the strategies that we would be working with in the Guide. The inside of the Guide typically features a student-friendly explanation (or reminder if the strategy has been taught before) of the strategies that will be covered in that unit and how students will be practicing their use in the Guides. Figure 38 features inside front covers of two Guides we've created based on different strategy combinations (see Appendix A). The student-friendly explanations featured on the inside front covers are the same as those featured in the Student-Friendly Chat on the Importance of the Strategy sections found in chapters 2 and 3. Both the cover and the inside front cover of the Guides are often used during a prereading minilesson to familiarize students with the instructional unit and are particularly helpful for both students and teachers. Additionally, the inside front cover serves as a reference point for students so that they are able to review the descriptions as needed. Just as you will select prompt pages for each Guide, you can also select and tweak these descriptions to fit your needs.

FIGURE 37
Views of Two Versions of the Read-Along Guide Cover

A. Read-Along Guide Cover for Unit on Immigration

_____'s Read-Along Guide on Immigration

Title: _____

Author: _____

In this Read-Along Guide, we'll be working on three strategies:

1. Finding the Important or Main Idea
2. Identifying Facts and Details
3. Finding Word Meaning and Building Vocabulary Using Context Clues

B. Read-Along Guide Cover for _Samuel's Choice_

_____'s Read-Along Guide

Theme: The Revolutionary War

<u>Samuel's Choice</u> by Richard Berleth

In this Guide, we'll be working on three strategies:

1. Drawing Conclusions and Making Inferences
2. Comparing and Contrasting
3. Finding Word Meaning and Building Vocabulary Using Context Clues

FIGURE 38
Views of Inside Front Covers for Various Read-Along Guides

A. Inside Front Cover for Nonfiction Read-Along Guide

In this Read-Along Guide we are going to work on three strategies that will help us become better readers. Each strategy has been described below. In addition to learning about these strategies, you also have some practice pages in this Guide to try them out.

1. **Strategy 9: Finding the Important or Main Idea.** Remember that the main idea is a pretty big idea that tells what a paragraph or an entire reading passage is mainly about. The main idea is not a small detail, although all of the small details together make up the main idea. Sometimes a main idea is stated, like in a topic sentence, a closing sentence, or somewhere else within the passage. Other times it is not. As you read your book, you will be asked to locate or summarize the main idea of a reading passage and to locate some specific details that support it.

2. **Strategy 10: Identifying Facts and Details.** Writers use facts and details for many reasons. Facts and details support a main idea and, in so doing, provide more information about the main idea. Facts and details may

    1. Describe a person, place, or thing
    2. Explain how to do something
    3. Tell the order in which things happen
    4. Share an experience, idea, or opinion

    An easy way to find facts and details is to look for sentences that tell about the who, what, where, when, why, and how of the main idea. As you read your book, you will be asked to create some questions (using <u>who</u>, <u>what</u>, <u>where</u>, <u>when</u>, <u>why</u>, and <u>how</u>) about the passage you read. Answers to your questions should highlight the facts and details that appear within the passage. You'll get the chance to ask your questions to classmates during guided-reading instructional time. See if your classmates can recall the facts and details!

3. **Strategy 2: Finding Word Meaning Using Context Clues.** While reading, you will usually come upon a word (or many words) that you don't know. It is important for you to try and figure out what the word means. Doing so not only helps you understand the passage, but it also helps to build your vocabulary. We will continue to practice this skill on the last page of our Read-Along Guide.

B. Inside Front Cover for Generic Read-Along Guide

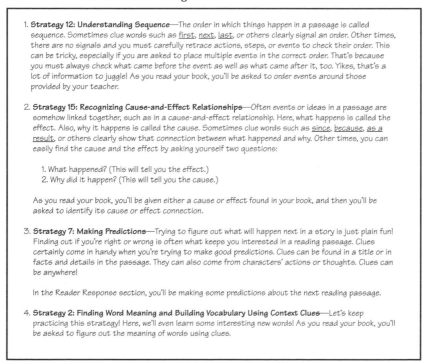

1. **Strategy 12: Understanding Sequence**—The order in which things happen in a passage is called sequence. Sometimes clue words such as <u>first</u>, <u>next</u>, <u>last</u>, or others clearly signal an order. Other times, there are no signals and you must carefully retrace actions, steps, or events to check their order. This can be tricky, especially if you are asked to place multiple events in the correct order. That's because you must always check what came before the event as well as what came after it, too. Yikes, that's a lot of information to juggle! As you read your book, you'll be asked to order events around those provided by your teacher.

2. **Strategy 15: Recognizing Cause-and-Effect Relationships**—Often events or ideas in a passage are somehow linked together, such as in a cause-and-effect relationship. Here, what happens is called the effect. Also, why it happens is called the cause. Sometimes clue words such as <u>since</u>, <u>because</u>, <u>as a result</u>, or others clearly show that connection between what happened and why. Other times, you can easily find the cause and the effect by asking yourself two questions:

    1. What happened? (This will tell you the effect.)
    2. Why did it happen? (This will tell you the cause.)

    As you read your book, you'll be given either a cause or effect found in your book, and then you'll be asked to identify its cause or effect connection.

3. **Strategy 7: Making Predictions**—Trying to figure out what will happen next in a story is just plain fun! Finding out if you're right or wrong is often what keeps you interested in a reading passage. Clues certainly come in handy when you're trying to make good predictions. Clues can be found in a title or in facts and details in the passage. They can also come from characters' actions or thoughts. Clues can be anywhere!

    In the Reader Response section, you'll be making some predictions about the next reading passage.

4. **Strategy 2: Finding Word Meaning and Building Vocabulary Using Context Clues**—Let's keep practicing this strategy! Here, we'll even learn some interesting new words! As you read your book, you'll be asked to figure out the meaning of words using clues.

Remember to number the pages. Guides can vary in length from 4 pages to 20 pages, although most average about 10 to 12. As student may be practicing their strategy instruction in up to three or four different areas in their Guide, you will want to remember to include page numbers on the Guide so that students can quickly get to areas as you work with them during small-group instruction. Figure 39 shows a thumbnail sketch of a sample Guide layout. This Guide would include four strategies and a response section and would be used for a six-day instructional unit. When creating master Read-Along Guides for your classroom, you may want to make similar sketches to help you plan for what you will include in your Guides.

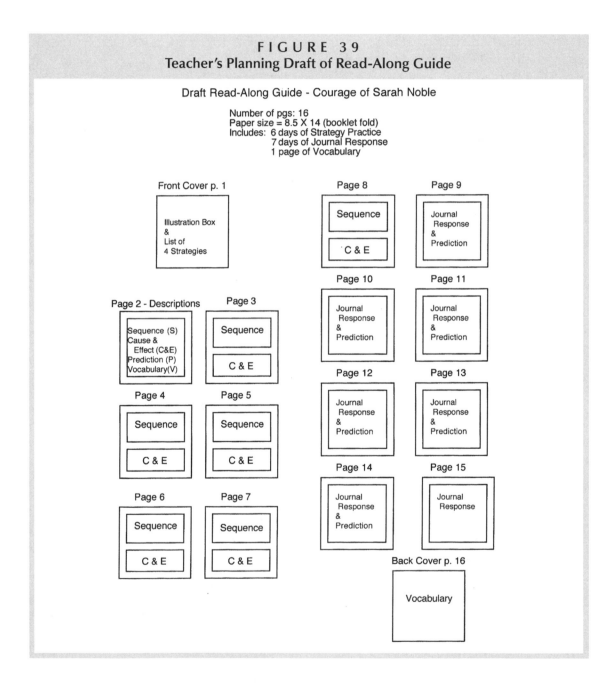

FIGURE 39
Teacher's Planning Draft of Read-Along Guide

Draft Read-Along Guide - Courage of Sarah Noble

Number of pgs: 16
Paper size = 8.5 X 14 (booklet fold)
Includes: 6 days of Strategy Practice
           7 days of Journal Response
           1 page of Vocabulary

Front Cover p. 1
Illustration Box
&
List of
4 Strategies

Page 8
Sequence
C & E

Page 9
Journal
Response
&
Prediction

Page 2 - Descriptions
Sequence (S)
Cause &
Effect (C&E)
Prediction (P)
Vocabulary(V)

Page 3
Sequence
C & E

Page 10
Journal
Response
&
Prediction

Page 11
Journal
Response
&
Prediction

Page 4
Sequence
C & E

Page 5
Sequence
C & E

Page 12
Journal
Response
&
Prediction

Page 13
Journal
Response
&
Prediction

Page 6
Sequence
C & E

Page 7
Sequence
C & E

Page 14
Journal
Response
&
Prediction

Page 15
Journal
Response

Back Cover p. 16
Vocabulary

Format. As your Guide begins to take shape, you will have to make a decision about the format, including the size of the Guide. For example, the reproducible Guides featured in Appendix A are 8½ × 11 inches and would be printed on both sides of the paper and stapled in the upper left-hand corner, yet you could also create a Guide using 8½ × 14-inch pages folded in half and stapled in the center. Though the latter sized booklet can easily be tucked into most student books or reading folders for safekeeping, it is important to note that the space available for student writing is significantly less in this format than in one measuring 8½ × 11 inches. Keep in mind that the size of your Guide will affect the amount of space students have for writing, either as they practice writing responses to practice prompts or while writing a responses to their reading, so depending on the need of the group, full-size pages may work best.

If you work with an 8½ × 11-inch Guide, you might consider trying to include an even number of pages so you do not end up with a blank page (if this matters). If you work with the booklet format (8½ × 14-inch page that is folded), you will have to try and work with groups of four pages. Although this is a bit trickier, it is a skill that is quickly mastered. Additionally, the 8½ × 11-inch format may be the desired one to use if you plan to make different Guide masters for each of your reading groups and tailor them with ideal space for prompt practice, written responses, and writing. Often we quickly sketched out the format of our Guides, especially if using the booklet format. As you explore these formats, should you encounter some mishaps as a result of miscalculations, know that you are in good company!

The Use of Sticky Notes. It is a good idea for students to use smaller sticky notes (one-inch size) as they are reading to mark an event or idea they might wish to record in their Guide later or to jot down information they want to share during group time. Often, theses are kept attached to the inside of their Guide so they can pull them as needed. We mention use of the sticky note here as there may be times when a student simply does not have enough room to record his or her thoughts or ideas. Having a supply of the larger, lined sticky notes (three-inch size) so these students can add information to their Guide is a perfectly acceptable solution to this problem.

Step 5: Tailor Your Guide to Specific Books and Uses

In many cases, you will want to tailor your Guides so they are a perfect match with your groups, their texts, and their needs. Our own Read-Along Guide collections contain generic Guides as well as ones that are tailored to different books we have used. If you wish to tailor your Guides to the individual books you have selected, you can simply follow the same steps discussed above and then electronically incorporate examples from a book into the practice prompts.

For example, some teachers like to select vocabulary words from the text for some of their reading groups, while leaving another group to identify them independently as a way to meet the specific needs of different students and groups. For example, Figure 40 features the vocabulary practice page from a Guide used with three different texts within a Revolutionary War instructional unit. In this example,

FIGURE 40
Vocabulary Page for Read-Along Guide With Teacher-Selected Vocabulary Words

Practice Using Our Word Identification Methods:

1. Sound Out the Word
2. "Chunk" the Word Use Context Clues
3. Link the Word to a Known Word
4. Look For Smaller Words That You Recognize

5. Use Context Clues
6. Think About What Makes Sense
7. Other: _____
8. Other: _____

Page #	New or Unfamiliar Word	Method(s) Used	Definition
4	master		
6	marshes		
8	currents		
10	fifes		
11	liberty		
12	servants		
12	Africans		
14	buttermilk		
14	bayonets		
16	Liberty Boys		
16	ordinary		

the teacher has selected vocabulary words for students to work with, but if you feel your students are ready for more independent practice, you could leave the prompt pages blank and instead allow students to locate the vocabulary words. Similarly, Figure 41 features the tailored prompts for one of the texts in this unit. Here, brief quotes from the text were included in the Guide, and students were able to use them to practice drawing conclusions and making inferences. Although this type of tailoring can be done for three different works within an instructional unit, it can also be done if only one book is used. Such is the case in Figure 42, where students were responsible for completing a graphic organizer tailored to events from the text the students were reading, *Toliver's Secret* (Brady, 1976). In this example, students were asked to compare themselves to Ellen Toliver using a Venn diagram; other ideas for this text could include having students use this graphic organizer to compare and contrast Ellen's chores and chores children do today, early colonial life and modern times, Ellen's family and students' own families, or Loyalists and Patriots.

Text Quote: " <u>Work you do not choose to do is always tiring</u>

_____

_____ ." (p. <u>8</u>)

Meaning:
(I think... because...)

_____

_____

_____

_____

_____

_____

Text Quote: " <u>That's the sound of people going free</u>

_____

_____ ." (p. <u>10</u>)

Meaning:
(I think... because...)

_____

_____

_____

_____

_____

_____

Text Quote: " <u>I could not think how the ordinary Americans I had seen, fresh from their farms and</u>
<u>shops, could ever drive away an army of real soldiers</u>

_____ ." (p. <u>16</u>)

Meaning:
(I think... because...)

_____

_____

_____

_____

_____

_____

From Berleth, R.J. (1990). *Samuel's choice*. New York: Scholastic.

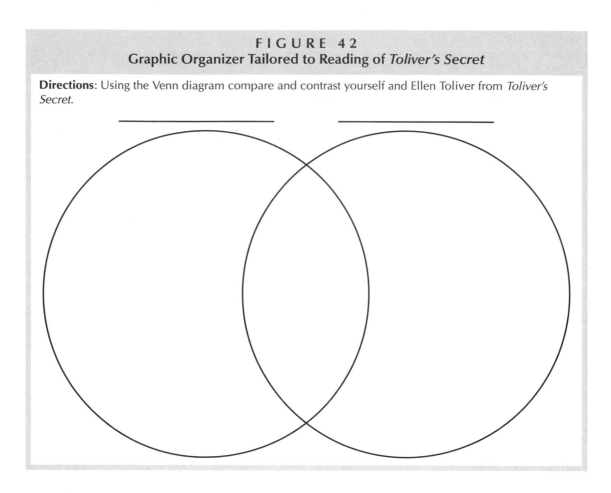

FIGURE 42
Graphic Organizer Tailored to Reading of *Toliver's Secret*

Directions: Using the Venn diagram compare and contrast yourself and Ellen Toliver from *Toliver's Secret*.

Adapting the Read-Along Guide

There are many other ways you can use the Read-Along Guide. For example, you might wish to use them as Listening Read-Along Guides to support instruction during a read-aloud. Here students can practice applying their strategies while listening to a text rather than reading a text. Another use of the Read-Along Guide is to have students work with single strategy pages to strengthen individual skills. Guidelines are provided in the following sections.

Listening Read-Along Guides

Read-Along Guides may also be used for books that are read aloud. When there is a book that is lengthy or difficult but worthwhile to share with a class, you can create a Listening Read-Along Guide. This Listening Guide is similar to the Guide used during guided reading. It may have a vocabulary section, a prediction section, a response space, and compare and contrast activities—the same strategies you would use while reading. If the content is historical, you may have the class listen for old-fashioned words. If it is fantasy, you may have students record those events considered imaginary. Some teachers provide students with their own copy of the book and encourage them to follow along and use sticky notes on areas they will want to return to for recording in their Listening Guide, while others have them only listen. These Listening Guides can be prepared with the same flexibility as the print text–based Read-Along Guides. This is a great way to expose all reading levels to content area information, difficult genres, or fantastic literature that may be too intimidating for them to tackle independently.

Single-Page Read-Along Guides

At times, you might wish to have groups or specific students continue to practice a strategy that has proven difficult for them. Although we have provided a rating scale in chapters 2 and 3, each student will have his or her individual ability to grasp the different strategies. As such, you might wish to use the single prompt pages for additional practice by simply copying one page only from a Guide.

Finding the Time for Creating Read-Along Guides

This is the single greatest concern everyone has, and it is a big one! However, it is relatively easy to find the time for Read-Along Guides if you start slow, collaborate, and adjust and reuse the materials. To help you do this, we have provided pointers on teamwork, electronic storage and retrieval, and some additional timesavers. Additionally, many teachers find that using the Read-Along Guide actually *saves* time, especially in the areas of preparation and planning.

Teamwork

Teamwork enabled us to get to where we are today. Though over time team members changed and the number of team members fluctuated, we were fortunate in working closely with anywhere from 4 to 20 colleagues who eagerly contributed to building this strategy-based comprehension instruction into what it is today. This collaborative or team approach greatly affected the process of creating the initial Guides. Without having the assistance to divide and tackle the workload, the process would not have been as smooth and unencumbered as it was. Although we are now beyond the initial start-up stage, teams continue to work together and split up the workload to alter or create new Guides. Some examples of this are as follows.

- Two classroom teachers may wish to create a new prompt to use for instruction on Strategy 15, Recognizing Cause-and-Effect Relationships, replacing the one that already appears in a Guide.
- Some teachers may want to select vocabulary words from a text (for use with Strategy 2, Finding Word Meaning and Building Vocabulary Using Context Clues) and add these to pages in a Guide, while other teachers may opt to leave

the vocabulary page blank and require students to find their own words as they read.

- A group of three teachers may chose to make multiple adjustments to a Guide based on the needs of different reading groups in their classrooms.
- Several teachers involved in cross–grade-level teams may wish to tailor a Guide to better address the needs, concerns, and developmental abilities of students at their particular grade levels.

Although these are just a few of the typical types of team-alteration sessions that occur today, having this kind of flexibility is most likely the desired outcome you will want as well. As such, now might be the time to initiate the development of a collaborative team so that no matter how you decide to work with Guides, there is an eager audience ready to pitch in. A final thought on this collaborative approach is that we have always found that working in this manner has—undeniably—helped to continually improve the Guides. Having input from several professionals enables each participant to consider possibilities that might otherwise not have been considered. Certainly in the case of creating and tweaking the Guides, the contribution of many voices has made a stronger product.

Working in teams with your colleagues can also help you more effectively tailor your Guides to specific texts or student needs. Working together in small groups with one or two other teachers allows team members to share tasks so that the workload is performed quickly. Figure 43 shows sample pages of teacher-prepared materials for *The Courage of Sarah Noble* (Dalgliesh, 1954). One teacher provided a list of vocabulary words, another identified two examples of cause-and-effect relationships that could be used, a third provided information on sequencing, and a fourth fed information into prompt pages of the Guide. Each teacher spent about 30 minutes completing these tasks and attached the sheets to their planning guide so that each could rely on them during instruction as necessary.

Electronic Storage and Retrieval

Being able to manipulate information quickly and easily will make the process of tailoring the Guides easier. As you begin to work with your own Guides, you might wish to consider how to build and maintain your collection electronically, as this will prove to be a time-saving device in the future. Feel free to copy the samples in Appendix A frequently, as you can cut and paste as necessary to create your own tailored Guides. Alternatively, you can retrieve electronic files and manipulate samples as you wish by visiting the webpage for this book on IRA's website at www .reading.org, where all Guides in Appendix A are featured. Working with information electronically will allow you to pick and choose, add or delete, and move or adjust materials as you feel necessary. At first, we worked largely with hard copy and relied on cutting and pasting to create a master. Today, we have stored our Guides electronically and frequently e-mail Guide materials back and forth between classrooms,

FIGURE 43
Sample Pages of Teacher-Prepared Materials for *The Courage of Sarah Noble*

Instructional Unit Plan

Title/Theme *The Courage of Sarah Noble*   Level(s) *0*
                                                    Approximate Time *6-7 days*

Strategies: 1. *Sequencing*
             2. *Cause & Effect*
             3. *Making Predictions*
             4. *Word Meaning in Context (voc.)*

Chapter Breakout: (Title/Level)

1. *Courage...all groups*   2. _____   3. _____

1/25 Intro. & chap. 1, pp.1-5	
1/26 Chap. 2&3, pp. 6-18	
1/30 Chap. 4&5, pp. 19-28	
1/31 Chap. 6&7, pp.29-38	
2/1 Chap. 8&9, pp. 39-46	
2/2 Chap. 10&11, pp. 47-54	
2/3 Final review/Guide assessment	

Instructional Plans

Before	During	After
· *timeline*	· *vocabulary development* · *discusses responses* *(*All students will be studying* *colonial times in S.S.)*	· *Colonial assessment*

Notes on Read-Along Guide Use: *Prediction section appears in Reader Response section*
_____

Attachments: *suggestions—sequencing/cause and effect/ vocabulary*
_____

The Courage of Sarah Noble   Vocabulary

Chapt. 1	Chapt. 2	Chapt. 3
comfortable cloak journey fastening courage wilderness	heathen savages	coarse

Chapt. 4	Chapt. 5	Chapt. 6
hollowed Johnny Cake porridge wove settlement	steadily palisade petticoats	lively mortar pestle

Chapt. 7	Chapt. 8	Chapt. 9
scarlet squaw mounting solemn	willing	dew wailing raided crinkled amused tiresome

Chapt. 10	Chapt. 11	
waded fretful quivers outlandish goods	cozy queer wigwams securely fastened	

The Courage of Sarah Noble   Cause/Effect
                                   (Possible prompts/responses)

		Cause	Effect
Chap. 1 pp. 2-3		*Sarah hears strange noises in the forest.*	*She calls out to her father.*
p. 4		*Sarah's mother could not bring the baby on a long journey.*	*Sarah said, "I will cook for you, Father."*
Chap .2 pp. 10-11		*The Robinson children told Sarah frightening stories about the Native Americans.*	*Sarah felt a little sick while at Mistress Robinson's.*
Chap. 3 p. 15		*Sarah begged her father not to shoot the deer.*	*Her father put down his gun.*

The Courage of Sarah Noble   Sequencing

Chapter 1
1. *Sarah drew her warm cloak close because the spring night was cold. (p. 1)*
2. *Sarah hears a strange sound from a nearby tree. (p. 2)*
3. *Sarah reminds her father of her offer to cook for him. (p. 4)*
4. *Sarah's father wonders if he should have brought Sarah into the wilderness (p. 5)*

Chapter 2
1. *Sarah and her father know on the door of a cabin. (p. 7)*
2. *Abigail offered to hang up Sarah's cloak. (p. 8)*
3. *Lemuel and Robert teased Sarah about the Indians. (pp. 10-11)*
4. *Sarah closes her eyes and wonders whether she sees Indians. (p. 12)*

Chapter 3
1. *Sarah picked wild flowers and stuck them in Thomas's harness. (p. 13)*
2. *Sarah begs her father not to shoot a deer. (p. 15)*
3. *Sarah gazes beyond the valley where the green hills stretched on. (p. 17)*
4. *Sarah holds her father's hand as they arrived to where their home would soon be. (p. 18)*

Chapter 4
1. *Sarah and her father unloaded the items from Thomas. (p. 19)*
2. *Sarah hears a branch snap and thinks it is an owl. (p. 20)*
3. *Sarah smells a strange odor. (p. 22)*
4. *It was morning and the sun was shining. (p. 22)*

---

grade levels, and buildings within our own district, as well as to colleagues in other districts and workshop participants who are making use of the Guides.

In addition to storing whole Guides, which are often named according to the theme-based instructional unit for which they were originally created (such as Revolutionary War or Tall Tales), many of us also store individual "strategy pages" that feature pages of the prompts we created for use with specific strategies (such as Strategy 15, Recognizing Cause-and-Effect Relationships, or Strategy 8, Synthesizing to Gain New Meaning, both of which are the same prompts featured in chapters 2 and 3).

The purpose for storing these strategy pages separately is twofold. First, you might provide instruction in the same strategy several times throughout the school year and simply use the same or a similar strategy page in different Guides. As an example, we typically included a vocabulary page in just about every Guide so that students could practice applying skills for Strategy 2, Finding Word Meaning and Building Vocabulary Using Context Clues, throughout the school year. Additionally, as Strategy 8, Synthesizing to Gain New Meaning, is one of the more difficult strategies for students to grasp, we often featured it several times throughout the school year. Cutting and pasting it electronically into a Guide helps prevent wasting time. A second reason why we store each strategy page separately is so teachers can easily match strategies to texts or texts to strategies, depending upon their needs. As we continually built our book collections, we also changed the texts we used within an instructional unit. For example, books that we used to provide instruction on government might have changed from year to year as new titles were published or as we located additional sources that might have better addressed the multiple reading levels of students within our classrooms. As the texts changed, we might also have wished to change strategies, having determined that another strategy or strategies were better suited for the new text. Having the flexibility to work with the strategy practice prompt pages for these purposes is another timesaver.

Additional Thoughts

While presenting workshops on the use of the Read-Along Guide, we have learned that some districts have allowed teachers staff development time or time outside of the school day to create materials. Find out if your district provides staff development time for creating curriculum materials. Another suggestion is to propose working on a summer curriculum project in which Guides for content area themes can be created. If these options are not available, try setting a realistic goal to create a small number of Guides per year, during planning or lunch time, while working in teams. This has also worked for some of our participants, though we would like to believe that your district will eventually come to value the benefits and will allot time, as our district did. (Your requests should be repeated year after year.) We also encourage you to seek grants to help cover some of your time used to create these materials. Begin with regional grants that might be available through your teaching center and national reading associations, and become familiar with others through independent

Internet searches. Your regional teaching center may also provide a good beginning to initiate your search.

Your work in creating these Guides will be evident when you see your students demonstrate their ease in using them. Figures 44 and 45 illustrate what the Guides will look like when you put all of the Guide components together and have your students work in the Guides during their readings. Figure 44 is a Guide completed by a student when the class read a selection of tall tales, and Figure 45 is a Guide completed by a student during the reading of *The Courage of Sarah Noble* (Dalgliesh, 1954). Each example demonstrates the students' strong ability to use the strategies and clearly show their level of understanding.

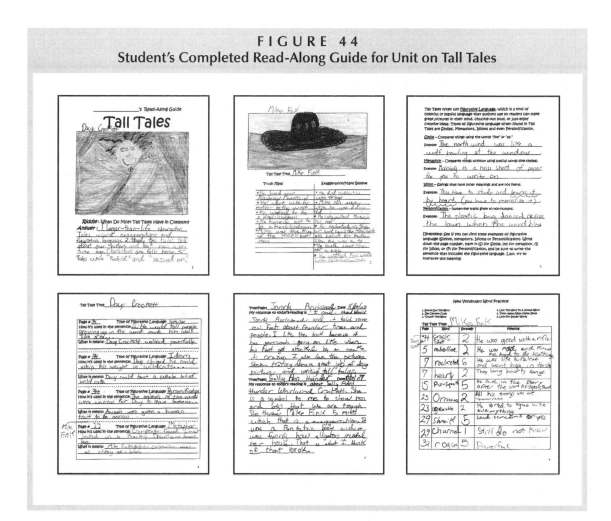

FIGURE 44
Student's Completed Read-Along Guide for Unit on Tall Tales

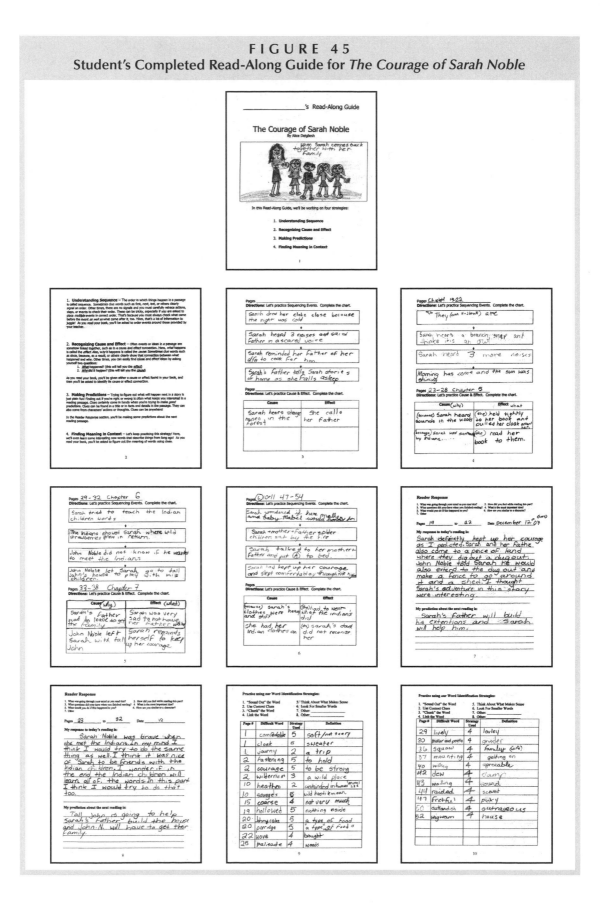

CHAPTER 5

The Written Response Section of the Read-Along Guide

"When students are asked to respond to their reading, it allows them to engage in a way that is unique and authentic. Including the response section together with the strategy-based practice in the Read-Along Guides represents a well-rounded instructional approach."

—Mrs. Ghanli, reading specialist

"Writing my responses helped me understand the book more because I had to think and write about how I felt. I liked making connections."

—Erika L., fifth-grade student

Most teachers find that allowing students to have the time to think about what they have read and then to explore how best to express those ideas in writing are valuable tasks, and the written response component of the Read-Along Guide provides students with this opportunity. Teachers asking for written responses in their Guides will find that these sections provide valuable glimpses into a student's overall comprehension. Rather than focus on the use and application of a single comprehension strategy, the written responses yield a broader perspective of a student's ability to comprehend. Written responses tend to be wider in scope than individual strategy practice responses and often demonstrate a student's use of multiple strategies, a concept that although difficult to capture during independent strategy practice, is a more authentic reading behavior.

However, reflecting and writing about what they read are tasks that students approach very differently. Therefore, in addition to practicing comprehension strategies on their own, students will most often also compose their written responses independently. For example, some students may be able to respond immediately to their reading, while others may spend considerable time thinking about their reaction or contemplating ways to express their ideas prior to writing them down. Allowing students to approach these tasks in a manner with which they are comfortable is the main reason why most teachers using this Model consider the written response element as an independent activity.

Certainly teachers will want to model writing a response several times when it is first introduced and may choose to provide this instruction in their small groups or even as lesson designed for the whole class. However, once students understand the basics and have also grasped the teacher's expectations for related issues such as spelling, length, detail, and so on, most students can complete this activity independently. Teachers will want to monitor student progress with this written activity to assist those who may struggle with either comprehension or with writing. Likewise, teachers can also determine if some students might benefit from completing their responses during their small-group instruction where immediate and ongoing assistance can be provided.

At first, we didn't consider including a written response component in the Read-Along Guide, as we focused on more direct strategy instruction. As such, the contributions students shared during our group instructional time were geared toward how they had applied a strategy, how they arrived at the meaning of a word using context clues, or other strategy-related, comprehension matters. Still, it felt awkward not knowing if students liked or disliked the reading, if they found certain parts interesting or unusual, or if they had questions about something that didn't make sense. Certainly, these topics often crept up, but we were not able to spend an ideal amount of time on them. As a result, we didn't really know how students were engaging with the reading. We then decided that including a response area would enable us to glean insights on some of these unknowns.

It turned out that the written response section provided us with some crucial insights on students' thinking as we diligently worked toward building their strategy-based comprehension skills. Additionally, students enjoyed sharing their responses and seemed to welcome finding their voice, particularly on matters that were new to them and engaged them in ways that they had not been previously engaged. Over time, we grew to appreciate that the written response section provided us with perhaps our best insights on a student's ability to comprehend and another outlet for individually assisting students with their comprehension.

Just as there are many ways to introduce and provide instruction in the comprehension strategies, there are also many ways to introduce and make the most of the written response section that appears in the Read-Along Guide. This chapter provides guidelines on ways teachers might wish to include a written component along within their reading strategy practice, an important and unique facet of the Quality Comprehension Model. In addition to providing prompts for the written response section, dialogue for introducing it to students and key indicators teachers might wish to look for are outlined. Our experience suggests that while instruction in the strategies is important, information gained from student response writing was indicative of their overall comprehension.

What Is the Written Response Section?

The written response section of the Read-Along Guide typically includes writing prompts which are used to launch student thinking and writing (although many students quickly develop an ability to initiate and focus their own writing and no longer rely on the prompts). In addition to the prompts, an ample amount of space is provided so students can respond daily or intermittently throughout the duration of their instruction in a given unit or text.

We discovered—as you will likely discover—that having a written response section in the Read-Along Guide is more effective than having students respond to their reading in journals. Despite the fact that most of the students we taught over the years had prior experience journaling in a spiral notebook or a composition book, we decided that asking students to bring a separate journal to use specifically for their written responses could be problematic and time-consuming for many reasons. Furthermore, students were already bringing a book, their Guide, a pencil, and often times sticky notes to a table where group instruction would take place; bringing another item could be cumbersome. Having everything in one place seemed practical. It would help students who might struggle with organizational skills, and teachers (as well as students) could more easily make connections between a student's practice with comprehension skills and their written response. Although we were concerned that the Read-Along Guides might become too lengthy, this didn't become an issue based on our observations of the students' ease with using them.

We found it beneficial to include the written response section toward the back of the Guide and to include other organizational aids such as a space for the date, chapter number, and page numbers. It's also interesting to note that, despite including a written response section in the Guide for use during reading instruction, many who use the Quality Comprehension Model still use a separate journal for morning writing activities or for writing instruction; the use of a separate journal for other writing activities remains a common practice.

Some teachers choose not to include the written response section in the Introductory Read-Along Guide, as they feel introducing students to the comprehension strategies and the use of the Guide is a formidable undertaking in itself. Still, others choose to include it from the start, wanting to expose students to the components and method of working with the full Read-Along Guide all at once.

Similarly, some teachers choose not to include the written response section in every Guide or may not have students write a response to every reading. Likewise, teachers may choose to coordinate the written response section with the strategy practice. Remaining flexible with how you choose to use the written response section fits with other elements of this approach, such as grouping, materials, and amount of teacher support. When to use the written response section and how often to use it are decisions best left to the teacher.

Read-Along Guide Written Response Prompts

The written response component of the Read-Along Guide provides students with an assortment of writing prompts or cues. These are designed to help jump-start those students who may be "stuck" or can't think of what to write. We tried to devise prompts that were based on authentic responses from skilled student writers and spent much time poring over years' worth of entries in students' journals to identify patterns, ideas, and common topics that seemed to reflect a natural engagement. We also tried to include a variety of prompts that were very broad in scope so that virtually any way in which a student connected to the text would easily fall within one of the selections provided. Therefore, the written response section offers the following collection of prompts, which represents strategies from the higher levels of Bloom's Taxonomy (teachers may adjust these or use their own):

1. What was going through your mind as you read this?
2. What questions did you have when you finished reading?
3. What would you do if this happened to you?
4. How did you feel while reading this part?
5. What was the most important idea?
6. How are you similar to a character?
7. What predictions do you have about the next reading?
8. Other

Including "Other" as the last prompt allows students flexibility, especially for those who wish to respond in ways they feel may not fit into one of the teacher-provided prompts. Having used these prompts for nearly 10 years, we never had reason to believe that they were too confining or stifling for students who wished to express their views uniquely and creatively. We even found that the prompts not only helped those students who had difficulty expressing ideas in writing but also could be used to encourage skilled writers to consider writing on topics they might not have otherwise considered. In addition to these benefits, we also began to use this section to enhance our comprehension-based instruction. For example, while working on Strategy 13, Comparing and Contrasting, some teachers choose to assign writing prompt 6 because the student responses could be used within a compare and contrast practice section located elsewhere in the Guide. Having flexibility with the prompts is key, and you can determine if you wish to assign them or have students select their own.

For example, Figure 46 shows one of the daily reader responses while reading *Love That Dog* (Creech, 2001) during a unit on poetry. Following their daily reading, students were required to summarize events, react to the events, and then identify poetic features they found. Here, teachers are not only able to determine if students clearly understood what was happening in the passages, but they can also identify

---

FIGURE 46
Reader Response During a Poetry Unit Featuring Three Required Writing Prompts

Responses
Your response should include three paragraphs.
1. The first paragraph should summarize the main events in the pages we read.
2. The second paragraph should be your response to those events. How did you feel about the events? Use good emotion words and explain fully and clearly.
3. The third paragraph should list 2–3 poetic features found in the pages we read. They may be from Jack's poem or from one of the other poets' poems. Be sure to list the feature (use the inside from cover), where you found it (ex. In the poem "The Tyger" by William Blake...), indicate what page you found it on, and give the example.

Date __2–4__   Pages Read __31–41__

The first main event that happened in this reading was Jack and his class are reading "Street Music" by Arnold Adoff. Jack liked this poem and then described his street and how it is thin and quiet, and there is not much traffic. Shortly after Jack and his class read the poem "The Apple" by S.C. Rigg. Jack like the fact that the poem was in the shape of what the author was describing. Then Jack tried to write his own poem about his yellow dog. He even made it in the shape of his dog. I don't think you're going to believe this, but Jack finally stepped up to the plate and told his teacher that when she types it up she can put his name on it! In Brief, these are some of the main events that happened in this section.

As I read pages 31–41 I think I was finally proud of Jack. He understood the poems and finally took a big risk to put his name on his poem. By the way the Yellow Dog was very good, but a little hard to read. To sum up, I was very happy for Jack and the progress he made, but let's just hope he stays on a role.

I found a big number of poetic features today. Some were repetition, a simile, and looking different because of space. There was a lot of repetition in the poems "My Yellow Dog" and "The Apple". Words just kept on repeating themselves until you just couldn't say the word any longer. I found a simile in "Street Music" when it said, "Hot, metal language combinations as plains overhead roar." In that same poem I found space features between the text. It looked fairly different from a poem with stanzas. In conclusion, these are some of the poetic features I found.

if students are engaging with and connecting to the characters, plot, events, or emotions. Lastly, teachers are also provided with glimpses into a student's ability not only to detect poetic features, such as similes, but also to interpret their meaning. Clearly this student demonstrates use of multiple comprehension strategies, such as Strategy 9, Finding the Important or Main Idea; Strategy 5, Making Connections to Aid Understanding; and Strategy 14, Interpreting Figurative Language, among others. (As these responses are lengthy, teachers may choose to have students select one of the three paragraphs to share during small-group instruction.)

In another example, Figure 47 features a student response to either prompt number 4 or number 1 during a reading of *The Courage of Sarah Noble* (Dalgliesh, 1954), which were among the optional seven prompts provided by the teacher in this unit. (Note that this teacher did not require the student to indicate which response they selected). Here the student demonstrates her ability to grasp the magnitude of the event taking place in the story and empathize with the main character, despite this event taking place outside of the student's realm of experience. Evidence suggests that this student has used many comprehension strategies while reading and thinking about ideas within this passage, such as Strategy 15, Recognizing Cause-and-Effect Relationships; Strategy 5, Making Connections to Aid Understanding; and Strategy 16, Drawing Conclusions and Making Inferences. Also shown in this example is one way in which the Strategy 7, Making Predictions, can be practiced by linking it to the written response section of your Read-Along Guide.

Multiple daily responses are shown in Figure 48, where the student, while reading *Harriet Tubman: The Road to Freedom* (Bains, 1996), describes her feelings as she works hard to consider what life would have been like for Harriet Tubman.

FIGURE 47
Reader Response During a Unit on the Colonial Period Using Historical Fiction

Reader Response

1. What was going through your mind as you read?
2. What questions did you have when you finished reading?
3. What would you do if this happened to you?
4. How did you feel while reading this part?
5. What was the most important idea?
6. How are you similar to a character?
7. Other _____

Pages __33–51__ Date __1–25__

My response to today's reading is:
When I was reading this part of the story I felt sad for Sarah because her father left her with the Indians because he had to go get the family. Sarah is scared and sad. I felt bad for her when I was reading.

My prediction about the next reading is:
That maybe the Indians from the north will come at night and Sarah will be very scared.

FIGURE 48
Reader Response During a Biography Unit

Reader Response

Each time you read, you will respond to what you have read. Choose one or more of the ideas listed below to respond to your reading. Be sure to be specific and write neatly.

Possible ideas for reading responses:
What was going through your mind as you read this?

1. What questions did you have when you finished reading?
2. What would you do if this happened to you?
3. How did you feel while reading this part?
4. What was the most important idea?
5. What predictions do you have about the next reading?
6. Was there anything about what you just read that surprised you?
7. What did you find out that you didn't know before?

Date ___Feb. 2___ Pages ___7–14___

My response to today's reading is:
If I went through the same things Harriet Tubman had to go through I would feel awful. I would be afraid of geting whipped most of all. I also wouldn't be able to care for a babie at age seven. That is how I would feel if I went through the same things as Harriet Tubman did when she was a little girl.

Date ___Feb. 3___ Pages ___16–21___

My response to today's reading is:
I would be determined like Harriet is to be free and to help other slaves be free as well. I would also not be afraid to show my feelings, like Harriet. I would also think that carring for a babie when you are weak and a very young age would be extremely difficult to do. I would hate to do the chores that Harriet had to do.

Date ___Feb. 4___ Pages ___22–27___

My response to today's reading is:
Just like Harriet and the other slaves I read the Bible and am very religious. I would think that after recovering for her injury it would be hard cutting a rail with an axe, then haul wood and many other heavey objects. Finally, it would be hard working in the hot sun in the fields every day after recovering just a few weeks ago.

Here, the student has been able to empathize with someone who was not only very different from her but who also had a very different lifestyle. Still, she was able to grasp connections that ranged from childcare concerns to working in the hot sun. Some other examples of strategies this student may have used to compose her journal response include Strategy 13, Comparing and Contrasting; Strategy 16, Drawing Conclusions and Making Inferences; and possibly Strategy 6, Visualizing to Support the Text.

In another example, Figure 49 presents reader responses to *If Your Name Was Changed at Ellis Island* (Levine, 1993) and *New York's Melting Pot Culture*, (Wilson, 2003). By including prompts 6 and 7 as optional, the teacher had the opportunity to extend her students' thinking by suggesting they make connections between their

FIGURE 49
Reader Responses During a Unit on Immigration

Possible ideas for your journal entries could be
1. What was going through your mind as you read this?
2. What questions did you have when you finished reading? Explain why you have these questions.
3. What would you do if this happened to you?
4. How did you feel while reading this part?
5. What was the most important idea? Explain.
6. Was there anything about what you just read that surprised you?
7. What did you find out that you didn't know before?

Date ___5/31___   Pages ___13–15___

I feel sad for the people who didn't pass the test at Ellis Island because they came to America hoping for a better life and they have to go back because they didn't pass the test. If there were Irish who didn't pass the test they have to go back to Ireland where there is a famine and they will most likely die. More people immigrated from Ireland because of poverty and overcrowding. Almost 4 million Irish came to America.

Possible ideas for your journal entries could be:
1. What was going through your mind as you read this?
2. What questions did you have when you finished reading this part? Explain why you have these questions.
3. What would you do if this happened to you?
4. How did you feel while reading this part?
5. What was the most important idea? Explain.
6. Was there anything about what you just read that surprised you?
7. What did you find out that you didn't know before?

Date ___6/1___   Pages ___17–18___

When I read this passage I wondered what Harlem Renaissance meant. I read more and found out that means African American writers, musicians, and artist living in Harlem who gained worldwide recognition in the 1920s. I learned that about 200,000 Jewish people came to America hoping for a better life. I learned that immigrants came to America for many reasons.

reading instruction and their social studies instruction (in which they were also learning about immigration). In the first example, the student has understood the severity of one outcome if Irish immigrants were turned away from the United States. This outcome was not stated in the reading text. Instead the student developed this new understanding by making connections between information he learned during reading and social studies. In addition to making connections, the student also demonstrates use of finding facts and details, synthesizing, and more. In the second example, the reader is able to extend her understanding of immigration in New York State. New facts about the Harlem Renaissance as well as new details she learned about Jewish immigrants have helped reshape her pre-existing knowledge; she has synthesized her knowledge on immigration as she integrates these new reasons why people came to New York and her existing understanding.

Student-Friendly Chat on the Written Response Section

Unlike the strategy component of the Read-Along Guide, the written response section offers students broad possibilities for expressing their understandings and insights. Likewise, teachers can use the response section as a second avenue through which to determine a student's level of understanding. When introducing students to the written response section of the Read-Along Guide, you can use the following dialogue:

> Many of you have had experience writing in a response journal. Sometimes it may have been in the form of a letter to your teacher. Other times it may have been like a diary entry, and perhaps you shared your entries with classmates. Also, you may have responded to questions your teachers asked, whereas other times you were able to write whatever you wanted. As most of us already know, writing responses to what we've read lets us express and explore our ideas and opinions.
>
> Throughout our reading units, you're going to have an opportunity to write responses in your Read-Along Guides. The response will be your ideas and opinions. We'll plan to share these responses (or parts of them) with classmates as a way to open our group gatherings during our instructional time. If we can't squeeze everyone in, then we'll take turns. You can respond to questions that I've prepared or you can respond in ways that I didn't even imagine. We'll be able to react to your responses, and we'll also be able to see how they develop over time. Let's take a look at page X in the Guide, and we'll review the written response section.

There are also additional forms of dialogue that you can use when introducing the written response section to your students, depending on their experience with this type of written response and specific classroom needs. The following dialogue is often used when students rely on responding to only a couple of prompts while avoiding others. Although this is one of the reasons teachers may assign prompts, an alternative is to encourage students to explore the use of others:

> Now that we've had a chance to share ideas back and forth about your written responses, I've noticed something that I think we might want to talk about. Sometimes we get used to responding to just one or two of the writing prompts. When this happens, we miss out on exploring other ways to think about our reading. Sometimes, a new way of thinking about something sparks new ideas. As you write your responses in this next unit, try to think hard about the prompts you've selected in the past and consider exploring new ones. You might be surprised to find that you have a lot to say on ideas that you just hadn't thought about before.

Following this dialogue, teachers may wish to have a student model his or her response from a less frequently used prompt. Although one of the prompts asks students how they feel about their reading, capturing this experience authentically may result in a different experience for students. If you find that students rely heavily on the teacher prompts, you can use the following dialogue to help students authentically engage with the text and write their response based on that experience.

Now that we've had some time to explore the use of different response prompts, I'd like you to consider another approach to your response writing. At times I'm unsure how some of you feel about the reading. I know one of the prompts asks you about your feelings, but I'm unsure if you've explored this as much as perhaps you could. For example, at times I don't know if you're enjoying your reading. I don't know if something about it made you happy or if something made you sad. I also don't know if you find it interesting or not. For your next few responses, why not try to capture what you're feeling as you read. In addition to knowing how you're feeling, I'd also like to know why you're feeling that way.

The following dialogue can be used to encourage students to make cross-curriculum connections.

We've explored a lot of new avenues with our response writing, but I'd like to offer another that I think you'll have fun with. I want to encourage all of you to extend your thinking and introduce into your writing ideas that might connect with areas outside of language arts. For example, as we read the next set of books, keep in mind that we're also studying the same topic in social studies. Use this knowledge to ask questions or to share how you've used it to build a deeper understanding. Although we don't mean to, sometimes we limit our thinking and we need to remind ourselves that it's okay to think outside of the box (or the curriculum area).

To encourage students to use new vocabulary words that appear in the text in their response, you can use the following dialogue:

I know from our discussions that most of you enjoy trying to figure out new words that you come across as you're reading. Why not try and include some of these wonderful new words in your responses? Chances are, by including them in your writing, you'll not only learn them much faster but you'll also remember them longer. Also, your writing will probably sound stronger and well developed. I hope many of you will accept my challenge to include more new vocabulary words in your responses.

What to Look For—Key Indicators of Successful Student Performance

As you identify key indicators of success showing that students demonstrate proficiency with the comprehension skills in chapters 2 and 3, you will also want to determine some key features to look for in students' written responses. We found that beginning with the skilled readers and writers whose abilities seemed strong was a good starting point. What we learned was that these students' responses contained one or more of the following key indicators, each illustrated with a student sample that demonstrates successful performance.

• *Responses clearly showed that a student understood most concepts and ideas and had few misconceptions or misinterpretations.* In the following example, the student has responded to the prompt "How did you feel while reading this part?"

> I feel wonderful for Dryden and the rest of the African American airmen who finally received orders from the Army Air Corps.... I thought it was interesting that Mrs. Roosevelt flew with Charles Anderson to get citizens attracted to the army. (Response to *If We Had Wings: The Story of the Tuskegee Airmen*, Spann, 2002, chapter 5, p. 7)

Here, the student shares his feelings, which are directly related to an event that took place in the text. Also, his feelings appear in line with the events. For example, the student suggests that he is happy after the long-awaited orders from the Army Air Corps were received and likewise, he found it noteworthy that Mrs. Roosevelt flew with Anderson.

• *Responses demonstrated use of a particular or multiple comprehension skills that were practiced elsewhere in the Guide.* In the following example, the student responds to the prompt "What questions did you have when you finished reading?"

> I wondered how Jack felt about going back in time to the Revolutionary War since it would be dangerous. I cept reading and I understood that he has seen suffering during the Civil War and dose not want to see it again....
> I wondered what made Annie so cereous about those solgers that she got so close. (Response to *Revolutionary War on Wednesday*, Osborne, 2000)

In this example, the reader poses two questions about the events from her daily reading. It's interesting to note that she has adopted the style of the strategy-based prompt for asking questions (see Strategy 4 in chapter 2), which uses the phrase "I wondered...." It is also possible that the she has relied on another strategy—Strategy 5, Making Connections to Aid Understanding—to assist her with developing questions. For example, she recognizes that Jack's desire to go back to the Revolutionary War could be "dangerous" as a result of her text-to-world connection whereby she has some understanding of the hazards of war.

• *Responses included new, unfamiliar, or unusual vocabulary words from the text in their writing. Often these words were listed in the context vocabulary section of the Guide (see Strategy 2).* This student was eager to include his newly learned word *syllabary* in his written response for the prompt "What was going through your mind as you read this?" as follows:

> I wondered how long it took to develop an alphabet (or syllabary). (Response to *Cherokee Heroes: Three Who Made a Difference*, Hirschfield, 2001)

Clearly, the student did not have to include this word in his response, as the prompt he selected did not require it. Choosing to include this new word on his own is a great indicator that this student is participating in his own learning and is using this instruction to extend his skill. Teachers will want to be sure that students have a clear understanding of new words they use in their responses and are not just inserting them. In this student's example, he has clearly demonstrated his understanding of the word by including the word "alphabet" along with it.

- *Responses included written discussions that were connected to other content area classes such as science or social studies, another book, something they had researched on the Internet, or a project familiar to the student.* In the following example, the student responds to the prompt "What was going through your mind as you read this?"

> I would be scared of radiation or not being able to move when I got back to earth. (Response to *Welcome to the International Space Station*, Logan, 2001)

In this example, the student made a connection to science upon completion of the book.

- *Responses showed evidence of engagement, such as through connections or through new ideas or questions that were not previously considered.* In this example, the student responds to the prompt "What was going through your mind as you read this?"

> I felt sad when Harriet got sent to a different plantation. I also felt bad that she only got enough food to keep her living. I was happy when Harriet was sent home.... I would find it very hard to be away from my family or to only have enough food to stay alive. (Response to *Harriet Tubman: The Road to Freedom*, Bains, 1996)

As illustrated in her response, the student is clearly feeling compassion toward Harriet Tubman and describes her emotional reactions to events discussed in the biography. As evidenced through her emotion, the reader is engaged emotionally and is able to connect with Tubman through this emotional empathy.

- *Responses were thoughtful and reflective and typically didn't address a particular prompt. Instead, they captured the authentic manner in which a student engaged with the text.* In the following example, the student has decided to prepare a written response without using one of the teacher-prepared prompt options:

> I really liked how the Iroquois told stories instead of writing them down. If I was an Iroquois little girl I would really enjoy listening to storytellers....
>
> I think the Iroquois womens clothing was very pretty. I think it would be cool to decorate my clothes with beads or porcupine quills. (Response to *If You Lived With the Iroquois*, Levine, 1998)

It isn't clear that she is responding to a particular response, but instead simply wishes to describe what she liked about that day's reading. Still, it is clear that this student is comfortable making connections and is able to easily imagine herself as an Iroquois girl.

Certainly most intermediate-level students are not ready to demonstrate this level of engagement with their text, especially at the onset of the reading instruction. Yet many are quick to show extraordinary gains toward these goals as instruction progresses. However, there are others who are so overwhelmed by writing that adjustments may need to be made, such as in the length of the response or in the frequency in which responses are requested. This may be necessary as the intention of the process—to enhance a student's understanding and enjoyment of reading—could otherwise backfire, and the entire experience could be viewed as a dreaded chore. Careful reflection on a student's responses in the first Read-Along Guide will often provide great insights on ways in which students comfortably engage or disengage with the passages they have read. Likewise, a student's comfort level with expressing ideas in writing will be evident. Other information, such as the student's use of reading and writing support services or student performance with reading and writing tasks in other classes will also guide you in your decision to adjust the written response section as you deem appropriate. Other ways in which teachers have addressed students' individual needs in terms of the written response section follow.

Teacher Response

Just as the written response section provides students with an important method of engaging with their text, so, too, does it become a critical method for teachers to communicate with students. Although the concept of teacher–student exchange of ideas through response entries is not new, it is a critical component of the Quality Comprehension Model. This is largely because teachers may use their exchange of ideas to promote and encourage comprehension. Often the exchanges are not lengthy but are intended to be motivating and thought-provoking. Therefore, the following section outlines suggested types of responses for students. Teachers will also quickly learn about their students' reading and writing behaviors and therefore decide to monitor, extend, and support individual students in a manner consistent with each student's needs. This, too, supports the teacher's response as a critical tool of instruction.

It is important to note that the frequency with which you respond to your students is a matter of personal choice and time. Although many teachers like to respond in some manner as often as instruction takes place—either with a check mark on the student's paper, which is applied during small-group instruction, or with a lengthier comment, which is typically done about two times weekly when Guides are collected overnight. Still, other teachers who might have smaller groups or reluctant or struggling readers might try to respond more often. This is a decision best left to the teacher providing instruction.

Correct Student Misunderstandings

This type of response is especially helpful if students are reading nonfiction, content-based texts that contain difficult ideas and concepts such as war, slavery, revolution, and poverty, to name a few. The following example shows a teacher's response to an entry where a student has misinterpreted a character's action:

> My response for today's reading is that Samuel is going to run away and he is going to bring all the other slaves with him. I say this because he says "I looked at my hands, grown strong from pulling ropes and oars and sacks." "Then I knew my choice." "These hands were now going to pull people, pull them to freedom!" That is how I know Samuel is going to run away and make the others come with him. (Student response to *Samuel's Choice*, Berleth, 1990)
>
> You show some misunderstanding. Let's reread to find out about the decision Samuel has made. (Teacher response)

In the actual text, the character Samuel does not run away but instead remains behind to help others. This misunderstanding was discussed during small-group instruction, during which time the teacher conferred briefly with the student to check that she had arrived at a new level of understanding. Teachers may refer students back to the text as a starting point to clear up any misunderstanding. Additionally, further questioning from the teacher (such as asking, "What made you think that?") is another way to clarify misunderstanding.

Refer to Specific Pages in the Text or to a Student's Previous Work in the Guide

At times, students may need reminders about actions, events, or ideas that have taken place earlier in the text. Teachers can quickly note text pages to clarify matters like this. Additionally, students can be reminded about other sections in their Guide that may help them with tricky issues, such as in the following example:

> Some questions I have in this reading are that I wondered why we wanted to keep people from coming to the U.S. because of the "quota".... (Student response to *Coming to America: The Story of Immigration*, Maestro & Ryan, 1999)
>
> Go back to pages 15 and 16 to check this. (Teacher response)

Here the student was referred back to the text, which provided an explanation for the quota. The teacher continued to monitor the student's understanding of this concept.

Reinforce or Help Build a Student's Background Knowledge

Although it is extremely difficult to build a student's background knowledge, creating a foundation one block at a time seems a less daunting task. Including a brief factual note that is linked to a student's response is one way to approach this. The following is an example of this type of teacher response:

> I thought that Samuel did to much work. I though Samuel would be better off do different things than just work...he should tell Van Ditmas that he has to eat more and not do so much chores. (Student response to *Samuel's Choice*, Berleth, 1990)

> The slaves did have a lot of work. Perhaps their siding with the colonists will help them gain their freedom. (Teacher response)

Here the teacher is attempting to foster an understanding of something outside of the student's experience, helping the student realize that a slave asking an owner for freedom, at that time, was unlikely.

Similarly, the following example also illustrates this type of response:

> If I was an Algonquian or Iroquois I would not like to be in a war for silly things like beaver skins or trying to drive someone out of the area. (Student response to *Native Americans in New York*, George, 2003)

> I hope you now understand that things that may not seem important to you today may have been very important at that time. Sometimes these things were important for survival. (Teacher response, discussing in group)

Here, the teacher attempts to clarify what were important issues during that time period.

Make Connections for the Student

Through the response entries, teachers can make connections to other books and characters that may help students gain an understanding. Likewise, they can even suggest similarities or differences between the student and a character, such as through character traits or shared experiences, as illustrated in the following example:

> I am similar to one of the cowboys because I like to cook. I am similar because I like to cook food and serve it to people. (Student response to *African American Cowboys: True Heroes of the Old West*, Fuerst, 2002)

> I bet you have more differences than similarities. What do you think? I like to cook too! I wouldn't want the job of cooking for the cowboys though. (Teacher response)

> Another question I had was why did they have to stick together? (Student)

> How did you find the answers to your questions? (Teacher)

> If I was on that cattle drive I would probily get killed. In the cattle drive it tells what the dangers were like stampedes, snakes, and lightning. (Student)

> Let's see if you can add on to this by making some connections to your life. (Teacher)

The preceding examples illustrate a teacher–student exchange of ideas that took place over several days. Here the teacher encourages the student to search for meaning and make connections.

Encourage Students to Explore and More Fully Develop Their Ideas

Often in the intermediate grades, students have limited experience with difficult ideas and either lack confidence in or have difficulty expressing complete ideas. Encouraging them to further explore an idea through positive coaching is a friendly, safe, and effective way of asking them to take further risks with subjects with which they aren't completely comfortable. The following example shows a teacher's response to encourage a student to develop his idea of what it would be like to live as a Native American:

> I would like living as an Iroquois because I would be in one of the clans. If I was a turtle clan and I was married to someone from a bear clan then I could go to the bear clan and my turtle clan. (Student response to *If You Lived With the Iroquois*, Levine, 1998)
>
> Why? What are the benefits of belonging to two clans? (Teacher response)

Here the teacher asks the student to demonstrate his understanding by explaining the benefits of belonging to two clans.

Help Lead Students to a Higher Level of Understanding

Through teacher questions or comments, students can be encouraged to reconsider conclusions they may have drawn for the purpose of reaching a higher level of understanding. Although we often delight in having students become emotionally charged by something they're reading, it often becomes necessary to lead them beyond their emotions so they can consider other possibilities, such as multiple sides to an issue. The following example demonstrates a teacher response to a delicate issue having to do with the relationship between the Native Americans and the Europeans.

> I never knew there were such things as the Beaver Wars or that Europeans brought bad Illnesses too! I can't believe those Europeans because they were crule! (Student response to *Native Americans in New York*, George, 2003)
>
> Be careful. It is often hard to judge right from wrong from events that happened long ago. Let's discuss this. (Teacher response)

In this example, the teacher cautioned the student to avoid making harsh judgments on historical events and to instead consider that there may be more than one point of view on most issues.

Cater to Students' Individual Interests

When students express enthusiasm for a particular topic or issue, the written response section provides a great outlet for a teacher to jot down suggestions to foster that enthusiasm: Other books to read, movies to watch, Internet sites to visit, and even family field trips to take are some ideas to include. The following example features a teacher's comment in which she encourages her student to contact those in charge of the International Space Station to answer the student's question that was not answered in the text:

> If you don't get a mission done, then what happens? (Student response to *Welcome to the International Space Station*, Logan, 2001)
>
> Great question! Perhaps we can write a letter to the ISS and pose the question. (Teacher response)
>
> I would possibly want to go onto the ISS with our class.... I wonder if some day I can go to college in a space school...if there is any? (Student)
>
> That sounds like a fun class trip. I wonder what we would see. A college in space is a great thought. What would that be like? (Teacher)

In this example, the teacher encourages a student who demonstrated enthusiasm for learning more about the subject by providing suggestions for further study.

Monitor Students' Comfort Level With Sensitive Topics

Some issues, such as death, loss of a pet, and family relationships, may strongly affect some students. This is true whether you're working with works of fiction or nonfiction. Using the written response section to monitor a student's level of discomfort will enable you to intervene in an appropriate manner. In the following example, a teacher has addressed a student's sensitivity to war and death by offering the student an option of reading another work.

> I didn't feel comfortable reading this. The Idea of people dieing and war makes me feel uncomfortable also I might be overstating but I don't like people dieing.... (Student response to *Toliver's Secret*, Brady, 1976)
>
> Sorry this made you uncomfortable. Let's meet to discuss this further. If you do not wish to finish this book, we can move on to another book. (Teacher response)

In this example, the student expressed some discomfort and the teacher provided alternatives to reading the current text. It may be necessary to privately discuss concerns with a student, provide another text selection, or even discuss matters with parents.

Acknowledge Improvement

As students will often include a daily written response during the instructional unit, their progress can be monitored over time to check for improvement. This is true whether monitoring a student's understanding, development of ideas, or other areas indicated above. Following up with students on individual areas targeted for improvement is unquestionably one of the most critical uses of the teacher response. The following is an example of a string of follow-up comments:

> I could picture the soldier stopping and asking for something to drink... I am similar to Sam because I am giving and kind. While I was reading this I thought that Samuel was going to.... (Student response to *Samuel's Choice,* Berleth, 1990)
>
> Very nice response! Let's make all of them like this! (Teacher response)
>
> Washington's men had lots of problems. One is the British are to good and inocent people are being captured...I am different from Samuel. (Student)
>
> Thanks for trying to add more detail. Keep up the effort. (Teacher)

Here, the teacher recognizes through a written a comment where the student has shown more effort and has made improvements.

Encourage, Motivate, and Have Fun

Providing positive feedback serves as a good motivator for students. It not only helps them gain confidence in their ability and skill development, but it also encourages them to continue using their best effort in their responses. Responding to their written expression assures them that their thoughts matter. This is demonstrated in the following example:

> When I read about going to the YMCA I wished I could have a birthday party there because there's a pool there. (Student response to *Who's Who in a Suburban Community,* Miller, 2005)
>
> Yes! The YMCA has many fun activities. Possibly we will have a chance to visit there in the spring. (Teacher response)

In this example, the teacher provides a comment that corroborates the student's sense of fun and adventure. Simply sharing these types of comments promotes reading as an enjoyable, worthwhile activity. In addition to this type of response, teachers can also reply to students to encourage and motivate them.

Do I Correct Spelling and Attend to Other Technical Matters?

Certainly the decision to correct or not correct errors of spelling, sentence structure, grammar, and other technical issues is a tricky matter. You can recognize that as students expend their effort to consider and then express their ideas in writing, these technical matters often take a back seat. Ideally you would like them to do both, yet rarely does this happen. Even the highly skilled students who are being challenged to consider new ideas and to express these ideas using a more sophisticated vocabulary or sentence structures are sometimes unable to do both. This is true even as you encourage them to always go back and proofread their writing. You can recognize that if you choose to make spelling an issue, then students will not take risks with their word selection, and one-syllable words will typically be selected in place of three-syllable words. Likewise, if you choose sentence structure as an issue, then students will opt to write simple sentences instead of working their way through more interesting compound and complex sentence structures. As such, the question we considered when trying to address a plan of action for this difficult issue was, If we can't address content *and* technical matters in a student's response with the same level of priority, what guidelines can we follow?

The answers to this question first led us to another: What criteria have been established in standardized state-testing practices for written responses? The answer to this helped us create broad parameters. Many state tests considered content and technical control separate categories with different grading rubrics designed for each. For example, in New York State, two rubrics are provided for scoring some lengthier written responses, separating content from technical control (mechanics). Keeping this in mind, teachers will want to weigh their concerns based on overall classroom instruction.

In our classrooms, we felt comfortable isolating content and considering it separately from mechanics. The only universal exception to this was when the technical issues interfered with readability. If errors in spelling, punctuation, grammar, and handwriting caused readers to struggle to decipher words, reread sentences for meaning, and pause to infer meaning, then lower scores must be given to content. When your objectives are to encourage students to develop their ideas, take risks, and challenge them in often-difficult areas, following state guidelines will enable you to set broad parameters and ignore technical errors in student responses unless they interfere with readability. At some point, you may wish to further refine your criteria so that it better aligns with your objectives. However, we offer the following guidelines:

- Initially provide the correct spelling for new and difficult content words that appeared in the vocabulary section of the Guide. However, if the student makes no subsequent attempt to use their Guide to spell these new words correctly, encourage them to do so through a comment, as shown in the following example:

  When I was reading I had some questions. here are some. I wonder if thay get to meet GeoRGe washiNgton. I think thay will. I think ANNie and Jack will follo the trops. The trops will follo GeoRGe.... (Student response to *Revolutionary War on Wednesday*, Osborne, 2000)

  I know you are working hard on spelling. Remember to go back to your book to check some of these words. (Teacher response)

- Circle any misspelled common sight words. For example, we circled misspelled words if they appeared on our Sight Word List, which was a component of spelling instruction that took place at another time. These words needed to be fixed.

• Handwriting must be legible. If students have serious difficulty with letter formation, spacing, and size of their writing, consider allowing them to use lined, raised-ruled, or other paper instead of working directly in the Guide.

Although concerns for sentence structure and grammar may be placed on hold, students may be given the opportunity to read their responses aloud. Beginning instruction in this manner not only provides everyone with a good review of the text, but it also ensures that students will read their responses in advance to check that there are no missing words, no awkward sentence constructions, and that the responses make sense. Knowing that their time with a captive audience is brief, they may become more conscientious of their reading fluency.

Providing lessons on proper mechanics during writing instruction can add value to the importance of technical control. However, in our case, we attempted to hold fast to our objectives of ensuring student comprehension and authentic engagement with the text.

In revisiting the Student-Friendly Chat for this chapter, you'll notice that it is brief and doesn't establish all expectations immediately. For example, there are no discussions on spelling and mechanics. The idea that, as a group, students and teachers react to responses and focus on content sends the message of the importance of comprehension. Many teachers are able to interject comments regarding spelling or mechanics (if need be) without detracting from the goal of comprehension.

CHAPTER 6

Reading Selections: Locating Materials for Use With the Read-Along Guide and Comprehension Strategy Instruction

"The Quality Comprehension Model isn't prescriptive and allows you to use a variety of reading materials in so many different ways. I like that I can mix different kinds of texts within reading groups, or I can even decide that using one text for all groups might work best. Selecting my reading materials carefully, lets me really address my students' needs and interests so I can provide them with best instruction possible."

—Mr. Deluna, fifth-grade teacher

"I liked practicing synthesizing in my Guide. I learned how to pull things out of a book and tell about it all in my own way."

—Dominique P., fifth-grade student

Teachers are inherently concerned about material and having enough materials, the right materials, an appropriate variety of materials, an acceptable range of materials, and so on. The good news about launching your strategy-based comprehension instruction is that you most likely will be able to get started using materials you already have. As you are aware from having read through the Text Suggestions sections in chapters 2 and 3, there are many types of sources that you can use for instruction including the following:

- Student newspapers and newsmagazines
- Content area–based textbooks (old and new)
- Existing book collections
- Materials from your library including encyclopedias; biographies; multiple books by the same author; and books within the same genre, such as poetry, fairy tales, and more
- Electronic resources, author websites, and more
- Basal readers (old and new)

Figure 50 features a selection of texts used in a fourth-grade classroom. The variety of topics spans content area curricula as well as many language arts genres. Although you might not have a diverse and well-rounded selection of multiple-copy sets of books, this should not be a barrier that prevents you from getting started. Keep in mind that although your starting point may not be ideal, it is nonetheless a starting point from which improvement can be made. Whether or not you have been given a budget to begin your strategy-based instruction, the following steps may prove helpful in guiding your initial actions toward building your collections:

Step 1: Survey What You Have
Step 2: Level What You Have
Step 3: Identify Needs—Content, Level, and Suitability
Step 4: Fill Gaps

Step 1: Survey What You Have

Your Classroom Collections

The best starting point for an initial survey is in your classroom. You are already familiar with your own collections, and it will not take you a lengthy amount of time to scan your shelves and jot some notes about your books. If you are a seasoned teacher you probably already have classroom libraries consisting of single-copy books that may be organized according to theme or genre. As this process should not be cumbersome and overly time consuming, you might wish to scan your shelves or bins quickly, noting works that you feel might have strong instructional potential. For example, current works, high-interest titles, well-liked books, or quirky

FIGURE 50
Selection of Book Covers for Fourth-Grade Texts Used for Strategy Instruction

Cover from *Native Americans in New York* by Lynn George. © 2003 by The Rosen Publishing Group. Reprinted with permission.

Cover from *Love That Dog* by Sharon Creech. Text copyright © 1998 by Sharon Creech. Jacket art © 2001 by William Steig. Used by permission of HarperCollins Publishers.

Cover from IF YOU LIVED WITH THE IROQUOIS by Ellen Levine. Copyright © 1998 by Ellen Levine. Reprinted by permission of Scholastic Inc.

From SKINNYBONES by Barbara Park, copyright © 1997 by Barbara Park. Jacket art copyright © 1997 by Jeff Walker. Used by permission of Alfred A. Knopf, an imprint of Random House Children's Books, a division of Random House Inc.

Cover from IF YOU WERE THERE WHEN THEY SIGNED THE CONSTITUTION by Elizabeth Levy. Copyright © 1992 by Elizabeth Levy. Reprinted by permission of Scholastic Inc.

Cover from TOLIVER'S SECRET by Esther Wood Brady, illustrated by Richard Cuffari, copyright © 1976 by Esther Wood Brady. Cover art copyright © 1993 by Dan Andreasen. Used by permission of Crown Publishers, an imprint of Random House Children's Books, a division of Random House, Inc.

Cover from *Cherokee Heroes: Three Who Made a Difference* by Laura Hirschfield. © 2001 by Wright Group/McGraw-Hill. Reprinted with permission.

Cover from *Floating and Paddling* by Leon Strebor. © 2001 by Wright Group/McGraw-Hill. Reprinted with permission.

Cover from *Colonial Life and the Revolutionary War in New York* by Kerri O'Donnell. © 2003 by The Rosen Publishing Group. Reprinted with permission.

titles are some ideas that will help you find works that stand out from the others. There is no need to record everything if you can select those that, based on criteria such as those suggested above, have more potential than others. If you are currently working with basal readers, they may or may not be housed in your classroom. Still, keep record of them.

Consider taking inventory not only of what you have but also of how many copies of each title you have. Over many years of collecting books through various channels, it is not unusual to have two or three copies of many titles. Likewise, you may work with a specific book that you keep in your classroom for content area instruction. For example, one teacher on our team typically introduced the biography *Thomas Alva Edison: Great Inventor* by Nancy Smiler Levinson (1996) as a read-aloud when students began studying electrical circuits during science instruction. As such, she had 25 copies of this title stored in her classroom. (Always keep in mind that working as a team and sharing resources will not only enable you access to more materials but will also help hasten the preparation of the Read-Along Guides; this was discussed in chapter 4.)

Beginning your survey in your classroom may also help you quickly call to mind many of your favorite titles. Planning to include some of your favorites in your instruction is an ideal way to share and authentically model your enthusiasm for reading, for specific texts, and for subject areas with your students. Students will recognize your reader attributes and may glean new perspectives on reading from them. As discussed in earlier chapters, some favorites, particularly the lengthier ones, may be best included in your reading program outside of your strategy-based instruction. You will quickly learn which ones fit easily into this format of instruction and which are better reserved for others.

As you are taking inventory of the titles and the quantities you have, you will also want to keep in mind categories or themes that might provide logical groupings for your titles (if your books are not already organized in this manner). For example, if you have a number of titles that might fall within a genre such as poetry or biography, make note of this. Even if an assortment could loosely be considered to comprise a theme-based collection, such as "Environment Texts" or "Grade-Level Fiction," this could help you devise collections for instructional units while your resources are limited. Also, it makes sense to keep in mind flexible methods of grouping your resources; texts you originally considered for instruction in one particular unit might work well within another. For example, a work on James Audubon could be appropriate for instruction in a unit featuring multiple biographies as well as a unit covering the arts or nature. Many seasoned teachers already have some form of organizing their personal collections in their classroom libraries, whether they are grouped into bins by broad subject, genre, curriculum connections, or otherwise. If you have a beginning, use it. There is no need to reshuffle. Teachers new to the profession may still be building and organizing their classroom libraries. One way to begin organizing your titles might be by using categories outlined in your school library, which are typically organized according to the Dewey Decimal Classification System. You could also use categories aligned with the Library of Congress Classification System. As a third alternative, you could create your own categories or borrow a category system from a colleague. Any of these methods will serve as a useful guide to help launch this process.

Pooling Resources Together With Other Teachers

Another method that has worked well for many teachers when trying to build their libraries is to pool their books together to create loaning libraries. These collections can be housed in one central location, or if that is not feasible you may decide to create one inventory list. These libraries can have very informal sign-in and sign-out cards. As many districts' book budgets are limited, pooling and sharing texts may be a good solution. An added bonus to sharing materials is the burden of storing large quantities of texts is lessened.

Another method of locating classroom texts is to e-mail colleagues with a call for copies of specific titles. Often, locating even two more books will enable all students within a group to have their own copy. This may be particularly handy, because you may need texts that span different grade levels, and although teachers within your own grade level might not have copies, teachers in other grade levels could.

Your School Library

Once you have the texts in your classroom inventoried, you might then want to review your school's library to determine if there are additional copies of texts you are interested in using for instruction. Many school libraries have multiple copies of popular titles. Electronically accessing titles or working together with your librarian to locate additional copies or to identify titles suitable for a theme-based instructional unit will greatly help supplement your own collections.

Even now, we rely on our library for copies of books, especially as our classroom numbers change and books within our own collections become lost or damaged. We also try to work with the same editions of books so locating information by referencing page numbers (which is often done during small-group instruction) doesn't become problematic for students who might have been working with another edition of the text. Before having to work with mixed editions of a text for your instruction, determine if your school library may be able to provide the one or two extra copies of the same edition you prefer to use.

In addition to supplementing your classroom sets, your library may have sources that would be useful for your strategy-based instruction. Journals, periodicals, and even reference works such as encyclopedias may be incorporated into your lessons. *National Geographic for Kids, Highlights for Children, Odyssey, Cobblestone,* and *Muse* are just a few examples of a number of well-written newsmagazines for children that many school libraries carry. Suggestions for using some of these types of materials are presented in chapters 2 and 3. Although your library may receive only one copy of a particular periodical, you might have access to technology such as a digital projector, or your subscription may include electronic access to the periodical that will enable you to share the single issue. Alternatively, you might find ways to incorporate using different volumes of a subscription with your lesson. Just as your school library is a great resource for you, so, too, is your school librarian. Although we tend to rely on our school library, public libraries can also be an excellent source.

Your Bookroom or Shared Collections

This set of materials is probably the largest collection that will be available to you for instructional purposes. Just as there have been new approaches in reading instruction and new trends in the publishing industry over the years, there will be evidence of them in your school's collections. There may be many whole-class sets of a single title to accommodate whole-class instruction across multiple classes of a single grade level. Basal readers, as well as particular trade publications that might align with the curriculum (trade publications are books with broad appeal that are typically published by "trade publishing houses" and purchased through large chain bookstores; there may be subsequent school editions published often with another cover or a paper cover so that bulk purchases are more affordable), might also fall into this category. There might be smaller sets of basal readers that are no longer used; collections of assorted holiday books grouped together; collections by genres; books set aside for use by particular grade levels, such as collections on science fair experiments that are used by the grade levels that will be judged for regional science competitions; books on author studies; and so on.

Certainly our bookrooms reflect our instructional habits over time, not to mention the distinct personalities of those responsible for keeping them orderly. No matter how materials in your district's collection are organized (for example, our lists were organized alphabetically by title and also included for each title the number of texts available, whether or not a teacher guide existed, if there was a curriculum tie-in, and the genre or theme), be sure you have access to the most up-to-date listings possible. When we began working with our district's collection, we were unaware that our lists only contained titles housed in our building. Meanwhile, a separate list existed for our lower elementary grades—K through 2—as these students were located in a separate building. Also, we had another building in our district that housed grades 3–5, which was located some distance from our own. That building, too, had a separate list of titles. Although one master list containing everything did exist, we did not initially know this. Having a complete list gave us more options to pull together collections that were better tailored to our students' needs. We had access to more as well as different texts. Knowing what materials other grade levels and other buildings in your district have on hand will be helpful and may increase your options.

Moving Forward

Though perhaps placing the cart before the horse, another point to keep in mind is that it is important to consider how to stay on top of all the new materials that become available from the sources described above. As you begin your inventory, it would be a good time to consider how to keep your collections current lest you have to repeat the process on a yearly basis. Just as your own classroom sets will grow, so will your library's holdings as well as the district's collections. Perhaps your school librarian might be encouraged to provide book talks about or display new titles ordered that year, or an appointed individual might be in charge of maintaining electronic versions or distributing hard-copy lists of your district's updated collections, and you might wish to keep a running list of new titles you acquire for your classroom.

Step 2: Level What You Have

Once you have an idea of the materials and the quantities available to you, the next step is to level the materials. Today many hard-copy as well as electronic sources are available that already provide levels for thousands of books. This will greatly help you level your collections. Books such as *The Fountas & Pinnell Leveled Book List, K–8* (Fountas & Pinnell, 2006) provide multiple methods of locating titles that already have a level provided—alphabetically by title, by subject, by level, and so on.

In addition to reference books, electronic sources are available. Scholastic provides an electronic leveling guide (the "Scholastic On-line Levelled Library" found online at guidedreading.scholastic.ca) for the works they make available through their book clubs. The Library lets you search all of Scholastic's educational resources by grade level, curriculum area, and other criteria. Although not all books have guided reading levels, a grade level is always provided as a guide. Fountas and Pinnell have a site that includes leveled collections at www.fountasandpinnellleveledbooks .com. In addition to these two websites, there are many other independent websites that can be accessed through any search engine using a keyword search, such as "leveled books" or "leveling guides," or others.

Finally, many books that you purchase today have levels indicated on the back cover or on the inside jacket. Many even include information that helps you interpret levels according to three different leveling systems. For example, the alphabetical guided reading levels developed by Fountas and Pinnell is the one on which we relied most often and used to level our own collections; however, we purchased some small-format guided reading texts several years ago that, at that time, relied on the Developmental Reading Assessment Levels. This system was developed by Joetta Beaver in connection with her assessment tools for the lower elementary levels. There are also other well-known leveling systems, such as the Lexile Levels (developed by MetaMetrics) and the levels used in a Reading Recovery approach. Today, many books have been reviewed by educational experts and feature several leveling systems (although some are only now beginning to extend into the middle and upper-elementary grades). Still, working with any of these systems and knowing how to interpret their classification methods will become second nature.

As discussed in the Introduction, we leveled many books—roughly 80% of our titles—within our district collections in an afternoon using one of the Fountas and Pinnell resources available at that time. Following this initial leveling activity, a cross-grade–level team was compiled to participate in a leveling workshop provided by the reading specialists in our district entitled *How to Level Books in Your Classroom*

Collection (Clarke & Birkel, n.d.). There, we followed a procedure outlined by Fountas and Pinnell (2002) and proceeded to level many of the texts for which we could not locate a level, including selections from one of our basal readers, some of our favorites that were not in the leveled reference libraries (for example, *The Matchlock Gun* by Walter Edmonds—published in 1941—is not only an older work, but it also takes place in New York and might have been considered too regional to include in reference libraries), or others that were new (for example, *Holes* by Louis Sachar [2003] and *Because of Winn-Dixie* by Kate DiCamillo [2000] were not yet leveled in the reference texts at the time we wished to use them). The following sequence of activities we used during this process may serve as a guide for you during your own classroom leveling systems:

1. We identified several core texts generally agreed upon by teachers as appropriate exemplars for grades 3, 4, and 5.
2. We identified specific characteristics within those exemplars covering broad categories as recommended by Fountas and Pinnell (2002), such as vocabulary, sentence complexity, length, illustration support, text structure, suitability, prerequisite content knowledge, among others.
3. We then established parameters or "gradients" within grade levels using our exemplars. Here, guided by the work of Fountas and Pinnell (2002), we created our own descriptions within a structure provided by these experts. For example, grade 3 gradient includes level L–P, grade 4 gradient includes level O–T, and grade 5 gradient includes level S–W. This gave us ownership of a process we felt certain would be successful and well grounded. What we ended up with were descriptions for all levels encompassing grades 3–5 (and above and below), a selection from which is featured in Table 4.
4. Once these descriptions were established, we broke up into small groups and leveled our remaining texts for which we could not locate levels.

Depending on where you are in the leveling process, we would recommend these two steps:

1. Rely on the reference texts or electronic sources available to level a bulk of your books.
2. Convene some leveling teams and level the remaining books using parameters based on suggestions from experts.

There will continue to be some books that may be difficult to level (for example, regional texts and works constituting new genres, such as Brian Selznick's [2007] *The Invention of Hugo Cabret*, which is largely composed of black and white illustrations but contains some subject matter as well as sentence constructions that might be considered more advanced). Remember, you can adjust the level just as quickly and as easily as when you originally assigned a level. Approximations are key.

We are often questioned about the appropriateness of students knowing their own reading level. When we first started working with our leveled texts, it didn't

TABLE 4
Book Difficulty Levels and Parameters for Grade 3–5 Students

Level M
Variety of formats
Different styles of text organization
Variety of topics
Longer chapter books/shorter "new info" books
More complex themes
Biographies with photos
More print, fewer pictures
Smaller print
Greatly expanded vocabulary
Text requires more interpretation and background
    knowledge
Character development and expanding plots
Vocabulary words specific to content
Vocabulary creates feelings or moods
Writer's style apparent
Documents within text to go along with text

Level N
Chapter books, 100 pages plus (shorter chapters)
More complex themes
Nonfiction, shorter—social issues
Irony used to create interest in characters
Mystery/suspense
Complex picture books illustrate themes
Variety of info books emphasized
Uses variety of strategies for understanding
One main plot, episodes take place over time
Vocabulary expands/more challenging
Topics beyond readers' experiences
Cultural/historical content

Level O
Longer chapter books
Range of problems
Sophisticated themes require more interpretation
    and understanding
Multiple characters whose development is shown
    through what they say and do
Continue to expand experiences through
    empathizing with characters
Realistic, historical fiction, biography, science
    fiction, humor, legends and fables
50–200 pages with black-and-white illustrations
Sophisticated and varied vocabulary
Multisyllable words included
Highly complex sentences
Full range of punctuation
Readers required to analyze new words

Level P
Variety of literary and informational texts
Chapter books explore problems of
    preadolescents and early adolescents
Text reads on a literal and figurative level
More text, more complex ideas and language
More sophisticated vocabulary
Longer descriptive narratives
Texts long
Three factors to be considered for understanding:
    1. Complexity of text structure
    2. Sophistication of theme
    3. Amount of background experience
Retain and recall information to support ongoing
    comprehension
Plays on words (metaphor and simile)

Level Q
Few illustrations
Complex sentence structure
Difficult vocabulary
Memorable characters
Complex plots
Humor
Analyze illustrations/text
Foreign language introduced
Long
Themes—problems in society, effects on kids

Level R
Fiction/nonfiction
Range of time in history
Long
Sophisticated vocabulary
Simile/metaphor
Biography/autobiography
Mature themes, death, politics

Level S
Complex ideas
Cultures
Multiple meanings
Complex sentences, paragraphs, punctuation
Historical fiction
Biography
Unusual settings
Many genres
Picture books/complex ideas/info

seem necessary to share this information with students. Today, our bins as well as the individual books contain easily recognizable letters representing a reading level or span of levels of the bins. It seems that what was once taboo has now been replaced by the notion that it is better to enable students to help themselves select titles. They can decide for themselves if they wish to choose a book that they can easily read independently, mildly struggle with independently, or require assistance from a parent or teacher to read successfully. They are empowered to choose. Likewise, it is now a mode of sharing information with other professionals and parents. Leveled books are available to students in the summer to continue academic growth. Leveled booklists are also available to parents to aid them in helping to select books with their child. Our concern about sharing reading levels is no longer an issue.

Step 3: Identify Needs—Content, Level, and Suitability

Once you have your list of available source materials, you certainly are ready not only to begin your instruction but also to build your library. As mentioned earlier, there is no reason to postpone your instruction because you don't have ideal material. Begin working with materials you have, knowing that this is a work in progress.

In building your library, it is important to keep in mind that you are working with three parameters: content, level, and suitability for strategy instruction. Further, you might wish to distinguish the content into two additional subdivisions: language arts and content area/informational, the latter of which would coincide with science, social studies, or even math instruction. As you have already identified available resources and have leveled them, many features of your current resources will become known, including gaps in your collections.

For example, the first feature we immediately recognized about our collections was that we typically had full class sets of roughly 25 copies or more of a single title, with very few smaller collections. Though this was not considered a problem, we knew that we would not be building our collections by filling gaps with full class sets. Instead, we more typically considered purchasing smaller units of 6 to 10 copies of a work to better accommodate our small-group instructional approach. We then used a quick tally system and determined we had very few titles at level R or above, and we were also heavily weighted with titles at levels O and P. To fill gaps, we would therefore need to acquire titles that represented the higher levels. This was our first step. We later returned to this process and reviewed our collections by subjects, using the classification provided in our original listing. We then determined that we were heavily weighted with works of folk literature (folk tales, fables, fairy tales, pourquoi tales) and were in need of more mysteries, fantasy, and science fiction. We therefore knew we might not want to initially purchase our higher level titles (identified as a gap through our first analysis) from works of folk literature (identified as a well-represented category in our second analysis, although we would return to fill level gaps at a later point in our collections-building process). Our historical fiction collections, typically aligned with our social studies curriculum, were strong for some grade levels but not necessarily for others. Our nonfiction collections contained titles most typically related to our science curriculums. Lastly, we noticed that we did not often have multiple levels represented within nearly all of these genre or subject collections. Although we had a good beginning, and in some cases had wonderfully curriculum-tailored titles in our collections (that we might otherwise not have easily located), we also were able to see where we would need to fill gaps. This was helpful and enabled us to make wise purchasing decisions.

Noticing the format of the resources in your collection is another factor you will want to consider. For example, our collections were—not surprisingly—comprised mainly of books. Still, we knew that print features unique to newspapers, such as headlines or political cartoons, and to informational texts, such as sidebars and captions, needed better representation within our collections so that our students were well versed in and felt comfortable working with and interpreting these types of features. This finding is what initiated our review of the final parameter in our collections-building criteria—the Suitability for Strategy factor. As indicated in chapters 2 and 3 within the Text Suggestions sections, there appeared to be some texts better suited for instruction in some strategies. We wanted to be sure we had a good cross-section so that our strategy instruction could be delivered using what we considered to be the best possible sources for instruction.

Step 4: Fill Gaps

Filling gaps in your collections may tax your creative problem-solving skills; yet as this is a problem you may be all too familiar with, you likely have experience managing this issue. Rarely are teachers given unlimited funds to purchase enough texts to create the perfect library. Also, as any teacher is fully aware, your collections are forever being built and are forever in need of strengthening. You will always be in search of ways to fund this ongoing evolution. The following are some suggestions, many of which might come in handy now, while others will be more effective down the road.

1. Ask for a budget from your reading department.
2. Ask your principal about any additional "book" or "text" funds available.
3. Ask your librarian about a yearly budget for new purchases that you can offer selection ideas.
4. Ask your Parent–Teacher Association about available funds that may be used toward book purchases.
5. Pool your book points through book club offerings, and purchase texts using points or other book club award incentives.
6. Create a wish list that parents can pull from to contribute to classroom collections, especially during in-school book sales. Often, the representatives from the sponsoring publisher will help to set this up and manage it entirely for you.

7. Write some grants to secure funds. Grants might be available through regional teaching centers to which your school belongs. Other grants are available through associations such as the International Reading Association or through the private sector or businesses. Searching the Internet for available grants is another way to secure funds.

8. Host school-based book sales or swaps.

9. Attend special book sales or swaps held by publishers, your local library, or within your community.

10. Ask book representatives if they have a review copy (or copies) available (which you should do anyway to determine if the book is appropriate for your needs). Call the publisher, who will put you in touch with the representative in your area. Ask for samples or multiple copies of samples.

At one time or another, we used every one of these methods to build our libraries. In addition to these methods for purchasing books, our district also began subscribing to an electronic book service that allowed us to print books on demand. Their collections are vast, leveled, and very easy to work with.

Methods of Monitoring and Assessing Your Students' Small-Group and Independent Activities

"I like the idea of having different types of assessments—some patterned after the state tests and others that are more project based. Together they represent a nice balance—we help students prepare for required state testing and also present some alternatives so they can show us what they've learned in other ways."

—Workshop participant, Central New York Teaching Center

"I think the questions in the unit tests are good because they're based on the strategies we practiced in our Guides, and the questions are good because they related to topics we studied."

—Kenny G., fourth-grade student

Two major questions that are addressed through the assessments in the Quality Comprehension Model are (1) "When should students be assessed?" and (2) "How should they be assessed?" We addressed these questions through the use of both project-based assessments and formal end-of-unit assessments, the latter of which are modeled after state tests. Monitoring and assessing student success with the strategies enables teachers to effectively tailor instruction to the needs of the students and also presents a systematic method of holding students accountable for instruction. You will want to consider which type of monitoring devices and methods of assessments align best with your objectives. Additionally you might find that in terms of the assessments, you can alternate between project-based and the more formal assessments as your objectives change. For example, if you are responsible for preparing for state assessments, you might want to use the more formal end-of-unit test some of the time.

Throughout this chapter, we have provided brief descriptions of our experience with assessments should you wish to integrate any stage of our assessment journey and your own. Initially, we often assessed students upon the completion of an instructional unit and recorded only informal observations of their performance during small-group instruction. As the units varied in length, depending upon the size of the book and the difficulty students had with the comprehension strategies that were covered, we were typically assessing students after five days of instruction for the shortest unit and nearly two weeks for some of the longer units. We also enjoyed the idea of project-based assessments and activities that included artistic and creative forms of expression. For example, students created teaching books where they were considered "specialists" on the topics covered in the book they had just completed reading (Harvey & Goudvis, 2000). As specialists, they were responsible for making a "teaching book" that included highlights of what they had learned. They would then this share with classmates. Another favorite was producing a dramatic book commercial they performed for classmates.

With project-based assessment, you might decide to provide students with a choice of two or more projects, as they might be motivated to do their best on a task over which they had some say. In a unit we covered on heroes, for example, students could either write a persuasive letter to the National Stamp Advisory Committee and convince them that a particular historic figure (discussed in their reading book) should be featured on a stamp or research the accomplishments of another heroic individual (not discussed in their reading book) and explore similarities among them. Likewise, in a unit on modern-day explorers, students who read Vanessa Marchetti's (2001) *Maurice and Katia Krafft, Volcanologists* could choose to either write a help wanted advertisement for a volcanologist (a scientist who studies volcanoes) or research the eruption of Mt. Vesuvius and create a safety brochure on the hazards of volcano eruptions. Considering choices like these might be something you wish to incorporate.

Though we had addressed the questions of when and how to assess students, we didn't feel we had enough concrete evidence to determine if our strategy-based approach to reading comprehension was working or not. Students typically performed well on our end-of-unit assessments, and we generally didn't have difficulty assigning grades that worked with our numeric 1–4 system. Still, we recognized that a glaring gap in our assessment system was our neglect of determining exactly *what* should be assessed. Though we believed the assessments would reflect whether or not students grasped a thorough knowledge of what they had read, we recognized the need to better align our assessments with our instruction. If we were focusing on the instruction of comprehension strategies—practicing them, talking about them, and sharing experiences using them—then we should be assessing students' overall ability to use them. We were not convinced these project-based assessments were doing this. We also felt we needed more concrete data on students' performance in the other components that made up our approach: How were students performing during small-group instructional activity and on their Read-Along Guide (especially those parts that were completed independently)? Having this knowledge would enable us to further identify students' needs and also monitor the success of our approach. As such, we refined our procedures and now have assessments that we use following each instructional unit as well as a monitoring process that is used intermittently during the instructional process. Suggestions for modifying both types of assessments for meeting a wide range of student abilities are also included. Therefore, this chapter will show you how to use the following assessment methods with the Quality Comprehension Model:

- Project-based assessments
- Formal end-of-unit assessments modeled after state tests
- Rubric-based assessments for Read-Along Guides
- Monitoring methods

Project-Based Assessments

Project-based assessments may be done individually or in groups and may address a wide range of modalities. Some project-based assessments could include:

- Oral presentation skills
- Poster features—design, color, catchy slogans
- Slideshow or PowerPoint presentations
- Dramatic representations

For example, Figure 51 shows an example of a project-based assessment in which students created a "teaching book" for *If We Had Wings: The Story of the Tuskegee Airmen* (Spann, 2002). This unit was an introduction to nonfiction and featured two strategies particularly important to nonfiction text: Strategy 3, Using Visual Text Clues to Figure Out Meaning, and Strategy 9, Finding the Important or Main Idea. Additionally, students were learning how to write a response to nonfiction in this Read-Along Guide. Because this instructional unit fell in the month of February, we decided to honor Black History Month, and for our three groups of readers, we

FIGURE 51
Project-Based Assessments for Nonfiction Texts

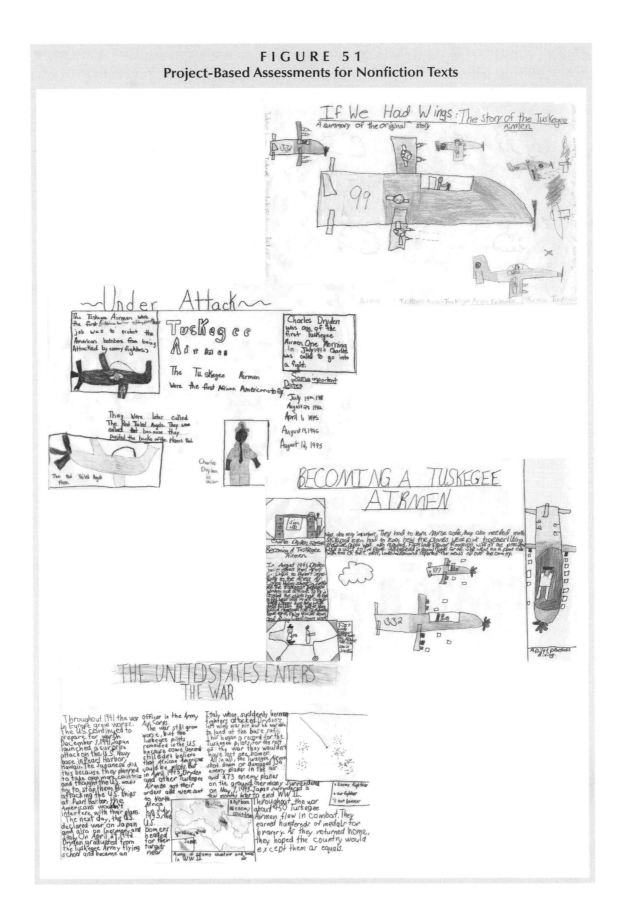

selected three texts that each cover the life and accomplishments of famous African Americans:

- *African American Cowboys: True Heroes of the Old West* (Fuerst, 2002) Level 3/L
- *North to the Pole with Matthew Henson* (Marsh, 2002) Level 4/H or R
- *If We Had Wings: The Story of the Tuskegee Airmen* (Spann, 2002) Level U

Here, each group of students was responsible for making a teaching book that covered the main ideas in their text, and in Figure 51, the group created the book for *If We Had Wings*. Each person contributed at least one page to the group's book. Additionally, students could use information from some of the features (such as sidebars) they read in their text to further support the main ideas they included in their teaching books. As is evident, even in the project-based assessments, aligning the assessment device with the instruction provided remained key.

You may also want to create rubrics to evaluate your project-based assessments. To do this, you may elect to incorporate a writing rubric based on your state's standards if you wish to grade the writing separate from the other components of the project-based assessments. These writing rubrics may already be available to you, and your students may already be familiar with them if you have previously used them in your writing instruction. For an example of a project-based assessment with a rubric, see the Book Review Brochure Instructions in Appendix B.

There are many excellent resources available that provide good ideas for project-based assessments. *Making Nonfiction and Other Informational Texts Come Alive* (Pike & Mumper, 2004) is a particularly good book for nonfiction project-based activities.

Test Modifications

There are numerous ways to modify the project-based assessments. For projects like these, students can draw concepts while a classmate or teacher scribes written captions, or students can use word processing to capture main ideas; students can also work in pairs or small groups to help support one another. Reminding students to rely on information that appears in their Read-Along Guide as well as the prompts is ideal, as this information has already been reviewed (during small-group instructional time). Having students use sticky notes to mark ideas and information they may wish to use in their project is another way to aid students who may benefit from this type of support. Depending on the project, ways to minimize writing or drawing, provide extra support through peer or teacher assistance, or adapt requirements to the special needs of individual students can be readily found. It is important to remember that the objective of the project-based assessment is to determine if the student has been able to grasp the content of the instruction.

Formal End-of-Unit Assessments Modeled After State Tests

Our formal assessments typically include reading passages, multiple-choice questions, short- and extended-response questions, and a lengthier essay. You may want to create an assessment that aligns with your state guidelines in both format and content. Rubrics that align with those used in our state testing program provide guidelines for assigning numeric grades.

Figure 52 shows an example of an end-of-unit assessment used at the completion of our Revolutionary War instructional unit. In this unit, students practiced the following strategies:

- Drawing Conclusions and Making Inferences (Strategy 16)
- Comparing and Contrasting (Strategy 13)
- Finding Word Meaning and Building Vocabulary Using Context Clues (Strategy 2)

Additionally, they read one of three different level books:

- *Revolutionary War on Wednesday* and the accompanying Research Guide (Osborne, 2000) level M
- *Samuel's Choice* (Berleth, 1990) level S
- *Toliver's Secret* (Brady, 1976) level T

Despite having read different books, students received the same assessment because they worked on the same strategies. Our test was designed to measure students' understanding of the strategy—not the content of the book. Each test included multiple reading passages that we made every attempt to determine were equivalent to those appearing on state tests. Each test also included multiple formats for assessing students' skills: multiple-choice questions, short-response questions, and an extended-response essay. Here, too, we modeled these formats after those appearing on our state English/Language Arts (ELA) tests.

In Figure 52, students were first asked to read passages from Kerri O'Donnell's (2003) *Colonial Life and the Revolutionary War in New York* and then answer 12 multiple-choice questions about the reading. Questions were designed to assess a student's ability to use the three reading strategies covered in the instructional unit. For example, questions 1–4 relied on students using context clues to figure out the meaning of vocabulary words (Strategy 2); questions 5–8 required that students compare and contrast information provided in the reading (Strategy 13); and questions 9–12 were questions where students needed to make logical conclusions and inferences based on information provided in the reading (Strategy 16). After the multiple-choice section, students read other passages on the Fourth of July celebration (which we created from readily available sources) and completed a compare-and-contrast graphic organizer and short-answer response that required inferential skills. Lastly, students were asked to write a five-paragraph friendly letter to a Japanese pen pal in which

FIGURE 52

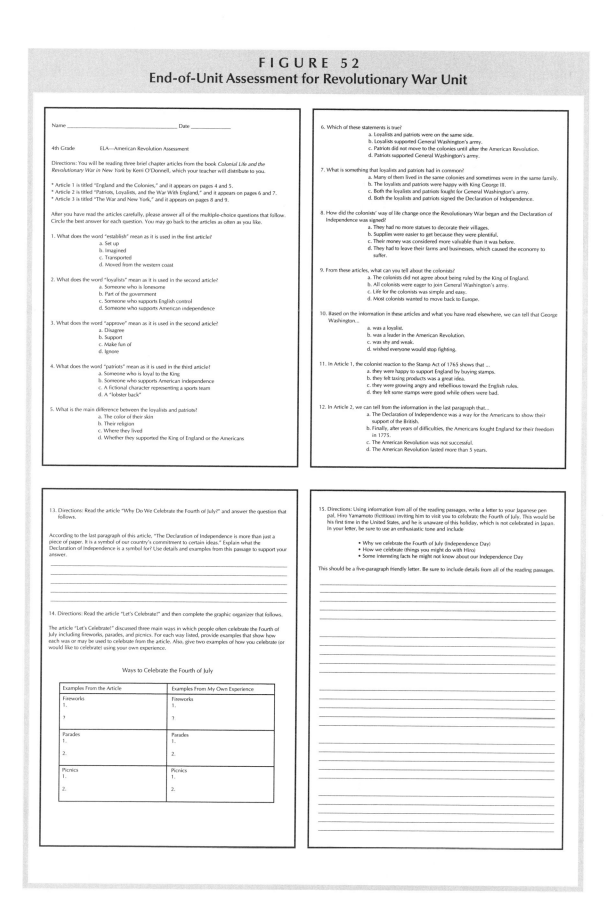

Name _____ Date _____

4th Grade   ELA—American Revolution Assessment

Directions: You will be reading three brief chapter articles from the book *Colonial Life and the Revolutionary War in New York* by Kerri O'Donnell, which your teacher will distribute to you.

* Article 1 is titled "England and the Colonies," and it appears on pages 4 and 5.
* Article 2 is titled "Patriots, Loyalists, and the War With England," and it appears on pages 6 and 7.
* Article 3 is titled "The War and New York," and it appears on pages 8 and 9.

After you have read the articles carefully, please answer all of the multiple-choice questions that follow. Circle the best answer for each question. You may go back to the articles as often as you like.

1. What does the word "establish" mean as it is used in the first article?
     a. Set up
     b. Imagined
     c. Transported
     d. Moved from the western coast

2. What does the word "loyalists" mean as it is used in the second article?
     a. Someone who is lonesome
     b. Part of the government
     c. Someone who supports English control
     d. Someone who supports American independence

3. What does the word "approve" mean as it is used in the second article?
     a. Disagree
     b. Support
     c. Make fun of
     d. Ignore

4. What does the word "patriots" mean as it is used in the third article?
     a. Someone who is loyal to the King
     b. Someone who supports American independence
     c. A fictional character representing a sports team
     d. A "lobster back"

5. What is the main difference between the loyalists and patriots?
     a. The color of their skin
     b. Their religion
     c. Where they lived
     d. Whether they supported the King of England or the Americans

6. Which of these statements is true?
     a. Loyalists and patriots were on the same side.
     b. Loyalists supported General Washington's army.
     c. Patriots did not move to the colonies until after the American Revolution.
     d. Patriots supported General Washington's army.

7. What is something that loyalists and patriots had in common?
     a. Many of them lived in the same colonies and sometimes were in the same family.
     b. The loyalists and patriots were happy with King George III.
     c. Both the loyalists and patriots fought for General Washington's army.
     d. Both the loyalists and patriots signed the Declaration of Independence.

8. How did the colonists' way of life change once the Revolutionary War began and the Declaration of Independence was signed?
     a. They had no more statues to decorate their villages.
     b. Supplies were easier to get because they were plentiful.
     c. Their money was considered more valuable than it was before.
     d. They had to leave their farms and businesses, which caused the economy to suffer.

9. From these articles, what can you tell about the colonists?
     a. The colonists did not agree about being ruled by the King of England.
     b. All colonists were eager to join General Washington's army.
     c. Life for the colonists was simple and easy.
     d. Most colonists wanted to move back to Europe.

10. Based on the information in these articles and what you have read elsewhere, we can tell that George Washington...
     a. was a loyalist.
     b. was a leader in the American Revolution.
     c. was shy and weak.
     d. wished everyone would stop fighting.

11. In Article 1, the colonist reaction to the Stamp Act of 1765 shows that ...
     a. they were happy to support England by buying stamps.
     b. they felt taxing products was a great idea.
     c. they were growing angry and rebellious toward the English rules.
     d. they felt some stamps were good while others were bad.

12. In Article 2, we can tell from the information in the last paragraph that...
     a. The Declaration of Independence was a way for the Americans to show their support of the British.
     b. Finally, after years of difficulties, the Americans fought England for their freedom in 1775.
     c. The American Revolution was not successful.
     d. The American Revolution lasted more than 5 years.

13. Directions: Read the article "Why Do We Celebrate the Fourth of July?" and answer the question that follows.

According to the last paragraph of this article, "The Declaration of Independence is more than just a piece of paper. It is a symbol of our country's commitment to certain ideas." Explain what the Declaration of Independence is a symbol for? Use details and examples from this passage to support your answer.

_____
_____
_____
_____
_____

14. Directions: Read the article "Let's Celebrate!" and then complete the graphic organizer that follows.

The article "Let's Celebrate!" discussed three main ways in which people often celebrate the Fourth of July including fireworks, parades, and picnics. For each way listed, provide examples that show how each was or may be used to celebrate from the article. Also, give two examples of how you celebrate (or would like to celebrate) using your own experience.

Ways to Celebrate the Fourth of July

Examples From the Article	Examples From My Own Experience
Fireworks 1. ?	Fireworks 1. ?
Parades 1. 2.	Parades 1. 2.
Picnics 1. 2.	Picnics 1. 2.

15. Directions: Using information from all of the reading passages, write a letter to your Japanese pen pal, Hiro Yamamoto (fictitious) inviting him to visit you to celebrate the Fourth of July. This would be his first time in the United States, and he is unaware of this holiday, which is not celebrated in Japan. In your letter, be sure to use an enthusiastic tone and include

• Why we celebrate the Fourth of July (Independence Day)
• How we celebrate (things you might do with Hiro)
• Some interesting facts he might not know about our Independence Day

This should be a five-paragraph friendly letter. Be sure to include details from all of the reading passages.

_____
_____
_____
_____
_____
_____
_____
_____
_____
_____
_____
_____
_____
_____
_____
_____
_____
_____
_____
_____
_____

they were to include details from all of their reading passages. Here, students were synthesizing information, pulling together the acquired knowledge they gleaned from having used all of the comprehension strategies tested in this instructional unit. Students were given up to one and a half class periods to complete the assessment.

Test Modifications

There are many ways you can modify these formal assessments. For example, you may reduce the number of multiple-choice questions for each strategy. You might also direct students to highlighted reading passages or paragraphs where answers can be located. The number of ideas you wish students to include in the graphic organizer can be specified. If you choose to include a writing piece, such as in Figure 52, you can provide options to ensure each student will have a connection he or she can write about. For example, ELL students may meet with more success writing about another historically based celebration they are familiar with instead of the Fourth of July. In the letter within Figure 52, students struggling with written expression can write shorter letters. Likewise, students can be instructed to write to a teacher, family member, or friend. Certainly more time can be given, and test components can be eliminated or shortened. Higher level students can be encouraged to create a project in addition to their formal assessment.

Rubric-Based Assessments for Read-Along Guides

Here, students are assessed on the degree to which they are able to demonstrate in writing the use of each of the strategies covered in the instructional unit (see Appendix B for a reproducible version of the Read-Along Guide Rubric). Clearly, being able to use a strategy and being able to demonstrate its use in writing may be considered two separate issues. Still, encouraging students to do the latter provides us with a sense of whether or not they have grasped a concept, and it is the method used in the Read-Along Guides. Likewise, students are assessed on their written responses within each of four categories: addressing the topic, details, organization, and language use. Students are familiar with these key criteria as they are the same ones that appear in our district's writing rubric used for nearly all of the students' writing assignments. Here, too, the writing rubric is also patterned largely on the state rubric. The 1–4 numeric system we use for grading purposes for the strategies section and the written response section is aligned to our schoolwide grading systems, including our report cards, which are further patterned on our state assessments. Comments sections are included to provide students with further feedback on their performance.

Typically these rubrics are completed at the end of an instructional unit and are often used for different purposes. For example, relying on the grades from these rubrics may be considered subjective largely because some reading groups may have continuous teacher support in completing the entire Read-Along Guide, while other groups might complete sections independently. Still, as a vehicle to relay information to students and parents, it is a useful feedback device as teachers can interject helpful and insightful comments such as on the amount of support needed for specific strategies or on areas that students may need to strengthen.

When using these assessments, we typically create one master copy and write the titles and strategies on it and then copy enough for a class set. This saves writing the same information on each student's assessment. For example, Figure 53

FIGURE 53
Sample Read-Along Guide Rubric Used With One Book

Read-Along Guide Rubric

Name _____ Date _____

Title _Colonial Unit—The Courage of Sarah Noble_____

Strategies & Skills-Practice
Degree to which student is able to demonstrate in writing
use of strategies & skills.

Strategy 1: _Sequencing (12)_	4	3	2	1
Strategy 2: _Cause & Effect (15)_	4	3	2	1
Strategy 3: _Meaning in Context (2)_	4	3	2	1
Strategy 4: _____	4	3	2	1

Comments _____
_____
_____

Written Response (Journal Entry)

Addressing the Topic—main idea present, task answered
                     4   3   2   1

Details—ideas developed with support details
                     4   3   2   1

Organization—logical, orderly, with transitions
                     4   3   2   1

Language Use—descriptive with content vocabulary
                     4   3   2   1

Comments _____
_____
_____

4—Consistently exceeds expected performance
3—Demonstrates successful performance
2—Is progressing toward successful performance with difficulty
1—Is not showing progress toward successful performance

---

features a rubric that is suitable for assessment when one book is used (*The Courage of Sarah Noble* [Dalgliesh, 1954]), yet this same rubric could be applied when multiple books are used, providing the same strategies are taught.

Monitoring Methods

In addition to the assessments that typically fall at the end of an instructional unit, monitoring methods are used to ensure that each student's progress is followed carefully. By doing this, we can provide students with assistance that aligns to their particular difficulties.

In addition to these monitoring methods, we also checked students' Read-Along Guides during small-group instruction. We found that commenting in some way on the students' work in the Guide daily was critical. During our small-group instruction, we would sometimes use a quick and simple check mark or "OK" on the page, which could indicate that the student's information was presented and discussed orally. In other cases, we might jot notes to encourage students or assist them by briefly clarifying matters. Certainly, if the teacher comments were given during small-group instruction time, they had to be brief (with a one-on-one follow-up discussion made for another time, if needed). On the other hand, if a group completed practice in their Read-Along Guides independently, we might periodically collect and provide more detailed comments on them, especially as we were often unable to thoroughly review all practice areas in the Guide during our group time. We quickly learned how to adjust the depth of our comments and our instructional pace to keep everyone moving, and we also developed a sense for when and where we should interrupt a routine to assist a student independently. Chapter 5 provides more detailed information on providing comments on the response section of the student Guides. Monitoring methods are described as follows.

Student Daily Checklist

These assessments are used during small-group instructional time to note a student's strengths or weaknesses, whether or not the student was prepared for class, and the degree to which the student participated in shared discussions and demonstrated a good ability to comprehend the reading materials. Typically, these were used each time the small groups met. A reproducible version of the Student Daily Checklist can be found in Appendix B. This checklist may be shared with the student if the teacher deems it appropriate to do so.

Formal Observations of Student Oral Reading Practices

These assessments are recorded periodically during small-group instructional time, noting students' abilities with practices such as pace, pitch, phrasing, and decoding. Typically, we recorded this information about each student once during each instructional unit, as illustrated in Figure 54 (see Appendix B for a reproducible ver-

FIGURE 54
Sample Oral Reading Practices Assessment

Oral Reading Practices Assessment

Title: _If You Lived With the_ Date: _11/18_ _Iroquois_ Name: _Emily E._	Title: _Revolutionary War_ Date: _2/11_ _on Wed_ Name: _Emily E._
N = Not at all S = Some of the time C = Consistently	N = Not at all S = Some of the time C = Consistently
Reads fluently (pace, pitch, phrasing) _S_	Reads fluently (pace, pitch, phrasing) _S_
Reads with expression _S_	Reads with expression _S_
Reads punctuation _S_	Reads punctuation _C_
Identifies sight words _C_	Identifies sight words _C_
Substitutes meaningful words _S_	Substitutes meaningful words _S_
Decodes _S_	Decodes _C_
Self-corrects _S_	Self-corrects _C_
Notes _Emily is making good progress. She uses strategies while reading and rereads when answering comprehension questions._	Notes _Emily works hard to read punctuation and is making gains with fluency and expressions._

sion of this assessment). During the small-group instruction, a teacher records information on each student's reading practices. Forms are copied onto sticky notes so that data can easily be reorganized by student (instead of by the reading group) and a student's progress over time can be seen.

Other School-Based Assessments and Monitoring Activities

In addition to these assessments and monitoring methods, we were required as a districtwide initiative to perform Rigby Running Records (Nelley & Smith, 2000) on each student four times per year, to coincide with the four marking periods. This information enabled us to note changes in their reading level, which we considered another critical piece of information to add to our data. We were also required to maintain a portfolio for each student, which contained specific writing samples and standardized reading comprehension tests.

Collectively, these assessment and monitoring methods enabled us to keep a close check on all of our students' progress in both their group and independent activities. Likewise, they provided us with keen insights on our approach to reading instruction so that we could make adjustments to the materials, the format, the length of time, the pace of instruction, or any other facet that needed mild tweaking. Lastly, as none of us had formal training in test construction, we felt that the standardized assessments we were required to keep in the student portfolios served as a "check" to help support our independent assessment methods.

Creating Assessments and Monitoring Methods

As discussed earlier, you may use a team approach for locating and creating your assessment materials. We found this to be helpful during the preparation of the Read-Along Guides, as well as the end-of-unit assessments and monitoring forms. You may begin by quickly assessing what you already have available. Then, one person can locate appropriate reading passages. Here, we relied on sources that we could reproduce in our tests, that we had ample copies to distribute to all students, or that we could easily and quickly create. Next, some team members can tackle the multiple-choice questions, while other members can prepare the short-response and essay questions. You might then gather to assemble the assessment, make adjustments as necessary, and merge the components electronically. Working in this manner, you can quickly create test materials. If you do not have a team to work with, you may be able to cross grade levels or even school districts to find others with whom you can collaborate. Even if you take on this task independently, you can build up your collection of assessment materials over time.

CHAPTER 8

The Quality Comprehension Model: Frequently Asked Questions

"I will definitely use the [Quality Comprehension Model] to enhance my writing and comprehension lessons."
—Teacher, Cherry Road School, Westhill Central School District

"I can use Read-Along Guides with texts I am using right now."
—Workshop participant, Central New York Teaching Center

This chapter provides answers to some of the most frequently asked questions we receive during our workshops as well as some of the more puzzling questions we struggled with while shaping our Model. We have always allowed time for a question-and-answer period at our workshops, as we typically find that participants are at various stages of exploring or implementing their own comprehension improvement initiative (even when participants are from the same district), and many have specific questions they need addressed so they can continue moving forward.

Question: Where do I get the materials to create thematic Read-Along Guides? How do I get started?

Answer: Everyone is surprised at how easily sources can be found in their own school. For example, old basal readers often have stories that meet your needs. Working with content-based textbooks is another good idea. Additionally, your librarian might also be able to help you find multiple copies of a text. Starting a collection of leveled trade books is ideal, but it takes time. Publications for students, such as *Weekly Reader* and *Scholastic News* are great sources of reading material that you might have in your classroom or in your library.

As you collect reading materials, keep in mind the reading levels, genres, and content matter that you teach. You'll want to select texts with varying reading levels, and you'll also want to fill gaps in your existing collections. When ordering new material, we suggest brief trade books or the small-format guided-reading texts that relate to the content curriculum. Favorite chapter books are good sources, but they may use much instructional time. Still, you might want to consider using them during reading instruction and also during read-aloud time. Online sources, such as A–Z Books, offer a great selection of leveled books with a variety of subjects and genres.

Question: What can I do if my school district requires that I use a basal reader or other reading series?

Answer: You can still create Read-Along Guides to accompany materials you're required to use. Remember that the goal is to improve reading comprehension. Match up the comprehension strategies with appropriate stories, and continue to offer varying amounts of support as needed. You could also supplement the required reading with other material.

Question: Do you provide instruction in all 17 comprehension strategies?

Answer: Yes. Although our district requires that we provide instruction in 12, we have found the others critical for helping students improve their reading comprehension. We might only provide formal instruction in some of the strategies during one instructional unit, with all supplementary instruction taking place informally through teachable moments or during content area instruction. However, we provide direct instruction in each of them at least once and still provide a balanced literacy program that includes other forms of reading activities.

Question: My class has a wide range of reading abilities. How can I make the Quality Comprehension Model work in a very diverse classroom?

Answer: How you group your students when using the Quality Comprehension Model may change each school year. If you have a specialist or teaching assistant available to you, consider having him or her instruct a reading group (even if it is only a few days each week). Reading groups can be flexible, so some days you might work with a larger group, while other days your group could be smaller. Try to cluster together students with similar needs for instruction. Allowing students to read with a partner or a tape recorder is also a possibility. Look carefully at your schedule, instructional range, and sources of support to decide what will work best for you.

Question: How can I fit in several reading groups in one day?

Answer: Some teachers see each of their reading groups every day, while others meet on alternating days. There may even be some days you have only whole-group instruction. Review the block of time you have for reading instruction and determine what will work best. You might decide to have four reading groups and see each group every other day for 30 minutes.

As an alternative, you may have four groups for 15 minutes each day. If support resources are available, a reading specialist may take one group for 45 minutes while the classroom teacher has two groups for 20 minutes each. If an arrangement isn't working well, try something different.

Question: What can I do if one of my groups of students finishes reading a book a day or two before the other groups?

Answer: Students who finish early may work independently using a single page Read-Along Guide as described in chapter 4. They may also do extended vocabulary work, write an extra journal response, read a book from another group, create a book review brochure (see Appendix B), or create a commercial relating to the book they have read. As you grow comfortable using the Instructional Unit Plan, you may be able to anticipate when a group may complete their reading and Guide early. You can easily add extra practice pages and prompts or other extension activities to help you align your groups.

Creating Literacy Bins containing activities to build or extend student background and to provide for practice in fluency might be a solution that you could work with in a couple of ways. You could either build activities like these into the schedule and integrate the activities with the reading instruction or you could simply have students work through some fluency-building or extension activities once they have completed their reading unit. We have found that students enjoy the activities and are eager to tackle them.

Question: Does everyone in my school need to follow the Quality Comprehension Model in their instruction?

Answer: No, it is not necessary for every teacher in your school to follow this format. Increasing your students' awareness of their own comprehension will help students long after they leave your class. Even one consistent year of working with the Quality Comprehension Model will be beneficial to students and provide them with a foundation for future skill growth. As the four components of the Model cover methodologies that are universal, classes that may not follow the Model will still likely address many of the concepts. Working with colleagues and having support within your building is very helpful. Because students feel comfortable with the repetitive format and support built into the Read-Along Guide, using the Guides throughout the year offers them many opportunities to succeed.

Question: Are there any common problems with or drawbacks to using Read-Along Guides?

Answer: Many of the comprehension skills are difficult for intermediate readers, and they may have some trouble with the concepts and application. The first several experiences with the Guides may require more modeling and sharing. Because the format is similar with each Guide, the students quickly embrace the style and use it with growing success.

We have made adjustments to the size and spacing of the Guides to better suit the amount of space our students need to complete their practice responses as well as their journal entries. You will want to plan and space your Guides to best meet your students' needs.

Question: How can we fit in traditional "favorite" literature if we use leveled texts or shorter nonfiction books for reading groups?

Answer: With the Quality Comprehension Model, you may use any literature selections that you feel are appropriate for this approach to reading instruction. We try to limit the use of lengthy novels because they may take several weeks or more to complete due to the strong focus on comprehension strategies. Even if your favorite novels are not used for this instruction, you can incorporate them into your lessons in other ways. Classroom read-alouds, author studies, and independent silent reading offer the opportunity to include other literature into your balanced reading program.

Question: How do students react to the Read-Along Guide?

Answer: Students really enjoy the Read-Along Guide. The written response section, opportunities for illustrations, and various extension and assessment activities are very popular. Students also find the repetitive format and clear directions comforting. Because there are many opportunities for students to practice their skills and the expectations for using the Guides are clear, students are generally successful when working with them.

However, here are a few helpful hints for ensuring that students will enjoy working with the Read-Along Guide:

- Avoid using the same strategies back to back.
- Be sure to offer enough writing space for students to write comfortably.
- Always allow students the chance to share and respond to one another's work.

Question: Can I assess students based on their performance in a Read-Along Guide?

Answer: The Read-Along Guide will offer much valuable assessment data. Because the skills are practiced and repeated, you will be able to identify students who are progressing and those who are having difficulty (and in which areas they're having difficulty). Through these, you'll be able to assess the students' independent use of the strategies. For some of our instructional units, we've also created end-of-unit assessments that are modeled after state tests. For other units, we rely on project-based assessments, such as making a commercial, a teaching book, or a book review to assess the students' progress. We are careful to balance our assessments and also keep in check our objective of helping our students improve their reading comprehension.

The Read-Along Guide will also help students prepare for state tests in many ways. Their exposure to a variety of genres (you must use a variety of genres to teach each of the specific strategies) and the vocabulary to identify these strategies will be advantageous to students. Repetitive practice and review of comprehension strategies will also aid students in all reading, including unfamiliar passages they may encounter on state tests.

Question: Creating material seems time-consuming. How do I create enough materials?

Answer: Collecting enough materials seems like an overwhelming task to some teachers we've met. Most have found collaborating with other teachers to be an ideal solution. If this type of collaboration is not possible, start slow and build over time. Setting a goal to create a set number of Guides per year works well. After a few years, you will have quite a collection.

Some schools offer their teachers extra time to do curriculum work or offer in-service credit for time spent working on classroom materials. This has also been an avenue some districts have taken, especially during a start-up phase.

Keeping your materials in electronic form makes it easy to cut, paste, and reuse previously created material. Like most anything, the process gets faster over time.

Question: Where do you see the future of teaching reading comprehension to intermediate readers heading in relation to the Model?

Answer: We continue to monitor our students' progress and believe that increased attention to fluency, motivation, and building background knowledge will keep us moving in the right direction. We are also interested in using new genres of books. For example, the use of illustrations in graphic novels can be incorporated into the visualization strategy. As new genres of text become available and technologies such as e-books introduce new and exciting methods of engaging with literature, these too can be blended into our Read-Along Guides. Additionally, we see there are many crossovers with the area of critical literacy. As students progress into the intermediate levels, the informational and content-driven nature of the curriculum welcomes the introduction of this into both their reading and writing.

Reproducible Read-Along Guides*

* Please note that you will need to make multiple copies of each page to align with the length of your instruction.

Introductory Read-Along Guide
(For Use With Strategies 1–8)

_____'s Read-Along Guide

Reading is an active process. It's kind of like skateboarding, playing soccer, or shooting hoops! You have to know the techniques and then you have to practice, practice, and practice some more to perfect them. Only then will you be a good athlete!

Like these sports, there are techniques or strategies that help you perfect reading. We are going to learn about the strategies that make good readers and we're going to practice, practice, and practice them!

Strategies Good Readers Use:

Strategy 1: Using Fix-Up Methods When Meaning Is Challenged

Strategy 2: Finding Word Meaning and Build Vocabulary Using Context Clues

Strategy 3: Using Visual Text Clues to Figure Out Meaning

Strategy 4: Asking Questions to Engage in the Text

Strategy 5: Making Connections to Aid Understanding

Strategy 6: Visualizing to Support the Text

Strategy 7: Making Predictions

Strategy 8: Synthesizing to Gain New Meaning

Title _____

Author _____

Introductory Read-Along Guide (continued)
(For Use With Strategies 1–8)

Strategy 1: Good Readers Use Fix-Up Methods When Meaning Is Challenged

Good readers pay attention to their ability to understand what they're reading. At times, even the best readers may be unsure of what they've read. Their thoughts might wander or maybe they get distracted by noises across the classroom. Before they know it, they're at the end of a page and can't remember what they've read. Other times, even the best readers might become confused by what they've read. "This doesn't make any sense," they might think silently. No matter which problem happens, whenever good readers don't get what they've read, they take action and do something to help fix this problem. They don't keep reading. Three good fix-up methods are:

1. Reread the passage—Rereading the passage after you've regained your focus might solve the problem. Also, if you read something incorrectly, rereading the passage might help correct the problem. Even rereading it aloud might help.
2. Go back to other parts of the text—Quickly scanning an earlier paragraph, page, or chapter, might help you find just the right detail that clears up a misunderstanding or confusion.
3. Read on for no more than two sentences—Often, a misunderstanding might become clear through something else that you read in the text. In this case, reading on might fix the problem. Still you have to be careful you don't keep reading and never clear up the problem. It's best to go only about two sentences before you stop and try another fix-up method.

Remember it's not only important to use one of these fix-up methods, but it's also just as important to recognize when you don't understand something, and take action!

Directions: Let's practice using these fix-up methods during our reading. Use the prompt below to record any confusing parts you read, and be sure to include the strategy you used to help fix the problem.

When I Read (Page #)	I Was Confused Because...	The Fix-Up Method I Used Was...

Strategy 2: Good Readers Find Word Meaning and Build Vocabulary Using Context Clues

Finding word meaning is a critical skill that will help you better understand what you're reading. Although it's one of the hardest strategies to master, it's also one of the most helpful. Being able to figure out new or unfamiliar words is kind of like good detective work. Often there are clues within the passage, and it's simply a matter of decoding them. Although it takes a lot of practice, it's a skill that will come in handy often. Also, it will make it possible for you to read and understand just about anything! Imagine never being stumped by a word again! Some of the methods are:

1. Sound out the word—You might know the word but not recognize it in print.
2. "Chunk" the word—Break up the word. Is there a root word, a prefix, or a suffix?
3. Link the word to a known word—Do you know other words that look or sound like this one? (Example: studious looks and sounds like study)
4. Look for smaller words that you recognize—Is the word made up of a smaller word you know? (Example: compound words)
5. Use context clues—Use clues from the sentence or surrounding sentences.
6. Think about what makes sense—Ask yourself, "What would make sense in the sentence?"
7. Other sources—Ask a teacher, use a dictionary, use a glossary, etc.

Directions: Let's practice using these methods during our reading. Use the space below to write your new or unfamiliar word, and try to use one or more of the methods to figure out the meaning of the word. Be sure to list the number of the method(s) you used and give a definition of the word.

Page #	New or Unfamiliar Word	Method(s) Used	Definition

Introductory Read-Along Guide (continued)
(For Use With Strategies 1–8)

Strategy 3: Good Readers Use Visual Text Clues to Figure Out Meaning

Good readers pay attention to any features of the page or the text. For example, good readers pay attention to when a character is speaking because of the quotation marks and the indented space. Also, good readers look at punctuation and read expressively (even silently to themselves) using the punctuation clues. For example, when coming across a comma, good readers will pause. Or, when seeing an exclamation mark, good readers know to add enthusiasm. Likewise, really good readers will notice that something has been written in boldface or italicized type and wonder why that is so—there is usually a good reason.

Directions: Before reading, scan the pages and try to find as many of these features as you can on the page and write down the page numbers where you found them. Then, try to figure out their importance.

Text Clue (Fiction)	Page #	Explain the Importance
Punctuation (. , ; : " " ... ! ? –)		
Boldface Text/Italics/Capitals		
Spacing Features or Unusual Spacing		
Titles or Subtitles		
Other		

Text Clue/Feature (Nonfiction)	Page #	Explain the Importance
Boldface Text/Italics/Capitals		
Titles or Subtitles		
Photographs/Illustrations		
Maps		
Captions		
Sidebars		
Table of Contents/Glossary/Index		
Other _____		

Introductory Read-Along Guide (continued)
(For Use With Strategies 1–8)

Strategy 4: Good Readers Ask Questions to Engage in the Text

Good readers ask silent questions (to themselves) before, during, and after reading. They question the content, the author, the events, the issues, and the ideas in the text. Sometimes your questions are answered immediately. Sometimes they are answered by the end of the book. Still, other times, you may need to research a little bit more to find an answer to your questions or you may need to think of them as open questions and hold onto them for the future. No matter when your question is answered, using this strategy makes you a better reader.

Directions: Let's see if you can catch yourself wondering about or even asking a silent question to yourself about something you've read. Use the prompt below to record times when this happened. Be sure to include what you wondered about.

When I Read (Page #)	I Wondered <u>Why</u>, <u>What</u>, <u>When</u>, <u>How</u>, <u>Who</u>, <u>Where</u>, or <u>If</u>...

Strategy 5: Good Readers Make Connections to Aid Understanding

Good readers use prior knowledge and experiences to better understand what they're reading. Sometimes it's helpful to think about how you "know" or "connect with" a character, event, or some part of the book you're reading. Your connection could be any of these three:

1. Text-to-Self Connection (T–S)—These include experiences you share from your background. For example, you might be a really good soccer or football player and share experiences with a character from a book who plays the same sport. Also, you might share a feeling with a character, such as being frightened or excited.
2. Text-to-Text Connection (T–T)—These include experiences you read about in other writings. For example, you may be familiar with fairy tale characters from reading books about them. Likewise, you may enjoy reading books that are in a series where you need to know what happened in earlier volumes. Also, you might have a favorite author who may write about similar things.
3. Text-to-World Connection (T–W)—These include experiences you know and share with others simply because of your common worldly experiences. These might be things you seem to know to do without being told, just like your automatic reflexes, such as blinking. Or it might be things that everyone just seems to know, like that the President's job is pretty important.

These types of connections may overlap, but it's fun to think about how you know or "connect with" something.

Directions: Let's practice thinking about connections we make during our reading. Use the prompt below to record your connection and label T-S, T-T, or T-W to identify what type of connection you've made.

When I Read (Page #)	I Thought About...	Type of Connection

Strategy 6: Good Readers Visualize to Support the Text

Good readers use this strategy to help them fully understand the words, actions, characters, setting, and other elements of the text they're reading. It's like having a movie playing in your head. Sometimes you can create a movie from some descriptive words the author has written. Other times, simply sharing an experience (such as through a connection) makes it easy to create a picture in your mind. Sometimes you get short, little movie pictures, while other times your movie might follow along with several pages of text.

Directions: Let's practice visualizing (creating pictures in our mind). Use the prompt below to record the times when you visualized.

When I Read (Page #)	I Could Picture...

Introductory Read-Along Guide (continued)
(For Use With Strategies 1–8)

Strategy 7: Good Readers Make Predictions

Readers are always guessing about what's going to happen next in their story. Guessing (or making predictions) about what's going to happen and then discovering whether the prediction is right or wrong is something that good readers do without thinking about it. It's like a game they play while they're reading. What's nice about the game is that you don't lose points if your prediction is wrong. When our predictions are wrong and we're surprised by something in a story, it often makes us enjoy the story that much more!

Readers' predictions are based on other events that might have happened in the story. They could also come from what readers know about a character. A reader's own experience might also help them make predictions. Making predictions and testing them helps us understand a story.

Directions: Let's practice making some predictions. Use the prompt below and write down your prediction.

When I Read (Page #)	I Predicted That...

Strategy 8: Good Readers Synthesize to Gain New Meaning

Synthesizing means that you actively collect and organize information you've learned from your reading. It's like filing information into folders you've stored in your mind. As you do this, you begin to discover ideas and even reshape your understanding to create new ideas. As you read, this process occurs continuously—you expand and reshape your ever-growing body of knowledge. It's like your knowledge is "morphing" into something new and exciting!

Synthesizing for Fiction
Directions: After we finish reading the text, let's practice synthesizing by thinking about the main character using information from all of the chapters. Using the graphic organizer, let's identify some of the main character's character traits and support our thinking with details from the chapters. This exercise will call on our synthesizing skills.

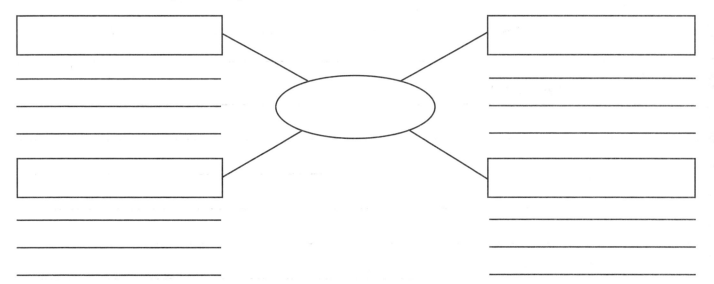

Synthesizing for Nonfiction
Directions: Using your sticky notes, identify 3–5 new, significant facts that you learned from your reading. Think about how these facts added to your understanding. Be prepared to complete your Read-Along Guide (after group instructional time) by considering how you would answer the following prompt:

On page _____ the significant fact I found was _____

_____.

I already knew that _____

_____.

What I didn't know was _____

_____.

This new fact is important because _____

_____

Read-Along Guide A—Nonfiction
(For Use With Strategies 9, 10, and 2)

_____'s Read-Along Guide for Nonfiction

Nonfiction tells about people, places, or events that exist, that are happening, or that have existed or happened in the past. Nonfiction can also express an opinion or true feelings.

Nonfiction Scavenger Hunt—Ask some friends, family, and other special people the title of their favorite nonfiction books!

Name	Title of Favorite Nonfiction Book

The nonfiction book I'm reading is

Title: _____

Author: _____

In this Read-Along Guide, we'll also be working on three strategies:
1. Strategy 9: Finding the Important or Main Idea
2. Strategy 10: Identifying Facts and Details
3. Strategy 2: Finding Word Meaning and Building Vocabulary Using Context Clues

Read-Along Guide A—Nonfiction (continued)
(For Use With Strategies 9, 10, and 2)

In this Read-Along Guide we are going to work on three strategies that will help us become better readers. Each strategy has been described below. In addition to learning about these strategies, you also have some practice pages in this Guide to try them out.

1. **Strategy 9: Finding the Important or Main Idea.** Remember that the main idea is a pretty big idea that tells what a paragraph or an entire reading passage is mainly about. The main idea is not a small detail, although all of the small details together make up the main idea. Sometimes a main idea is stated, like in a topic sentence, a closing sentence, or somewhere else within the passage. Other times it is not. As you read your book, you will be asked to locate or summarize the main idea of a reading passage and to locate some specific details that support it.

2. **Strategy 10: Identifying Facts and Details.** Writers use facts and details for many reasons. Facts and details support a main idea and, in so doing, provide more information about the main idea. Facts and details may

   1. Describe a person, place, or thing
   2. Explain how to do something
   3. Tell the order in which things happen
   4. Share an experience, idea, or opinion

   An easy way to find facts and details is to look for sentences that tell about the who, what, where, when, why, and how of the main idea. As you read your book, you will be asked to create some questions (using <u>who</u>, <u>what</u>, <u>where</u>, <u>when</u>, <u>why</u>, and <u>how</u>) about the passage you read. Answers to your questions should highlight the facts and details that appear within the passage. You'll get the chance to ask your questions to classmates during guided-reading instructional time. See if your classmates can recall the facts and details!

3. **Strategy 2: Finding Word Meaning and Building Vocabulary Using Context Clues.** While reading, you will usually come upon a word (or many words) that you don't know. It is important for you to try and figure out what the word means. Doing so not only helps you understand the passage, but it also helps to build your vocabulary. We will continue to practice this skill on the last page of our Read-Along Guide.

Quality Comprehension: A Strategic Model of Reading Instruction Using Read-Along Guides, Grades 3–6 by Sandra K. Athans and Denise Ashe Devine. © 2008 by the International Reading Association. May be copied for classroom use.

Strategy 9: Finding the Important or Main Idea

Directions: Summarize or locate the main idea for your reading passage and then find three examples from the passage that support the main idea.

The main idea in pages _____ to _____ is

_____

_____

_____

Support/p. _____	Support/p. _____	Support/p. _____

For this passage, create two who, what, when, where, or why questions to test your classmate's ability to recall facts and details.

1. _____

2. _____

Directions: As you read through the text, look for important details (names, dates, events) and record them in the Key Facts section of the chart. Decide which key facts seem most important and write a brief statement describing the main idea of this passage. This statement should explain the overall idea the author is trying to express.

Key Facts	Main Idea

Strategy 10: Identifying Facts and Details

For this passage, create two who, what, when, where, or why questions to test your classmate's ability to recall fact and details.

1. _____

2. _____

Possible Ideas For Your Journal Entries Could Be
1. What was going through your mind as you read this?
2. What questions did your have when you finished reading?
3. What would you do if this happened to you?
4. How did you feel while reading this part?
5. What was the most important idea?
6. How are you similar to one of the characters?
7. What predictions do you have about the next reading?
8. Other

Pages _____ to _____   Date _____

My response to today's reading is _____

_____

_____

_____

_____

_____

_____

Pages _____ to _____   Date _____

My response to today's reading is _____

_____

_____

_____

_____

_____

_____

Strategy 2: Finding Word Meaning and Building Vocabulary Using Context Clues

Practice Using Our Word Identification Strategies:

1. Sound Out the Word
2. "Chunk" the Word Use Context Clues
3. Link the Word to a Known Word
4. Look For Smaller Words That You Recognize

5. Use Context Clues
6. Think About What Makes Sense
7. Other: _____
8. Other: _____

Page #	New or Unfamiliar Word	Method(s) Used	Definition

Read-Along Guide B—Generic
(For Use With Strategies 12, 15, 7, and 2)

_____'s Read-Along Guide

Theme _____

In this Read-Along Guide, we'll be working on four strategies:

1. Strategy 12: Understanding Sequence

2. Strategy 15: Recognizing Cause-and-Effect Relationships

3. Strategy 7: Making Predictions

4. Strategy 2: Finding Word Meaning and Building Vocabulary Using Context Clues

Read-Along Guide B—Generic (continued)
(For Use With Strategies 12, 15, 7, and 2)

1. **Strategy 12: Understanding Sequence**—The order in which things happen in a passage is called sequence. Sometimes clue words such as <u>first</u>, <u>next</u>, <u>last</u>, or others clearly signal an order. Other times, there are no signals and you must carefully retrace actions, steps, or events to check their order. This can be tricky, especially if you are asked to place multiple events in the correct order. That's because you must always check what came before the event as well as what came after it, too. Yikes, that's a lot of information to juggle! As you read your book, you'll be asked to order events around those provided by your teacher.

2. **Strategy 15: Recognizing Cause-and-Effect Relationships**—Often events or ideas in a passage are somehow linked together, such as in a cause-and-effect relationship. Here, what happens is called the effect. Also, why it happens is called the cause. Sometimes clue words such as <u>since</u>, <u>because</u>, <u>as a result</u>, or others clearly show that connection between what happened and why. Other times, you can easily find the cause and the effect by asking yourself two questions:

    1. What happened? (This will tell you the effect.)
    2. Why did it happen? (This will tell you the cause.)

    As you read your book, you'll be given either a cause or effect found in your book, and then you'll be asked to identify its cause or effect connection.

3. **Strategy 7: Making Predictions**—Trying to figure out what will happen next in a story is just plain fun! Finding out if you're right or wrong is often what keeps you interested in a reading passage. Clues certainly come in handy when you're trying to make good predictions. Clues can be found in a title or in facts and details in the passage. They can also come from characters' actions or thoughts. Clues can be anywhere!

    In the Reader Response section, you'll be making some predictions about the next reading passage.

4. **Strategy 2: Finding Word Meaning and Building Vocabulary Using Context Clues**—Let's keep practicing this strategy! Here, we'll even learn some interesting new words! As you read your book, you'll be asked to figure out the meaning of words using clues.

Strategy 12: Understanding Sequence

Directions: Let's practice Sequencing Events. Complete the chart.

Pages _____

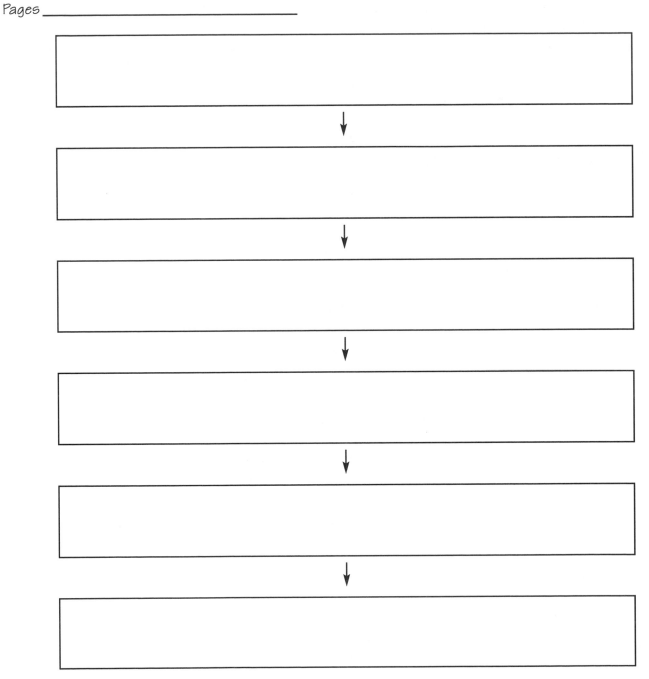

Strategy 15: Recognizing Cause-and-Effect Relationships

Directions: Let's practice Cause and Effect. Complete the chart.

Pages _____

Cause (Why)	Effect (What)

Strategy 7: Making Predictions

Reader Response
1. What was going through your mind as you read this?
2. What questions did your have when you finished reading?
3. What would you do if this happened to you?
4. How did you feel while reading this part?
5. What was the most important idea?
6. How are you similar to a character?
7. Other

Pages _____ to _____   Date _____

My response to today's reading is _____

_____

_____

_____

_____

_____

_____

_____

_____

My prediction about the next reading is _____

_____

_____

_____

_____

_____

_____

_____

_____

_____

Strategy 2: Finding Word Meaning and Building Vocabulary Using Context Clues

Practice Using Our Word Identification Methods:

1. Sound Out the Word
2. "Chunk" the Word Use Context Clues
3. Link the Word to a Known Word
4. Look For Smaller Words That You Recognize

5. Use Context Clues
6. Think About What Makes Sense
7. Other: _____
8. Other: _____

Page #	New or Unfamiliar Word	Method(s) Used	Definition

Individual Strategy Pages
(For Use With Strategies 11, 13, 14, 16, and 17)

Strategy 11: Telling Fact From Opinion

Distinguishing fact from opinion is sometimes harder then we imagine. Facts express ideas that can be proven, whereas an opinion tell us what someone thinks or feels. Often, there are keywords that help us determine if something is a fact or an opinion. For example, using words like <u>greatest</u> and phrases like <u>I believe...</u> or <u>I think...</u> or <u>I feel...</u> all signal an opinion.

As you read record a fact and an opinion found in the text, as well as your own opinion about what you have read.

Pages: _____

Fact: _____

_____

Opinion: _____

_____

My Opinion: _____

_____

_____

Pages: _____

Fact: _____

_____

Opinion: _____

_____

My Opinion: _____

_____

_____

Next, challenge a member for your group...

See if they can tell which ideas are facts and which are opinions (mix up the order sometimes).
Then ask them if they agree or disagree with your opinion. Try to stump them with some that do not use any key words.

Strategy 13: Comparing and Contrasting

Directions: Your teacher will provide labels for the items you're going to compare. Then you can complete the Venn diagram.

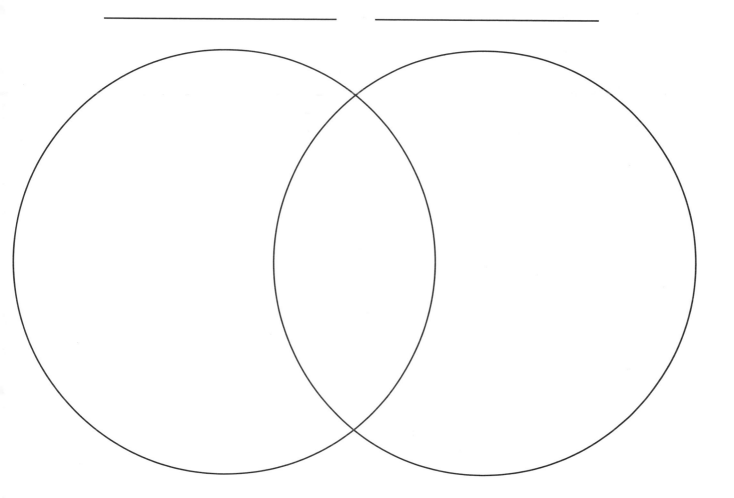

Strategy 14: Interpreting Figurative Language

Books of all kinds often use figurative language, which is a kind of colorful or playful language that authors use so that readers can make great pictures in their mind, chuckle out loud, or just enjoy creative ideas. Types of figurative language often found are similes, metaphors, idioms, and personification.

Directions: See if you can find some examples of figurative language (similes, metaphors, idioms, or personification). Write down the page number, mark it (S) for simile, (M) for metaphor, (I) for idiom, or (P) for personification, and be sure to write the sentence that includes the figurative language. Last, try to interpret the meaning.

Title _____ Page # _____ Type of Figurative Language _____
How it's used in my reading: _____
_____
What it means: _____
_____

Title _____ Page # _____ Type of Figurative Language _____
How it's used in my reading: _____
_____
What it means: _____
_____

Title _____ Page # _____ Type of Figurative Language _____
How it's used in my reading: _____
_____
What it means: _____
_____

Title _____ Page # _____ Type of Figurative Language _____
How it's used in my reading: _____
_____
What it means: _____
_____

Simile—phrase that compares things using the words <u>like</u> or <u>as</u>
Example: _____

Metaphor—phrase that compares things without using special words (like similes do)
Example: _____

Idiom—saying that has another meanings and is not literal
Example: _____

Personification—phrase with human-like traits given to non-humans
Example: _____

Strategy 16: Drawing Conclusions and Making Inferences

Directions: As you read your book, you'll be asked to practice using your ability to read between the lines (to infer) and explain the meaning of a passage or quotation from the text.

Text Quote: "_____

_____

_____ ." (p. _____)

Meaning:
(I think... because...)

_____

_____

_____

_____

_____

_____

_____

_____

_____

Text Quote: "_____

_____

_____ ." (p. _____)

Meaning:
(I think... because...)

_____

_____

_____

_____

_____

_____

_____

_____

Strategy 17: Summarizing

Pages _____ Date _____

In these pages,

_____

_____

_____

_____

_____

Pages _____ Date _____

In these pages,

_____

_____

_____

_____

_____

Pages _____ Date _____

In these pages,

_____

_____

_____

_____

_____

Pages _____ Date _____

In these pages,

_____

_____

_____

_____

_____

Reproducible Planning and Assessment Charts

Literacy Bin Tic-Tac-Toe Board

Name_____

Unit_____

Instructional Unit Plan

Title/Theme _____ Level(s) _____

Approximate Time _____

Strategies   1. _____

2. _____

3. _____

4. _____

Chapter Breakout (Title/Level)

1. _____   2. _____   3. _____

Instructional Plans

Before	During	After

Notes on Read-Along Guide Use _____

_____

_____

_____

Attachments _____

_____

Read-Along Guide Rubric

Name _____ Date _____

Title _____

Strategies & Skills—Practice
Degree to which student is able to demonstrate in writing
use of strategies & skills.

Strategy 1 _____   4   3   2   1

Strategy 2 _____   4   3   2   1

Strategy 3 _____   4   3   2   1

Strategy 4 _____   4   3   2   1

Comments _____

_____

_____

Written Response (Journal Entry)

Addressing the Topic—main idea present, task answered

                                      4   3   2   1

Details—ideas developed with support details

                                      4   3   2   1

Organization—logical, orderly, with transitions

                                      4   3   2   1

Language Use—descriptive with content vocabulary

                                      4   3   2   1

Comments _____

_____

_____

4—Consistently exceeds expected performance

3—Demonstrates successful performance

2—Is progressing toward successful performance with difficulty

1—Is not showing progress toward successful performance

Student Daily Checklist

Name _____

_____ ( ) prepared ( ) participation

_____ ( ) prepared ( ) participation

_____ ( ) prepared ( ) participation

_____ ( ) prepared ( ) participation

_____ ( ) prepared ( ) participation

_____ ( ) prepared ( ) participation

Name _____

_____ ( ) prepared ( ) participation

_____ ( ) prepared ( ) participation

_____ ( ) prepared ( ) participation

_____ ( ) prepared ( ) participation

_____ ( ) prepared ( ) participation

_____ ( ) prepared ( ) participation

Name _____

_____ ( ) prepared ( ) participation

_____ ( ) prepared ( ) participation

_____ ( ) prepared ( ) participation

_____ ( ) prepared ( ) participation

_____ ( ) prepared ( ) participation

_____ ( ) prepared ( ) participation

Name _____

_____ ( ) prepared ( ) participation

_____ ( ) prepared ( ) participation

_____ ( ) prepared ( ) participation

_____ ( ) prepared ( ) participation

_____ ( ) prepared ( ) participation

_____ ( ) prepared ( ) participation

Name _____

_____ ( ) prepared ( ) participation

_____ ( ) prepared ( ) participation

_____ ( ) prepared ( ) participation

_____ ( ) prepared ( ) participation

_____ ( ) prepared ( ) participation

_____ ( ) prepared ( ) participation

Name _____

_____ ( ) prepared ( ) participation

_____ ( ) prepared ( ) participation

_____ ( ) prepared ( ) participation

_____ ( ) prepared ( ) participation

_____ ( ) prepared ( ) participation

_____ ( ) prepared ( ) participation

Oral Reading Practices Assessment

Title _____ Date _____

Name _____

N = Not at all
S = Some of the time
C = Consistently

Reads fluently (pace, pitch, phrasing)_____
_____

Reads with expression_____

Reads punctuation_____

Identifies sight words _____

Substitutes meaningful words _____

Decodes _____

Self-corrects _____

Notes_____
_____
_____

Title _____ Date _____

Name _____

N = Not at all
S = Some of the time
C = Consistently

Reads fluently (pace, pitch, phrasing)_____
_____

Reads with expression_____

Reads punctuation_____

Identifies sight words _____

Substitutes meaningful words _____

Decodes _____

Self-corrects _____

Notes_____
_____
_____

Title _____ Date _____

Name _____

N = Not at all
S = Some of the time
C = Consistently

Reads fluently (pace, pitch, phrasing)_____
_____

Reads with expression_____

Reads punctuation_____

Identifies sight words _____

Substitutes meaningful words _____

Decodes _____

Self-corrects _____

Notes_____
_____

Title _____ Date _____

Name _____

N = Not at all
S = Some of the time
C = Consistently

Reads fluently (pace, pitch, phrasing)_____
_____

Reads with expression_____

Reads punctuation_____

Identifies sight words _____

Substitutes meaningful words _____

Decodes _____

Self-corrects _____

Notes_____
_____

Book Review Brochure Instructions

Name_____ Date_____

Fourth Grade   ELA-[book title]_____

Project Description—Create a Book Review Brochure

The Front Cover of Your Brochure Will Have

1. An Illustration (picture). Choose one of your favorite parts of the book and draw a picture of it. Please make this colorful by using colored pencils or crayons. Also, be sure that your picture is historically accurate.

2. The Book Title. Watch your spelling. Be sure the title stands out by using dark colors or fancy writing. Look at some of the books we've been reading and see how the titles are featured on the covers.

3. The Author's Name. Watch your spelling. Look at some of the books we've been reading and see how the authors' names are featured on the covers.

4. A Persuasive Statement to Encourage Others to Read Your Brochure.

The Inside of Your Brochure Will Have

1. A Book Review About the Book. In your book review, you will be sharing your understanding of and opinion about your book. You will be using the entries you have written in your Read-Along Guide and other factual information to write your review.

Book Review Brochure Instructions (continued)

Name _____ Date _____

Fourth Grade   ELA-[book title] _____

Collection Sheet For Your Book Review—After a short introduction, your book review should answer three basic questions:

1. What Is the Book About? _____

_____

_____

_____

_____

_____

2. What Do I Like About This Book? _____

_____

_____

_____

_____

_____

_____

3. What Is the Book's Theme or Message? _____

_____

_____

_____

_____

_____

Never tell readers everything that happens in your book or all of your reasons for liking it. Say just enough to help them decide for themselves if they want to read it.

Book Review Brochure Instructions (continued)

Name _____ Date _____

Fourth Grade   ELA-[book title] _____

```
┌─────────────────────────────────────────┐
│                                           │
│        Overall Grade  _____         │
│                                           │
└─────────────────────────────────────────┘
```

Book Review Brochure Rubric

1. Illustration shows careful thought and represents the book. Illustration is colorful and historically correct. _____

2. Book title shows complete title, written and spelled correctly, and is featured well. Author's name is spelled correctly and is featured well. _____

3. Persuasive statement is well-written, shows thought, and uses correct grammar and punctuation. _____

4. Theme of the book has been identified with support from the text, and sufficient details have been included to encourage others to read the book. _____

Ashmore, D. (2003, January). *Reading is thinking: A metacognitive approach to reading with an emphasis on non-fiction texts.* Paper presented at a seminar sponsored by Stephanie Harvey Consulting, Syracuse, NY.

Atkinson, E.S. (2000). An investigation into the relationship between teacher motivation and pupil motivation. *Educational Psychology, 20,* 45–57.

Clarke, J., & Birkel, R. (n.d.). *How to level books in your classroom collection.* Handout from inservice professional development, Chittenango Central School District, Chittenango, NY.

Curriculum Associates, Inc. (2000a). *Comprehensive assessment of reading strategies II* (CARS Series II). North Billerica, MA: Author.

Curriculum Associates, Inc. (2000b). *Strategies to achieve reading success: STARS series books 3, 4, & 5.* North Billerica, MA: Author.

Diller, D. (2005). *Practice with purpose: Literacy work stations for grades 3–6.* Portland, ME: Stenhouse.

Fountas, I.C., & Pinnell, G.S. (1996). *Guided reading: Good first teaching for all children.* Portsmouth, NH: Heinemann.

Fountas, I.C., & Pinnell, G.S. (2001). *Guiding readers and writers, grades 3–6: Teaching comprehension, genre, and content literacy.* Portsmouth, NH: Heinemann.

Fountas, I.C., & Pinnell, G.S. (2002). *Leveled books for readers grades 3–6: A companion volume to Guiding Readers and Writers.* Portsmouth, NH: Heinemann.

Fountas, I.C., & Pinnell, G.S. (2006). *The Fountas & Pinnell leveled book list, K–8.* Portsmouth, NH: Heinemann.

Gambrell, L.B. (2007, May). *Strategy-based instruction.* Breakfast meeting sponsored by Sundance/Newbridge at the annual convention of the International Reading Association, Toronto, ON, Canada.

Gardner, H. (2006). *Multiple intelligences: New horizons.* New York: Basic Books.

Harvey, S., & Goudvis, A. (2000). *Strategies that work: Teaching comprehension to enhance understanding.* York, ME: Stenhouse.

Heffernan, L. (2004). *Critical literacy and writers' workshop: Bringing purpose and passion to student writing.* Newark, DE: International Reading Association.

Leu, D.J., Jr. (2001). Internet project: Preparing students for new literacies in a global village. *The Reading Teacher, 54,* 568–572.

McGraw-Hill. (1998). *New York state testing program: English language arts sampler.* New York: Author.

McLaughlin, M., & DeVoogd, G. (2004). *Critical literacy: Enhancing students' comprehension of text.* New York: Scholastic.

Monroe, J. (2002, April). *Guiding reading: Teaching strategies for grades 3–8.* Paper presented at a seminar sponsored by Staff Development Resources, Syracuse, NY.

Nelley, E., & Smith, A. (2000). *Rigby PM benchmark kit: A reading assessment resource for grades K–5.* Barrington, IL: Rigby Education.

New York State Education Department. (1996). *Learning standards for English language arts.* Albany: Author. Retrieved February 5, 2008, from www.emsc.nysed.gov/ciai/ela/pub/elalearn.pdf

New York State Education Department. (2005). *English language arts core curriculum.* Retrieved December 6, 2007, from www.emsc.nysed.gov/ciai/ela/elacore.htm

Pike, K.M., & Mumper, J. (2004). *Making nonfiction and other informational texts come alive: A practical approach to reading, writing, and using nonfiction and other informational texts across the curriculum.* Boston: Allyn & Bacon.

Strickland, D.S., Ganske, K., & Monroe, J.K. (2002). *Supporting struggling readers and writers: Strategies for classroom intervention 3–6.* Portland, ME: Stenhouse; Newark, DE: International Reading Association.

Tomlinson, C.A. (1999). *The differentiated classroom: Responding to the needs of all learners.* Alexandria, VA: Association for Supervision and Curriculum Development.

Trehearne, M. (2007, May). *Literacy learning grades 3–6: What we know that works.* Paper presented at the annual convention of the International Reading Association, Toronto, ON, Canada.

West, T. (1998). *Teaching tall tales* New York: Scholastic.

Willingham, D.T. (2006/2007, Winter). The usefulness of brief instruction in reading comprehension strategies. *American Educator*, 39–50.

Literature Cited

Adoff, A. (1995). *Street music: City poems.* New York: HarperCollins.

Bains, R. (1996). *Harriet Tubman: The road to freedom.* New York: Troll.

Berleth, R.J. (1990). *Samuel's choice.* New York: Scholastic.

Blume, J. (1990). *Freckle juice.* New York: Macmillan.

Brady, E.W. (1976). *Toliver's secret.* New York: Random House.

Catling, P.S. (1988). *The chocolate touch.* New York: Yearling.

Cleary, B. (1990). *Muggie Maggie.* New York: HarperTrophy.

Creech, S. (2001). *Love that dog.* New York: HarperCollins.

Dalgliesh, A. (1954). *The courage of Sarah Noble.* New York: Simon & Schuster.

DiCamillo, K. (2000). *Because of Winn-Dixie.* New York: Candlewick.

Edmonds, W.D. (1941). *The matchlock gun.* New York: Dodd, Mead & Company.

Fuerst, J.B. (2002). *African American cowboys: True heroes of the Old West.* Parsippany, NJ: Celebration Press.

George, L. (2003). *Native Americans in New York.* New York: Rosen Publishing Group.

Griffin, J.B. (1977). *Phoebe the spy.* New York: Scholastic.

Hirschfield, L. (2001). *Cherokee heroes: Three who made a difference.* Bothwell, WA: Wright Group/McGraw-Hill.

Kellogg, S. (1992). *Mike Fink.* New York: Scholastic.

Klingel, C., & Noyed, R.B. (2001). *Ellis Island.* Chanhassen, MN: Child's World.

Levine, E. (1993). *If your name was changed at Ellis Island.* New York: Scholastic.

Levine, E. (1998). *If you lived with the Iroquois.* New York: Scholastic.

Levinson, N.S. (1996). *Thomas Alva Edison: Great inventor.* New York: Scholastic.

Levy, E. (1992). *If you were there when they signed the Constitution.* New York: Scholastic.

Logan, C. (2001). *Welcome to the International Space Station.* Bothell, WA: Wright Group.

Maestro, B., & Ryan, S. (1999). *Coming to America: The story of immigration.* New York: Scholastic.

Marchetti, V. (2001). *Maurice and Katia Krafft, volcanologists.* Bothell, WA: Wright Group/McGraw-Hill.

Marsh, J.P. (2002). *North to the pole with Matthew Henson.* Parsippany, NJ: Celebration Press.

Miller, J. (2005). *Who's who in a suburban community.* New York: PowerKids Press.

O'Donnell, K. (2003). *Colonial life and the Revolutionary War in New York.* New York: Rosen Publishing Group.

Osborne, M.P. (2000). *Revolutionary War on Wednesday.* New York: Random House.

Park, B. (1997). *Skinnybones.* New York: Random House.

Park, B. (2004). *The kid in the red jacket.* New York: Scholastic.

Sachar, L. (2003). *Holes.* New York: Dell Yearling.

Selznick, B. (2007). *The invention of Hugo Cabret.* New York: Scholastic.

Spann, M. (2002). *If we had wings: The story of the Tuskegee Airmen.* Parsippany, NJ: Celebration Press/Pearson Learning.

Strebor, L. (2000). *Floating and paddling.* New York: McGraw-Hill.

Wallace, B. (1989). *Danger on Panther Peak.* New York: Aladdin.

Wilson, N. (2003). *New York's melting pot culture.* New York: Rosen Publishing Group.

Note. Page numbers followed by *f, t,* and *r* indicate figures, tables, and reproducibles, respectively.

POSTERS: for assessment, 205; on strategy, 6, 6f
POWERPOINT PRESENTATIONS, 205
PREDICTIONS: making, 82–88, 229r, 237r, 240r
PROJECT-BASED ASSESSMENTS, 205–207, 206f; modifications to, 207
PROMPTS, 7; for asking questions, 68, 69f; for cause-and-effect relationships, 132, 133f; for comparing and contrasting, 120–121, 121f; for conclusions and inferences, 137, 137f; for figurative language, 125–126, 126f, 127–129, 128f; for finding main idea, 100–103, 101f, 103f; for finding word meaning, 55–56, 57f; for fix-up methods, 50, 51f; for identifying facts and details, 106–108, 107f; for making connections, 73–74, 74f, 75, 76f; practice with, 47; for predictions, 84–85, 85f; in Read-Along Guides, 153–154, 154f–156f; for sequence, 116, 117f; for summarizing, 141–143, 142f; for synthesizing, 90–93, 92f–93f; tailoring Guide for, 162, 163f; for telling fact from opinion, 112–113, 112f; for visual clues, 61, 62f, 63, 64f; for visualizing, 79–81, 80f; in written response section, 174–178, 175f–178f

Q

QUALITY: of independent work, concerns with, 30
QUALITY COMPREHENSION MODEL, 17–44; in action, 25–34; components of, 21–25; current status of, 11–12; and curriculum, 42–44, 43t; development of, 1–15; evaluation of, 13–15; FAQ on, 215–219; future of, 219; initial efforts toward, 2–5; intermediate efforts toward, 5–11; single-classroom approach to, 38, 39f–218, 217; strengths of, 12–13
QUESTIONS: for text engagement, 67–71, 226r
QUIET: importance of, 32–33

R

READ-ALONG GUIDES, 145–170, 147f, 169f–170f; adapting, 164–165; and assessment, 219; creating, 149–163; development of, 1–15; early version of, 7, 8f–9f; electronic storage and retrieval of, 166–168; format of, 161; Generic, 150, 159f, 236r–241r; Introductory, 150, 222r–230r; master, 153–161, 154f–157f; Nonfiction, 150, 159f, 231r–235r; planning draft of, 160f; problems with, 218; in Quality Comprehension Model, 12, 22–24; reproducible, 221–246; rubric-based assessments for, 210–212, 211f, 250r; student reactions to, 218; tailoring, 161–162, 163f–164f. *See also* prompts; written response section
READERS THEATRE, 60
READING TEACHERS: and Model use, 26–27
REPRODUCIBLES: online versions of, 24, 166; planning and assessment charts, 247–255; Read-Along Guides, 221–246
RESPONSE. *See* written response section
RIGBY BENCHMARK PROGRAM, 27
RIGBY RUNNING RECORDS, 213
RUBRICS: for assessments for Read-Along Guides, 210–212, 211f, 250r; for book review brochure, 255r; for project-based assessment, 207
RYAN, S., 184

S

SACHAR, L., 198
SCAVENGER HUNT: nonfiction, 231r

SUPPORT: and Model use, 26–27
SYNTHESIZING, 88–95, 230r

T

TEACHERS: pooling resources with, 195; reading, and Model use, 26–27; and written response section, 183–188

TEACHING BOOKS, 205–207, 206f; by student specialists, 204

TEAMWORK: and creation of assessments and monitoring methods, 214; and creation of Read-Along Guides, 165–166, 167f

TECHNOLOGY: challenges of, 20

TEST-TAKING TIPS: for asking questions, 70–71; for cause-and-effect relationships, 134–135; for comparing and contrasting, 122–123; for conclusions and inferences, 138–141; for figurative language, 130; for finding main idea, 104–105; for finding word meaning, 58–59; for fix-up methods, 52; for identifying facts and details, 109–110; for making connections, 77–78; for predictions, 87–88; for sequence, 118–119; for summarizing, 144; for synthesizing, 94; for telling fact from opinion, 113–114; for visual clues, 66; for visualizing, 82

TEXT SELECTION, 191–202; for asking questions, 67–68; for cause-and-effect relationships, 131–132; for comparing and contrasting, 120; for conclusions and inferences, 136; curriculum and, resources on, 43t; favorite books and, 218; for figurative language, 124–125; for finding main idea, 100; for finding word meaning, 54–55; for fix-up methods, 48; for identifying facts and details, 106; length and, 3; for making connections, 72; for predictions, 83–84; for Read-Along Guides, 149–150; resources on, 14t; for sequence, 115; for summarizing, 141; for synthesizing, 90; for telling fact from opinion, 111; for visual clues, 60; for visualizing, 79

TEXT-TO-SELF (T–S) CONNECTIONS, 71, 73, 227r

TEXT-TO-TEXT (T–T) CONNECTIONS, 71, 73, 227r

TEXT-TO-WORLD (T–W) CONNECTIONS, 71, 73, 227r

TIC-TAC-TOE BOARDS, 39, 41f, 248r

TIME: for instruction, and Model use, 28; for Read-Along Guides, 165–169; use of, in independent work, 31

TOMLINSON, C.A., 20, 39

TRADE PUBLISHING HOUSES, 196

TREHEARNE, M., 22

U–V

UNDERSTANDING: higher level of, teacher response and, 186

VENN DIAGRAMS: for comparing and contrasting, 119–121, 121f, 123, 243r; tailoring Guide for, 162, 164f

VISUAL TEXT CLUES, USING, 59–66, 225r

VISUALIZING, 78–82, 228r

VOCABULARY: building, 53–59, 224r, 235r, 241r; dialogue on, 180; tailoring Guide for, 161–162, 162f

W

WALLACE, B., 60

WEST, T., 55, 126

WILLINGHAM, D.T., 22

WILSON, N., 177

WORD MEANING: finding, 53–59, 224*r*, 235*r*, 241*r*

WORLD, 71, 73, 227*r*

WRITING: in small-group instruction, 29

WRITTEN RESPONSE SECTION, 171–190; definition of, 173–174; in Read-Along Guides, 155–156, 157*f*; teacher communication in, 183–188